BORN FEARLESS

BORN FEARLESS

*From Kids' Home to SAS to
Pirate Hunter – My Life as a
Shadow Warrior*

BIG PHIL CAMPION

Quercus

First published in Great Britain in 2011 by

Quercus
55 Baker Street
7th Floor, South Block
London
W1U 8EW

A CIP catalogue record for this book is available
from the British Library.

HB ISBN 978 0 85738 376 1
TPB ISBN 978 0 85738 377 8

10 9 8 7 6 5 4 3 2 1

Text designed and typeset by Ellipsis Books Limited, Glasgow

Printed and bound in Great Britain by Clays Ltd, St Ives plc

This book is dedicated to Martin White,
the father who I never met.

AUTHOR'S NOTE

Where necessary a number of names, dates and place names have been changed to protect people's identities and obscure sensitive information.

ACKNOWLEDGEMENTS

Thanks to Annabel Merullo, my literary agent, to Richard Milner, David North and Josh Ireland at Quercus, the publishing team who did such a superb job on the book, and to Digby Halsby, the publicist at Flint PR. Thanks to Damien Lewis, the military author, for teaching me how to drink copious quantities of beer – not! Thanks to Kaarisa, Chubbs, Logs and Podge, for all the hospitality and for allowing me to turn their daddy upside down in the pub and drag him home. Thanks to Mike Mawhinney, a good mate without whom this project would not have happened.

Thanks to John 'Ginge' Davidson, for all the help over the years and for being such a solid mate. Thanks to Jack Parnell, with whom I've spent so many hours watching Southampton Football Club getting kicked around the park. Thanks to Eddie, Jim Munro, Jase Woods and Trevor Arthey, for being such great muckers on the circuit. Thanks to Gary Brooks, for always keeping my bases covered at home when I'm away. Thanks to Wayne Batton, for helping keep my weary bones in some sort of shape. Thanks to Steve Allen and Marty Farrow at Risk Contained, for allowing me to manhandle their celebrities. Thanks to Roger Hildon and family, for showing me the ways of the Rupert.

Thanks to the staff past and present at Calshot Activities Centre, with special mention to Martin Dewey, Griff Watkins and Lawrence West. Thanks to all the staff at Hawk's Lease Church of England

Children's Society, who set me on the straight and narrow, and put up with my endless absconding, drunkenness and wayward ways.

Thanks too to all those in the Royal Hampshires and the Princess of Wales Royal Regiment of all ranks who shared with me many of the experiences of being a soldier, and who continue to commit themselves to the safety and security of this country. Thanks to all those with whom I undertook Para selection and Royal Marines selection – we had a good laugh and a few good punch-ups along the way. And thanks to all the ranks in the Special Air Service, who continue to lead the way in terms of elite forces operations world-wide, so making this country a safer place.

Thanks to former prime minister Tony Blair for the copy of your book, which will be reciprocated, and for the signed photos.

Thanks to Julie Davies, film producer and director, who came up with the title for this book. Nice one, Julie.

Thanks to all my family in London – Della and Tom, Tony and Mitchel, plus all the Whites and all the Christmases. And last but not least, heartfelt thanks to Woogle, Derek Dog, Jack-the-Hat Macvitie, Bibba Monkey, Gracadile, Ems, D, Rock and Gravel, Ugly Betty and Ikle D, and Carol and Mick – you who have put up with all the time I've spent away on work, or buried in the writing of this book.

Find out more about Big Phil at:
www.bigphilcampion.com

CHAPTER 1

I'm at the entrance to the tunnels. The closest you can get to hell on earth.

Ever since the years I spent growing up in kids' homes, I've had problems with enclosed spaces – being locked up, crushed, suffocated, trapped.

Going into the tunnels at Erez brings all of that back to me, and worse.

Like anyone wanting to cross this war-blasted border, we'll be fed into the tunnels one by one. Isolated. Alone. Deep under this flat, empty, sun-baked stretch of no-man's-land. Cut off from whoever might provide a little human comfort and security.

Erez is the only border crossing on foot into Gaza. It's a real man-stamp in your passport to have this one. Not a lot of blokes have been through this way, that's for sure.

Once on the far side it's not a question of who wants you dead. It's a Who's Who of Islamic militias in there. *They all want you dead.* And first in the queue are most likely our clients, one of the most powerful and feared terrorist outfits on earth.

Still, we've got a job to do. We've hit pay dirt big time with this one. And taking insane risks is something of a hallmark of the SAS, the unit I served with before moving onto 'the circuit' – the world of private security operations.

The Israeli border guards are used to the form by now. I go into the tunnels last – letting Jack, Eddie and Paul go first. That way I know the lads are through ahead of me when – if – I make it through to the far side.

We've already had the hours of body searching and abuse from the Israeli border guards. It's become like a ritual by now. They hate us for working with their arch-enemies, and I can't say that I blame them. If I was one of those border guards – getting shelled and sniped at every day by terrorists operating from inside Gaza – I'd hate blokes like me too.

Only today, they've got something new in store for us at the end of the tunnels.

A big surprise.

Something to really fuck us up.

The steel bars of the entryway hiss open, and I'm prodded into this narrow, floodlit underground passageway by a nervous border guard. He's pimply, and I can see that he's cut himself shaving. I'm probably old enough to be his father.

He's as edgy and trigger-happy as teenage conscripts are anywhere in the world on the edge of a hellish war zone. Ill-motivated. Volatile. Full of youthful anger and hatred.

Plus he's brandishing an M16. Seriously dangerous material.

I turn my back on him and wait for instructions. I feel vulnerable and exposed, but it's the worst thing ever to show it. Fear breeds power in those who detect it. *Show fear and you're finished.*

'Hands on your head.'

The disembodied voice echoes from speakers set above and behind me in the tunnel roof. I don't bother to search for them, just lift my hands and place them on my scalp.

I'm bareheaded. The UN tried issuing us with body armour and helmets, but the kit they had for us was next to useless. It consisted of misshapen plates of metal thicker than a whale omelette. They'd weight you down and make you a sitting target, then fragment into lethal projectiles when hit by the first round.

Instead, I've got my mate Francis at Guartel to ship me out a set of their space-age body armour. It's made of a light, composite Kevlar material. I've been out on the ranges and tested the stuff, firing fifty-odd rounds into it, and seen it survive.

In comparison, the UN kit dates from the Stone Age.

Still, I've no idea yet how thankful I'll be for Francis's body armour by this day's end.

Apart from the body armour, me and the lads are completely unprotected. No one is allowed through at Erez carrying any weapons.

I'm dressed in standard private-operator kit – desert-colour combat trousers and a dark blue polo shirt – as are Eddie, Jack and Paul. I've got a black grab bag with the bare essentials – water, rations and a torch. Plus I've got a Gerber Leatherman multitool slung on my belt.

As I await my next set of instructions, I tell myself that I've just thought up a new use for the Leatherman. When I get through to the far side I can use it to pull all my teeth out – that's before Islamic Jihad or whoever capture me get to do the same.

I've got a stupid smile on my face at the thought of ripping out my own gnashers, just to spoil Islamic Jihad's day. I can imagine the reaction of the Israeli spook at the other end of the surveillance camera who's watching me from the tunnel's ceiling. He's seeing me grinning insanely to myself. He must be wondering what drugs I'm on.

'Start walking. Slowly.'

I do as the metallic-sounding voice on the speaker instructs me. I've gone twenty yards or so in the suffocating silence when I reach the next gate.

'Stop,' the voice commands.

As if I could do otherwise. I'm hardly about to walk through a seven-foot-high barrier of steel bars.

There's a clunking and whirring from above, and the barrier slides open. I stare straight ahead, waiting. No instructions come. This is all part of the game, one designed to mess with your mind. And I know it'll get worse before I'm out of here.

Finally, after what feels like a lifetime but is probably no more than five minutes, I'm ordered to proceed.

I shuffle forward. Another twenty-five yards. Another barrier. Just as soon as it slides open I'm ordered through. Then I'm told to stop. The gate swishes shut behind me, and another closes just ahead of me, right in my face.

I'm trapped in a cage. The front and back walls are steel gates, the sides the tunnel walls.

Silence. Stillness. Nothing. Now the real mind games begin. From experience I reckon they'll keep me locked in here for thirty minutes or so, before trying some of their sicker stuff on me.

The lights go out. Darkness like the grave. Apart from the faint whir of what must be an extractor fan, there's not a sound to be heard. Or at least, so I think.

Then I catch it. A faint groaning. Human? Or could it be an animal? I hear it again. No doubt this time: a human noise. A human in agony. Or distress. Or both.

I search in the darkness, my natural vision adjusting from the glare of the spotlights to the gloom, and I can just make out a prone form, lying to the front side of the cage that I'm in. The figure is on a stretcher, the head wrapped in bandages. I can't tell if it's a man or a woman, or what nationality he or she might be.

Then a word: whispered, hoarse, delirious. '*Saa'adinil.*'

One of my specialisms in the military was languages. I've got a functional grasp of Arabic. '*Saa'adinil*': *Help.*

Another gasp in Arabic: '*Mariid*': *Sick.*

Then: '*Tabib*': *Doctor.*

I've heard all the stories. Medical emergencies that can't be treated in Gaza have to come through to Israel via the tunnels. But no one's allowed to carry the stretcher cases through, so they get dumped in the tunnels, waiting for the Israeli border guards to fetch them.

But now and then the figure wrapped in bandages isn't one of the genuine sick or dying. Now and then it's a suicide bomber. So the border guards are reluctant to risk collecting any of the stretcher cases. And this is the result.

I'm sharing the tunnel with either a traumatized, dying patient, or a suicide bomber. No telling which.

Question is, what do I do?

I know I'm being watched. My every move recorded. They've got infrared cameras that'll cut through the darkness, so they can scrutinize my facial expressions, my every action, and record my every word.

As well as specializing in languages, I also did medical training when in the military. But if I go to help that stretcher case, I'll land myself in a world of pain and hurt. Yet a part of me is sorely tempted to do so. It's one of the legacies of the years getting bullied and abused in the kids' homes: an inability to stand by and watch others get needlessly tortured, abused or hurt.

My instinct is to go and help the figure on the stretcher. But maybe it's not a sick and dying person. Maybe it's a fanatic with slabs of P4 strapped around his waist, his finger on the button.

I try to reason with myself, working it through in my head. Let's say the figure is a genuine medical emergency. To have made it into the tunnel, he or she must be in a very bad way. In need of serious medical treatment that only Israel can provide.

It's nothing my level of medical training will be able to help with.

Alternatively, if it is a suicide bomber and he or she decides to press the button, I figure there's nothing I can do about it. I've had a fine innings. I'm good to go.

Gradually, the groaning and pleading from the stretcher dies down. Maybe the figure thinks I've gone. In the suffocating silence and semi-darkness I consciously try to control my breathing, to keep a level of calm inside me.

Finally, a metallic voice rings out of the speakers: 'Proceed.'

The gate ahead of me swishes open. I take a step forward, not even glancing at the stretcher case, and I keep walking.

There's another set of gates that bar my way. Another chance for them to mess with my head. I'm ordered to strip to the waist. I do as instructed and stand there half-naked, as the cameras whirr and click.

I can just imagine the Israeli spook on the other end having a good laugh with the pimply border guard. *The stupid, juvenile bastards. I've forgotten more than these cretins know about security operations.*

They've done repeated body searches of me back at the border post. They know I've got nothing hidden on my person. This is all a game, one designed to humiliate and intimidate anyone passing through the tunnels.

Finally, I'm ordered to dress, and I figure I'm pretty much through. Sure enough the last gate opens, spitting me out into the blinding white light of the beating sun outside.

I hear a voice just ahead of me. 'What kept you, mate?'

As my eyes adjust to the glare I can see that it's Eddie. He grins. 'What kept you?'

'Gridlock,' I joke back at him. 'Tunnels were fuller than a fat girl's shoes. The Erez rush hour. Got a bit much when they asked me to bend over though . . .'

Eddie laughs. He's a big, stocky bloke with a drooping Mexican-style 'tache and a goatee. He's an ex-Para and ex-SAS, and a veteran of the Falklands. When he's not working the circuit he stands duty on a nightclub door in Aldershot, largely because he loves scrapping with Pikeys.

He's a proper hard bastard, and the dog's bollocks as far as operators go.

We turn to face the way ahead. Eddie points across the 200-metre patch of no-man's-land, stretching between the tunnel exit and Gaza proper.

'Guess that's our reception party.' He shrugs. 'At least there's someone here to meet us.'

I glance where he's pointing, towards a group of figures with vehicles. There are a couple of civvy vehicles, together with gunmen in dark fatigues: our terrorist employers. Plus a couple of white UN Toyota Land Cruisers parked towards the rear.

'Welcome to man-town,' says Eddie.

I have to agree. A blouse is not required here.

While the UN has refused to officially sanction this job – it's far too hot for that – they have agreed to loan us a couple of wagons, in case we have to evacuate under fire. The hope is that the UN logos on the vehicles might buy us a little protection.

It's heating up like a pressure cooker inside Gaza. I can sense it's only a matter of time before it explodes. Got to hope the UN ruse works, at least for long enough to get us out of the premises and on the move.

We start walking, the four of us alone and exposed on this flat, featureless patch of land that lies between two nations hell-bent on ripping each other's throats out. To make matters worse, the terrain is completely devoid of any cover.

I feel this horrible, tingling sensation running up and down my spine. It's a feeling that I recognize well from my days in the military elite. *Danger.*

Difference is, I have rarely felt as defenceless and vulnerable as I do now. During operations with The Regiment I knew I had the might of the SAS behind me. If it came to it, the entire British Army and our American allies might come riding to the rescue. Now I'm a private operator, and me and my fellow guns for hire are alone and unarmed out here. The odds don't stack in our favour: they never do as a civvy operator.

Plus we're sandwiched between two of the most battle-hardened fighting forces in the world. *Nice one. Welcome to Erez.*

We've made about twenty yards when the silence around us erupts into gunfire. All four of us freeze as the rounds go cracking past our heads and slamming into the vehicles on the far side.

A burst of automatic fire stitches a neat line of bullet holes through the windscreen of the nearest wagon, a fountain of glass glinting through the air. Further bursts of fire punch through the bodywork, chunks of metal spinning off in all directions.

It's like the final scenes from the movie *Heat*, when the bank robbers' vehicles are ambushed as they try to make their getaway.

The gunmen who make up our reception party aren't slow to react. They're piling out of the vehicles and taking whatever cover they can find behind the engine blocks of the wagons.

AK47s are raised, and muzzles spark, as rounds start screaming back towards the Israeli side. These gunmen consist of hardened Hamas operatives. They need little excuse to take on the Israelis in full-on warfare.

They're spraying off angry bursts on automatic, and pumping rounds into the Israeli border post behind us.

And the four of us are caught like dead men in the heart of the crossfire.

CHAPTER 2

It's obvious what the Israeli soldiers are up to. They've opened fire knowing that Hamas will retaliate, and hoping that in the midst of all the mayhem Hamas gun down the four of us.

That'll be a neat end to all the trouble that the Israelis say we've been causing, and no one can ever accuse them of having put the bullets in us.

So here we are, caught between two warring parties who hate each other's guts, a storm of lead zipping and snarling past. My mind is screaming one thing at me, over and over and over: *Find some fucking cover.*

I glance around. There's only one vague suggestion of a bolt-hole in the whole godforsaken patch of flat, shitty desert: a pile of humped boulders some thirty yards in front of us.

I glance at Eddie. We lock eyes. I can sense he's seen it, and we're both thinking the same thing.

I make a mad dash towards that boulder pile, Eddie right on my shoulder. We're screaming for Jack and Paul to follow.

'FUCKING MAKE FOR THAT COVER!'

For many, the natural human instinct when under fire is to freeze. Basically, limbs go to jelly, and you often find people pissing or shitting themselves in terror. Operators like Eddie and me have trained for years and years to get over that fear reflex, and force themselves to react differently.

We're fifteen metres short of the boulder pile when the Israeli border guards realize what we're up to. In an instant their aim shifts, and they're no longer ripping into the Hamas vehicles.

Instead, they're pouring fire into the cover just ahead of us. They drill in a murderous volley of rounds, bullets snarling and ricocheting angrily in all directions. Their message is crystal-clear: *Back the fuck off, or we'll kill you.*

I skid to a halt, Eddie cannoning into the back of me. Jack and Paul do likewise. I glance behind me and Eddie's got his hands in the air in the universal sign of surrender.

'Stand still, mate! Keep fucking still!' Eddie mouths at me, gesturing for me to get my hands up.

It's fair enough. There's sod-all else we can do. I raise my hands, and Jack and Paul follow suit. So there we are like four scarecrows in the middle of nowhere, with fire going in all directions around us.

We have no means of fighting back, for we aren't scheduled to pick up any weapons until we make our rendezvous with Hamas. Our only chance is to make it clear that whoever puts a bullet in us – Hamas or the Israelis – they'll be shooting unarmed civilians.

I stand there with my hands above my head, waiting to take a round. It's the worst possible feeling. At least with a weapon in your hand you can return fire. Like this we're sitting targets in a shooting gallery.

I see one of the Hamas vehicles edging forward, as if it's trying to reach us. The bizarre thing is that it's a yellow taxi. I've got this silly voice calling in my head: 'Taxi for Phil and his mates!' Just like the bloke does when he comes to pick you up from the boozer.

In an instant, the Israelis shift their fire, rounds kicking up the desert sand right in front of its wheels. The driver slams it into reverse and beats a rapid retreat, tyres spinning crazily as he does so.

I wonder how it can get any worse. I don't have to wait long to find out. Over the deafening noise of the gun battle, I hear the piercing scream of an incoming projectile. I recognize it instantly. We've got a mortar round in-bound.

The noise grows louder and louder, drilling into my head. Time seems to freeze. I hit the deck right where I am in slow motion, the other lads thudding down into the dust and sand next to me.

The mortar howls down, slamming into the desert not thirty yards away. Shrapnel and blasted rock zings past our ears, smoke and sand swirling all around us in a thick, blinding cloud.

An instant later the mortar operators begin to fire for effect. It has to be a Hamas mortar team, for the rounds are coming from deep inside Gaza. They'll have the mortar tube hidden amongst the rubble, and are lining up to slam a few dozen rounds into the Israelis.

They start walking the rounds towards the Israeli border post behind us. Trouble is, we are caught in the open and right in the path of the mortar's creeping barrage, whereas the Israeli border guards are in secure, sandbagged bunkers.

It sounds like a 2-inch mortar, a favourite weapon of Hamas. The light man-portable tube is easy to set up and move, so as to evade Israeli surveillance, and retaliatory air strikes. It's a smart weapon for terrorists and militias with no air cover. The key is to get as many rounds down the tube as quickly as possible, and to move position before you're detected.

These operators know what they're doing, and they're hammering out the rounds like there's no tomorrow. *Which for us there just mightn't be.*

The 2-inch fires a round not a great deal bigger than a 40mm grenade, but as the shells slam into the dirt all around us size doesn't really seem to matter. A direct hit from one of those and we're toast. All that'll be left of us is a few shreds of bloodied meat, plus a fine pink mist on the hot desert air.

The rounds creep closer. We're digging in with our eyelids. A mortar tears into the sand not ten feet from where I'm lying. The blast rips me away from the earth and slams me into Eddie lying next to me.

I'm a big bloke, but the explosion has punched all eighteen stone of me through the air. I must have blacked out, for I come to lying on my back with red-hot tracer rounds zipping past above me.

There's a smoking hole torn in the khaki material at the front of my body armour. It looks just the right size for a chunk of 2-inch mortar shrapnel.

When I check myself over I don't seem to be wounded. I'm not bleeding out. Francis's body armour seems to have saved the day. For now at least I'm still alive.

But I'm getting pretty close to using up every last one of my nine bloody lives.

CHAPTER 3

It was seven years before the Hamas job when I was first contracted to work on the private military circuit. It was the summer of 2001 and I was asked to do a specialist tasking for Hemley's, the international diamond company who advertise themselves as 'truly the world's finest jewellers'. A stupendously wealthy Arab sheikh was planning on having the wedding of the century – money no object – and he wanted some top rocks with which to impress his bride.

During my years in the SAS I'd earned myself as colourful a reputation as I had in the Green Army before that. One of my Green Army commanding officers had referred to me as someone who should be 'kept in a metal cage and only brought out at times of war'. I'd left The Regiment after some awesome operations, and with honour intact. I was a few months out by the time the Hemley's job came along, and I was hungry for some decent work on the circuit.

The phone call had come from a private security company called Omega One, run by an ex-SAS mate of mine. He'd refused to give me any details of the job over the phone. Instead, he'd asked if I was free for a specific set of dates, and if so to get my arse up to London.

I told him that I was, and headed to their Knightsbridge office. I learned that the job was to travel to Abu Dhabi, in the Gulf, with some £50 million worth of diamonds on my person. Apparently, the job was likely to turn into a pissing competition, to see which sheikh could spend the most money buying the biggest stones. Hemley's were intending to send out some seriously large rocks with which to tempt them. I was to be the mule carrying the diamonds from Hemley's London headquarters to the sheikh's palace.

I'd be doing the job accompanied by two of Hemley's diamantaires, as professional diamond dealers are called. It was their job to strike the deal with the sheikh; mine was to keep the rocks securely in my possession until they were sold, or safely back in Hemley's London vault.

I took the job and so began the waiting game. I had to sit by the phone with my bags packed, expecting a call from Hemley's at any time. I would be given a London rendezvous where I was to pick up the rocks, and I had to be ready to move at a moment's notice.

I guess all this cloak-and-dagger stuff was to prevent me from hiring a bunch of ex-military mates to knock off the diamonds before they'd so much as left London. And don't imagine for one moment that it hadn't crossed my mind to do so. There would be just the one bag stuffed with rocks, and it would have a street value of some £50 million. Divide the proceeds of selling that little lot, and me and whoever I'd brought in to help me knock them off could happily retire.

At first Hemley's had wanted me travelling with a codeword-protected titanium attaché case handcuffed to my wrist with the rocks inside it. I'd told them that was a total non-starter. I would be unarmed for the duration of the mission, and an attaché case with handcuffs would only advertise that I was carrying some-thing of immense value.

Instead, I wanted to keep as low a profile as possible – just as we always had done when on operations with the elite military units that I've trained and served with. I persuaded the Hemley's guys to purchase a dirt-cheap Adidas sports bag, and place the individual rocks, plus the rings, bracelets and tiaras, in there.

That way, I'd look like an average Joe off for a touch of sun, sand and whatever in the Gulf. I'd take the sports bag as carry-on luggage, and keep it with me at all times. It was my only precondition on taking the contract. If they insisted on the shiny titanium attaché case, I was out.

The telephone call comes late one afternoon, around a week after getting warned off for the job. I'm instructed to go imme-diately to an NCP car park, just off Hatton Garden, the gem-dealing heart of London.

I'm told the number of the bay that I'm to pull into, and where I'm to leave my car. On the right side of me will be the Hemley's vehicle, which will take me to the airport. It all seems simple enough, so I head down there right away.

I pull into the bay, and there's a sleek black Mercedes parked up on my right side. I can see a guy in the driver's seat waving at me. It strikes me as somewhat amateur hour. I figure the guy must know my number plate, and that he's positively identified my vehicle as I drove in. But what guarantee does he have that it's actually me driving it?

I walk over to the car and try the rear passenger door. Un-believably, it's unlocked. I slide into the seat, and the guy in front turns to me.

'Hi, mate, I'm Kelvin,' he says.

I stare at him for a second.

'Well done,' I reply, incredulously.

I presume he knows my name. If not, who the hell has he just let into his car? Hemley's have these security guards working on the doors of their retail branches, and I figure Kelvin must be one of them. He's got the badly fitting suit and the clip-on tie to match.

Kelvin proceeds to pass me two bulging sports bags, ignoring the fact that it could be anyone he's just let into his unlocked vehicle. Despite all their best efforts to make this cloak-and-dagger, it's more plastic mac and butter knife from what I can see.

'Couldn't fit them all in the one bag,' Kelvin remarks. 'You know, *the rocks*.'

I lock my door of the Mercedes, then reach over and do the same with the other rear door. It's before the days of central locking. I see Kelvin note my actions in his driver's mirror, and then he's doing likewise with the front doors.

'So there they are, mate,' Kelvin continues. 'Guard them with your life, like.'

He starts the car and we pull onto the road heading west for Heathrow airport. We're under way and Kelvin's giving me my instructions. He will deliver me to the airport, whereupon I'll make my way to the Concorde Lounge. There I'm to rendezvous with the two diamantaires.

I suppose I've been half expecting a team of super-suave James Bond types to do the handover. After all, it is £50 million worth of diamonds we're talking here. Instead, I've got just the one guy – Kelvin. He's the kind of bloke I could knock over with a beer fart. And I can see already that his plan is full of holes.

What's to stop me heading straight for the airport toilets and unloading a few of the rocks into my pockets in the privacy of a cubicle? I could even swallow them, and search through my own poo for the next few days until I find them.

I consider this for a few seconds, but eventually I decide to put temptation behind me. This is my first gig on the circuit, and even though I wouldn't trust Kelvin with half a pound of jelly babies, my professional pride makes me want to do this job right. My mate in the security firm has trusted me with this one, and if I run off with the rocks I'll have let him down big time. And that goes against the entire esprit de corps, and the brotherhood of where I come from.

I deliberately take a long hard look in Kelvin's rearview mirror, making sure he notes me doing so. I repeat it a few times, but whenever he catches me looking I act as if I wasn't. Increasingly, Kelvin's shifting around in his seat worriedly. It's cruel to torture him like this, but I simply can't resist making it look as if I've got someone tailing us.

Kelvin is a Scouser, and I'm an East End of London type of bloke. From what I've seen so far you could write what he knows about security on the back of a postage stamp with a twelve-inch paintbrush.

As we approach the terminal, he starts flapping again. He's speaking fast, gabbling words from the front seat. 'So, we're like almost there, mate. You know, at the airport like. So, d'you need me to watch your back, mate?'

I have this vision of him bomb-bursting through the terminal doors. I figure having Kelvin on the case will only draw attention to me, and that's the very last thing I need.

I shrug. 'It's hardly Rourke's Drift. I think I can handle it from here.'

Kelvin looks really disappointed, and for a moment I almost feel sorry for him. Then he's pulling up at the terminal and I'm out of the door, a bag gripped in either hand. I do one lap of the concourse on foot, just to ensure that I've not been followed.

Then I make a beeline for the rendezvous in the Concorde Lounge.

CHAPTER 4

The lady on the Concorde Lounge reception desk gives me the once-over. I'm hardly her normal business lounge fare. I'm dressed in smart desert-style fatigues and a clean white shirt, but I've still got the military-style buzzcut. And it's the thick Cockney accent that's the real giveaway.

I ask her for Sebastian Bellshire and Irani Alsour, the names of the two Hemley's diamantaires. She sends someone through to check, and a minute later two figures appear.

This tall, stooping bloke leads with the limpest handshake I've ever felt. It goes with his pinstripe suit and salmon-pink shirt. Irani's next, and she's short and delicate-looking, plus she's dressed in this ultra-expensive women's business suit that makes her look good regardless. Whilst Sebastian's all smiles and a posh stutter, Irani's gushing and kissing me on both cheeks, French-style.

Its hardly the kind of greeting that I'm used to, which is more of the 'how-you-doin'-you-old fucker' type. Still, I guess this is civvy street, and best I get used to it if I want to make it on the circuit.

It turns out that Irani is an Afghan by birth. She speaks Farsi and Arabic pretty fluently, and she's with us as the translator. We exchange the odd word in both languages, and I can see the surprise written on her face. It's the last thing she's been expecting from 'someone like me'.

I explain that I've served in both Farsi- and Arabic-speaking parts of the world, and there's something of a bond forged between us. As for Sebastian, his only concern is the 'four Cs' of the world of the diamantaire – the Cut, Clarity, Crystal and Colour – by which stones are classified and valued.

Sebastian is camper than Christmas, and we've got just about nothing in common. I reckon the crack between us will be about as good as a one-inch whip. Still, I'm not here to enjoy myself. I'm here for the money, and to start forging a reputation as an operator on the circuit.

After a polite chat over coffee, Sebastian asks if we can go into a side room that he's hired for the purpose of inspecting the stones. He seems excruciatingly embarrassed about having to check that they're all still there, as if I'll somehow object to his doubting my honesty.

In fact, I'd think him insane not to. But after Kelvin's performance, I'm ready for anything from these guys.

I place the bags on the table in the private room, and Sebastian goes to unlock them. As he does so he explains that before padlocking the bags and handing them to Kelvin, he compiled a list of the contents, so he can check they're all present and correct.

During the years that I spent in the kids' homes, I became an expert in stealing cars and joyriding. Picking locks is second nature to me, but I guess that wouldn't occur to the Sebastians of this world. Far from being a James Bond operation, it's beginning to feel as if I've signed up to a mission with Dad's Army.

Still, I'm fascinated to see the contents of the bags.

The nearest I've ever got to anything like £50 million worth of diamonds was when Princess Diana inspected the Royal

Hampshires, the Army regiment that I had joined when I was still in my teens. We'd been drafted in to drive a fleet of ancient Green Goddesses during a firemen's strike, prior to yet another Northern Ireland tour. For some reason Lady Di had paused before me on parade, so as to have a brief chat with Private Campion.

She asked me how I'd found it, doing the job of a fireman. I wasn't about to lie. I told her the nearest we'd ever come to putting out a fire was being called to rescue an old horse trapped in a Welsh bog. The Green Goddesses were so slow that by the time we'd got there, the nag had slid below the surface and was long gone. Lady Di appeared to see the humour in the story, and whilst she'd smiled and shaken my hand I'd admired the big rocks on her fingers.

Unfortunately, the RSM had failed to see the funny side of me telling Lady Di the dead horse story. It was yet another black mark that I'd earned for myself in the regular Army.

But compared to the rocks on Lady Di's fingers, the ones that Sebastian unloads in front of me are true whoppers. By the time he's emptied both bags there's enough bling on the table to get the knickers off a nun.

There are the individual rocks, the largest the size of a conker. There are a dozen or more necklaces and tiaras with hundreds of glittering stones set in them. Plus scores of diamond-encrusted watches displayed on individual leather rolls.

I have never seen anything remotely like it. I'm a 34-year-old ex-soldier who joined the Army at sixteen, after which the Army had quickly become the only real home that I'd ever had. I have never in my life been anywhere remotely close to wealth on this scale, and it's mind-boggling.

Sebastian checks over each of the pieces, and fills out these customs forms as he does so. Hemley's are temporarily exporting the rocks to Abu Dhabi, in the hope that they'll sell the lot, or at least a good proportion of them.

We make our way to the departure gate, and as we do so Sebastian hands me my boarding card. It's an overnight flight, and I'm hoping to be able to stretch out in business class. Then I take a look at my seat number: 59C. That puts me somewhere down the back in economy, probably one in front of the toilets and with less legroom. Again, it's hardly the James Bond champagne-and-caviar treatment that I'd been expecting.

I get a glance at Sebastian and Irani's boarding cards. They're in single-digit seats, which puts them somewhere in first or business class.

I catch Sebastian's eye and wave the boarding card at him. 'Jesus, mate, even the hostesses won't bother with me this far down the plane.'

He gives me this half-apologetic, half-embarrassed shrug, and up the steps into the aircraft we go. As we enter, he and Irani go to turn left, me right into cattle class, and Sebastian holds out a hand for the bags.

I shake my head. 'No, no, no, mate. I may be down in the Bronx, but the bags stay with me at all times.'

I can see that he's uncomfortable with this, but he really doesn't want to make a scene. He's dithering, and as he does so I turn left and hustle down the aisle. I reach my allocated seat, and sure enough I'm so far back the hostesses are only ever likely to venture down here in pairs.

To make matters worse I'm bang in the middle of the plane, with seats to either side of me. Somehow I squeeze my six-foot-two, eighteen-stone frame in there. I get the bags shoved under the seat in front of me, where I can keep physical contact with them at all times. But it leaves me zero legroom.

I start zoning in to my surroundings, maximizing my 'situational awareness'. Over many years' of elite soldiering I'd learned how your chances of identifying danger or threat are greatly increased if you are 'situation aware'.

At its simplest, young squaddies are taught to have some form of 'shark watch' whenever out and about on the town. Ideally, one member of the group volunteers to remain reasonably sober for the evening, so he can keep an eye out for his fellows.

That's the first rung of situational awareness. Jack that up to being alone, unarmed, bereft of any back-up, and with £50 million in diamonds in tow, and you have to ramp up your situational awareness accordingly.

I can't permanently 'patrol' life, as it's almost impossible not to switch off at some point. But it's vital to know when to be one hundred per cent switched on, and on your guard. And right now I need to be constantly alert to what's going on around me.

To know when something is wrong, you need to know how things are when all is normal. You need to scan your environment, and soak up how things are when they're all right – just as I'm doing now.

You then need to envisage what might happen if everything turns ugly. You need to play with scenarios and ask yourself the 'what-ifs'. You might not always come up with the answers, but at least you've made yourself aware of a potential danger or threat.

As I wriggle around in my economy seat trying to get comfortable, I consider the 'what-ifs'. What if someone near me drinks too much and a fight breaks out? If so, I don't get involved: I've got too much to lose in those bags.

What if one of the flight attendants asks me to change seats? It could happen that someone wants to sit near a friend or relative. If I'm asked to move I'll agree to do so, no fuss. To object and make a scene will only draw attention. People may start asking – what does that guy have to hide?

What if I have to go to the toilet? The total crass stupidity of booking me alone in economy class means I have no back-up – not even a Kelvin – to turn to. I can't exactly carry the sports bags into the toilet with me. Nothing like drawing attention to what I'm carrying.

The only option is to not use the toilet during the entire seven-hour flight: and that means no food or drink for the duration. This makes me doubly angry with Sebastian and Irani, the nobby diamond geezers sitting somewhere forward in gold-plated class.

What if I fall asleep? Not doable. I have to remain awake. Period. I can't exactly jack up on the coffee, as I can't use the toilet. I reckon I'll slip on my headphones, choose a good action movie and pump up the volume.

What if some bird tries to chat me up? I'm no oil painting, but the fairer sex has occasionally been known to go for my rugged maverick charm. But if it happens on this flight, the lady's going to be sorely disappointed. She can think that I'm Sebastian's type for all I care. The honeytrap is a standard weapon in the arsenal of intelligence agencies, mafias and thieves. Which is why truly professional criminals operate by keeping exposure to everyone outside of their gang to an absolute minimum.

My final 'what-if' is the aircraft getting hijacked. Unlikely. But then again, it is full of dodgy-looking blokes in turbans. If that happens, I'll endeavour at all times to remain the 'grey man' – the one who does nothing to get himself noticed, or to attract unwelcome attention.

If the hijackers are armed, and they order me off the aircraft without my luggage, I'll leave the rocks where they are. No amount of money is worth getting killed over, especially when it isn't your own.

I don't think this diamond-carrying mission has been compromised, but you never know. One of the diamantaires could be working for the bad guys. I figure Kelvin certainly could.

Either Kelvin, Sebastian or Irani could have tipped off their criminal associates. One or more of their number could be booked onto the aircraft. In a situation such as this there is every reason to be paranoid, and to use that paranoia to your advantage.

In the military we'd rendered down that paranoia into a three-letter motto: TNF (Trust No Fucker). Within your unit you could pretty much dispense with the TNF rule, for you knew that every bloke had made it there by hard graft and merit. But outside of my unit I could count the people that I truly trusted on the fingers of one hand.

In the military we'd all passed the same selection course; we'd achieved the same intensive level of training; we'd not been found wanting when adopting the warrior's mindset. Whoever was fighting on your shoulder you could pretty much rely on.

But now I was working the circuit, and I had no guarantee whatsoever of anyone's bona fides. I knew nothing about their backgrounds. One weak link in the chain, one rotten egg in the basket, that's all it would take.

With Sebastian and Irani as my 'team', I basically have zero back-up. I am alone and unarmed, carrying £50 million worth of diamonds into Abu Dhabi, an Arab sheikhdom that I've never visited before.

I've not been able to do a recce, and I have little or no intelligence about what it's like on the ground there.

It's the TNF rule that may just save my arse on a mission such as this one.

CHAPTER 5

We're preparing for take-off, and I'm still fuming about how the Hemley's cheapskates have put me in cattle class. Then I see a tiny little Indian-looking woman making her way towards the seat beside me. She's about the size of my left foot, and as she sits down it strikes me she smells like it too.

She proceeds to curl up on her seat like a cat, and she falls fast asleep. A sound rises from her like the wheezing of a badly tuned set of bagpipes. The volume of the whistling rises as she sinks deeper into her slumber. For her size, she is a snorer to rival any number I've come across in the Army.

For a moment I consider whether I could get away with murdering her, and stashing her body in the bogs. But I figure that's a short-cut to getting the diamond mission truly compromised. Instead, I grab my headphones and scan the menu for some movies.

I reckon I've got away with it to the left of me, as that seat's still free. The aircraft taxis onto the runway and takes off, and still it remains empty. I'm just considering moving into it, to get one place away from bagpipe-snoring catwoman, when these two loaded-looking Arab blokes come waltzing down the aisle.

They're dragging behind them this Arabic brother who looks two sandwiches short of a picnic. Sure enough, they shove him into the seat next to me. Then they turn around and fuck off back to business class. I see him fumbling with his seat belt, with a hand that's shaking so much that he can't make it work.

It's not fear of flying that's making him shake. He's clearly got some serious disability that he's struggling with here. I lean across and belt him up. As the aircraft continues to climb, he's shaking like a dog taking a crap.

I presume that he's going to keep it up all flight, and I resolve to bury myself in the make-believe world of the movies. I switch on my TV and settle down to watch. Almost immediately Abdul leans over to try to see my screen.

He has no English, so gently as I can I push him back to his side. I explain in broken Arabic how the TV works and get his screen set up for him. I get his remote out on its wire, and show him how to operate the movie menu.

But in spite of all my efforts, five minutes later Abdul's leaning over me again to watch mine. It reaches the stage where his head's flopped onto my shoulder, and he's dribbling all down my shirt. I decide there's nothing for it but to ring for a stewardess.

Eventually, one of the in-flight ladies comes down to me. She's a young, Arabic-looking lady, and quite attractive if you can get past the severe headscarf style of the uniform. But there's something hard and inscrutable about her face that doesn't bode well.

I try a winning smile, the kind I employed whilst telling Lady Di the dead pony story: 'I think you're going to need to move me. You see, this guy has his head permanently on my shoulder and he's dribbling all over my shirt. I've tried to set up his TV, but he's not interested. He just wants to watch mine.'

She shrugs. 'There are no free seats on the aircraft, sir.'

I know this is complete bullshit. There are always free seats in business and first class. What she means is no free seats in economy.

I try to remain patient and polite. 'Well, you either need to get rid of him or me, 'cause I can't travel all the way to Abu Dhabi with Bubbles here blowing dribble into my ear.'

She goes off to investigate, and returns ten minutes later. She tells me that there are no free seats for me, or for Bubbles for that matter. I get the strong feeling that whoever Bubbles's Arab relatives are, the hostess really does not want to do anything to upset or disturb them.

As she turns to leave, I can feel myself boiling up with rage. My ears are starting to turn red, which is a sure sign of an imminent eruption. You don't spend sixteen years being dragged through the mud in kids' homes, then make it into the most elite military force in the world, to take shit from air hostesses.

I know exactly what I'm going to do. The only problem is the two bags at my feet. But bugger it, no one's getting off this aircraft with a bag of rocks that's been entrusted to my possession, of that I'm certain.

I lift the bags into the overhead locker, where I will be able to keep an eye on them for most of the duration of what I'm about to do. They're more visible up there, so less chance of anyone sneaking a look inside.

I head up the aisle, keeping one eye on the bags, and go straight through the curtain into business class. Sure enough there are dozens of empty seats. I can feel my ears glowing redder by the second.

I spot the two Arab guys who dumped Bubbles on me, and I'm beside them in a flash. I shake the nearest of them awake.

'*Arabi? Ingli?*' I demand. Meaning – d'you want to do this in Arabic or English.

He tries a shrug. '*Mushkila?*' Problem?

I say: 'Yeah, too fucking right there's a *mushkila.*'

I can tell that the guy's recognized me, and I can see from the

29

shifty look on his face that he knows exactly what the problem is.

'The *mushkila*'s sat in the chair next to me, mate,' I continue. 'Whoever Bubbles is, I'm not here to babysit him. He's your responsibility, so you'd best come and fetch him. Pronto.'

I leave him in no doubt as to the consequences if Bubbles isn't shifted, and the guy confirms that he's on it. I return to my seat, ears a slightly less violent shade of red. I check in the overhead locker, and the bags are still there. I get them down under my seat again, and five minutes later the air hostess arrives and gets Bubbles shifted.

Result.

When he's gone, I take stock. Indian catwoman is still whistling like a kettle beside me, but at least I can wipe the spittle from my shirt, and enjoy a movie in peace. I settle down to watch the start of *Black Hawk Down* for the third time, the first two attempts having been scuppered by Bubbles.

I figure it's as good as it's going to get.

Hours later the jumbo goes into a holding pattern above Abu Dhabi. A few minutes' delay, the pilot tells us, and we should be on the ground. I glimpse palm trees and a beating sun through the aircraft window as it banks across the city limits.

Although I've had no sleep I'm feeling pretty much okay. My shirt's still just about presentable enough to meet the sheikh, in spite of Bubbles's best efforts. The two bags of rocks are present and correct.

I reckon I'm doing all right.

But I have zero idea what a whole world of shit is about to descend upon us. The one 'what-if' that I haven't prepared for is about to hit us, and almost as soon as we step off the aircraft. But being a diamond-running virgin, I have no chance of knowing the ropes at the delivery end of the business.

That is the diamantaires' responsibility – or at least it should be. Trouble is, Sebastian and Irani have been sat up front in diamond class, having a grand old time of things, as our flight jets onwards towards a world of trouble.

CHAPTER 6

I'm reunited with Irani and Sebastian at the arrivals gate. They both look impeccably groomed and very well rested, the bastards.

'How was the flight, old chap?' Sebastian purrs.

It's on the tip of my tongue to ask him how he'd like a bag of diamonds shoved up his arse. But I decide to let it go. It's my first gig on the circuit, and I want to make it work.

Sebastian takes the lead now, as we head for a desk inside the terminal building. It's got some lettering in Arabic above the entrance, from which I figure it has to be the customs hall.

Sebastian's telling me nothing about what's going on here, and it's starting to get to me. Being provided with accurate and timely intelligence is the very foundation upon which you build security into a mission. But I'm being treated like a bagman; like a mushroom that gets kept in the dark and fed on shit.

Given accurate intelligence, I can pre-prepare for a given situation. Given zero intelligence as I am now, I can prepare myself for jack.

We're received at the customs desk by this enormously fat bloke. You'd be hard-pressed to get a Rizla paper under his shirt, it's stretched so tight across his vast belly. And the designer sweat patches under his arms are to drown in.

I presume Sebastian's been through this process in Abu Dhabi dozens of times before, but there's no sign that he knows the fat geezer, or vice versa.

Sebastian hands across the paperwork – the list of stones stamped by the customs officials at Heathrow – whilst I keep a firm hold of the bags. I hope this is going to be a formality, much as it was at the London end, and shortly we'll be on our way. But there's a part of my brain that's screaming otherwise. I've been in enough Arabic shitholes to know to expect the worst from overweight guys in ill-fitting uniforms adorned with oodles of sparkly bits. And on that score, Bubba here takes the biscuit.

He gets his sweaty paws on the paperwork and runs his eyes over it. In no time he's practically dancing around with excitement. He starts calling out in Arabic to his buddies, and soon there's a group of eight clustered around his desk. Sebastian's starting to get a real flap on, which is hardly surprising.

Before us is an unbelievable mishmash of uniforms. It's as if these nine blokes have been given the keys to the fancy-dress shop, and chosen the most outlandish garb possible. There's a mixture of crooked peaked caps, misshapen dog-eared berets, and turbans big enough to land a helicopter on. Plus everyone's got acres of gold braid, with stripes to match. There's trousers sitting halfway up blokes' ankles, and a hotchpotch of pistols each holstered in a different way. In short, each and every one of these blokes looks like a complete sack of shit, Bubba first and foremost.

But that doesn't make our situation any the less worrying. Quite the opposite, in fact: there's no telling what this lot aren't capable of.

Operating on the basis of TNF I have to presume that any one of these blokes may have links into criminal gangs. Having an inside man in airport customs would be invaluable to the Abu Dhabi mafia, and for sure the country has one.

My heart sinks as Bubba motions us into a room to his rear, then signals for his motley crew to follow. Or more accurately, he tries signalling Sebastian and Irani into the room at the rear, whilst telling me to stay put. I let him know that I'm having none of that: I've got the rocks, and where they go I follow. Shortly, there are the nine of them and the three of us crowded into this small space, which is mostly filled with an executive-style table far too large for the room.

Bubba motions for me to empty the bags onto the tabletop. I glance at Sebastian. He's turned as white as a sheet at the very thought of these nine guys getting their grubby hands on the rocks.

It's clear this is rapidly going to ratshit, and unless someone takes a stand we're going to have hands filching diamonds left, right and Chelsea. But Sebastian's doing fuck-all. He's dithering, and seems hardly capable of speaking. There's no point looking to him for any guidance.

In a mixture of broken Arabic and English I ask to see Bubba and his band of brothers' IDs.

I don't doubt for one moment that every bloke in this room is a bona fide airport official. This is probably as good as they get in Abu Dhabi. But I figure that one of them at least will be playing for both sides – airport customs and the criminal gangs. By asking to see their IDs I'm trying to flush out who that individual might be, by looking for classic indicators. I'm also trying to show Bubba and his buffoons that they haven't managed to intimidate me. This is a game, a piece of theatre, and someone has to step up to play for our side.

But for sure, I'm worried. We could lose some serious chunks of rock and metal here. Yet I'd be amazed if any one of these guys has fired his weapon this side of Ramadan. If I had to take the nine of them on, I'd still put good money on me coming out on top.

Trouble is, there's nowhere to run in the midst of an Abu Dhabi airport. And I don't fancy spending the next twenty years in an Abu Dhabi jail cell, with only Sebastian and Bubba for company – both of whom would render my arse like a wizard's sleeve if they got half the chance.

I'm particularly alert to two guys in the room. Both seem anxious as they flash their IDs, especially when I grab them to take a closer look. I flick my eyes from their photos to their faces, and back and forth a good few times. Tongues moisten nervous lips. Eyes dart about uneasily.

But what really does it for me is when one of those two guys demands of Bubba that we be body-searched. We are obviously clean, as we've just come through airport security. A body search is totally irrelevant and unnecessary, and can only be designed to humiliate, and put fear into us. It's clearly an unreasonable request, and any 'official' who asks unreasonable things of you is sure as eggs not to be trusted.

I raise objections with Bubba on three counts. One, Irani is a woman and a fellow Muslim. No way can Bubba and his fellow male officers subject her to a body search. Two, we've been through security at Heathrow, so it's obvious that we're clean.

And three, the object of having us here has to be to check that the rocks in the bags match the UK Customs' temporary export list. And that doesn't require any body searches.

I offer instead to bring out the jewels one by one onto the table, so Bubba & Co can check them off the list. Unsurprisingly, that seems to win the day. It's obvious that's what all nine of these jokers are here for: to get eyes on the diamonds.

Sebastian is shitting himself as sweaty guys in a motley cast of uniforms crowd closer around the table. I draw out the first piece – a thick platinum diamond-encrusted bracelet. It is valued on Sebastian's list at five million quid.

There's an audible gasp from Bubba and Co, who immediately start grabbing at the shiny glitter of the thing like a flock of magpies. I keep palming back wrists and blocking grasping hands, so as to keep them back from the prize.

I pull out further lumps of rock and metal. There's a tiara dripping in crystals, a piece valued at double that of the bracelet. And then there come the individual diamonds in fancy pinks, yellows and violet shades, each of them worth a small fortune.

I get Sebastian working with Bubba ticking off the individual pieces on the list, whilst I keep forcing the rest of the guys away from the growing pile of bling. It's clear that only Sebastian and Bubba are needed to check the goods, and that the rest are here for the free-for-all.

Dodgy blokes keep trying to snaffle an individual rock or piece, and secrete it on their persons before it can be recorded as present. I have to keep forcing the clowns to put the stuff down. And with nine pairs of hands to keep an eye on, and keep shoving back from the table, it's proving a total fucking nightmare.

Finally, Bubba and his bros must get the message that I at least am not about to be intimidated, or pushed around. Plus Irani has been putting forth a good argument in Arabic about how this free-for-all is totally unnecessary and unacceptable.

She keeps quoting the name of the big sheikh who we're bringing the stuff to see. It's his name – and the threat of his sheikhly displeasure – that eventually makes Bubba and gang back off. We get the forms stamped, and finally we manage to cut away from their company.

I've got a bag in either hand as we exit the customs hall, and Sebastian blathering in my ear about how he needs to check every piece individually. Apparently, the rocks are mounted in some kind of paste, and they can literally be pulled out by hand. He's shitting bricks that Bubba and Co may have prised some stones away.

'We have to inventory every last piece, Philip, old boy,' he whines. 'Every last one of them.'

I tell him not here and now we don't. We may have got away from Bubba and the boys, but that's the least of our worries. The nine of them have dispersed to different corners of the airport, and I've seen one at least pulling out a mobile phone.

TNF: Trust No Fucker. No prizes for guessing who they'll be calling: some of their equally bent buddies, to alert them to how one shaven-headed Englishman is about to exit the airport with £50 million worth of diamonds clutched in a couple of holdalls.

As I hustle Sebastian and Irani towards the exit, I'm scanning what people are up to ahead of us, beside and to the rear. Do we have a reception committee to our front? Is there a watcher on a cellphone, calling through our movements to his accomplices? Is anyone following us? Are there any signs that a trap has been set – one that we're about to blunder into, without back-up?

As I scan the crowd, I'm upping my 'third-party awareness'. No one is above suspicion. I keep telling myself to expect the unexpected. I remind myself how in many parts of the world kids are used as the third party, to lure you into a trap.

The first time I'd come across this was in Kenya with the Green Army. I was out on the town having a bit of R & R, when some kids started hurling rocks at me. It was totally unprovoked, and I was tempted to chase the cheeky fuckers up a dusty sidetrack as they did a runner.

But my sixth sense warned me of impending danger. I stuck my head around the corner, and up ahead I could see a gang lying in wait in the bushes. Nice try. The kids had stoned me simply to lure me into a trap.

A little later on the same trip one of my fellow squaddies was offered a 'sherbet' by a local kid. Stupidly, he took it. Hours later he woke up in a strange place with only his underpants for company. The sweet was drugged, and he'd been robbed of everything. Worse still, he didn't have the slightest memory of who had done what to him.

I'm keeping very much 'third-party aware' as Sebastian, Irani and I near the airport exit. A supposedly innocent third party – a kid, an old granny, not to mention an Abu Dhabi customs official – could be the link into a criminal gang that's setting us up for the mother of all gem heists.

Bubba and his brothers will be aware of one further, vital factor concerning our team. As we've just come through airport security, they'll know that we are unarmed.

Due to my demeanour and my size, plus the way that I've behaved, they'll have figured that I'm the security element of the team.

But unarmed, I'm a piss-easy target.

CHAPTER 7

Sebastian can sense the urgency from me now. He assures me that there'll be a car waiting for us just outside the terminal building, together with a driver with name-card.

We exit, and I scan the name-boards being waved before us. There's no card reading 'Sebastian, Irina and Phil'. I give Sebastian a look: *Where the fuck's the vehicle, pal?* He's got this pleading, bewildered expression on his features.

'W-w-well they promised it'd be here, old boy,' he stammers.

'Not fucking good enough,' I fire back at him.

I scan for a taxi rank and find one, just to the right of the pickup point. I set off towards it fast, but not so fast as to be obviously hurrying. I flick my head around to Sebastian and Irani.

'You two coming, or what?'

I've got the bags with the rocks, so they're forced to follow after me.

'Where . . .' Sebastian tries.

'Listen, Sebastian, mate, you can stand around all day waiting to get hit, but count me out. I'm taking a cab.'

I haul open the door of the taxi at the front of the rank, and slide into the rear seat. I bum-shuffle across to the far side, and motion Sebastian in beside me. I signal Irani into the front passenger seat, as she's got some translating to do.

'Downtown,' I tell the taxi guy. 'Let's get moving.'

He glances in the mirror, reads the expression on my face, which is pretty close to murder, then pulls away from the kerb with a screech of rubber. I lock my door, and nod at Sebastian to do likewise.

The cabbie picks up the pace until he's haring along at a near-suicidal speed. We're beginning to stand out like a bulldog's nuts going this fast.

'Irani, tell the driver *downtown via the back roads*,' I add. 'Plus drop the speed to dead slow.'

Irani translates. I see the taxi driver eyeing me in the mirror again. Then he shrugs, eases off the gas, and pulls into a side road. Soon we're bumping along nice and easy.

It's a common myth that the best way of checking for a tail is speed. The opposite is true, especially in an Arab city where every bloke with a set of wheels tends to drive like a bat out of hell.

And it's the quiet roads that are the very best to stick to. It's easy for a tail to hide in built-up traffic. Far harder on a deserted Abu Dhabi side road.

I don't want to give the cabbie an address yet. Can't. I don't know exactly where we should be heading. I need some time to think. To plan.

How would we have handled a mission like this one, I ask myself, when I was serving with the military? Completely differently from this gang-fuck, that's for sure. We'd have manned it up properly for starters, having guys all along the route as watchers, making certain everything was secure.

But how would we have handled it if manpower was tight, say just as a three-person team? We'd have done what we always do:

keep a low profile, and blend into the environment, whilst carrying as much concealed firepower as possible.

The firepower bit is out for us, at least for the foreseeable future. But low profile maybe we can do. It'll mean scoring a local-looking vehicle, but this cab will do for now. Plus it'll mean the three of us making like locals.

I scan for any obvious vehicles following us, but there's nothing I can detect. With the speed we got out of the airport and on the road, I figure we've kept ahead of Bubba and his boys.

Then I check out the cabbie in his rearview mirror. He's sporting what I figure must be the standard kind of threads to be seen in here in Abu Dhabi: a chequered headscarf-cum-turban, an enormous pair of mirror shades, and a white dishdash-style robe reaching down to his ankles.

I can't see his feet, but no guessing there: sandals.

I tap Irani on the shoulder. 'Irani, ask the cabbie if he knows a local clothes market or a tailor's.'

'A what?'

'A market or a tailor's,' I repeat. 'You know, like a clothes shop the locals would use.'

Irani asks the question in Arabic. The cabbie makes some suggestions. Sebastian's glancing at me out of the corner of his eye, giving me a look as if I'm cracked or something.

I give him the eye back. I take a long hard look. Sixty-something; greying; perspiring profusely. Sebastian's close to retirement age I reckon, a fat Hemley's pension just around the corner. Last thing he needs is for one of his final diamond jobs to go pear-shaped in the twilight of his career. I reckon he'll let me take the lead. No choice but to. And the very thought of getting him out of his pinstripe suit and salmon-pink shirt and into some local Abu Dhabi garb is irresistible.

I can't help but laugh.

Unexpectedly, against all odds, I'm starting to enjoy myself. How fucked up is that?

Mohammed, our cabbie, heads for the souk. We park somewhere inconspicuous, whilst Irani and Mo' head off to score us some local gear approximately her size, and that of Sebastian and me.

Fifteen minutes later they're back, mission accomplished. We head for the Hilton, in Corniche Road, five minutes' walk from the commercial district. There's still no sign of anything suspicious, so I reckon we've shaken off Bubba and the Bubblets way back.

We check in. We've been reserved rooms on the same floor, adjacent to each other. No cattle class for me here then. We take the elevator, dump our gear, and Sebastian sets to checking out the contents of the bags. He scrutinizes every piece minutely, and it's a good forty-five minutes before he finally breathes a sigh of relief.

'Happy to announce they're all present and correct,' he beams. 'Not a single stone missing, old boy.'

Sebastian seems overjoyed. I guess that was always his biggest worry: that one of Bubba's gang might have ripped off and pilfered a rock. Maybe the entire bigger-picture threat – that of the diamond heist of the century – has escaped him. I can't quite believe that anyone can be so lacking in awareness, but with Sebastian anything's possible.

The two of us head straight for the lobby, where we check the sports bags into the hotel safe. Once locked in there they're fully covered by the hotel's insurance, Sebastian assures me. Safe as houses.

This is the first time since taking possession of those two Adidas sports bags that I've relinquished control. I feel like a massive weight's been lifted off my shoulders. I'm suddenly aware of how totally knackered I am.

We're not expecting the sheikh to show for several hours, so I head to my room for some kip. It's the first rule of being on operations: never miss the chance of a good feed or a good sleep. You never know when you might be getting your next.

I wake and it's late afternoon. I've slept most of the day and I'm feeling great. I go to leave the room, and for a moment I'm searching for those two bags of rocks. Then I catch myself. *Silly fucker. They're locked away in the hotel safe.*

Whilst waiting for the sheikh to show, Sebastian and Irani have decided to get some time in by the hotel pool. That's where I find them. I figure it's as good a moment as any to discuss the standard operating procedures (SOPs) we're going to adopt from now on with this job.

I explain to Irani and Sebastian that the next time we're heading out of the hotel with the rocks, we're going to make like locals. When sitting in a vehicle dressed in those headscarves, robes, and wearing dark shades, we'll be pretty much indistinguishable from your average Abu Dhabian.

And whatever car Sebastian has got lined up for us, it had better blend in with the local traffic. If not, I'm giving Mo'-the-cabbie a call again, and hiring him for the duration.

Sebastian tries to raise a half-hearted objection to what I'm suggesting, but in truth he seems glad to let me take the lead. But only so far.

I want them to consider the 'what-ifs', and take on board an agreed set of actions should a particular situation arise. I've compiled a list of the local emergency services, and I want to sort a series of actions-on with Sebastian and Irani – our collective responses to various scenarios.

I start with what-if there's a fire in the hotel. I suggest our actions-on should be that whoever is nearest to the hotel reception gets the diamonds out of the safe, as a first priority. We make sure we get that done before following the hotel fire drill.

Sebastian seems perplexed. 'Oh really? We do that, old boy? Why would we want to do that?'

'Cause the safe's in the basement,' I explain. 'And down there in a good fire all the jewellery'll get melted to fuck.'

Sebastian shrugs. 'Well, I must say I really hadn't thought about it. I was more worried about getting a tan, and the office getting all upset that I've not been working hard enough.'

Maybe this is Sebastian's attempt at humour. Either way I'm starting to get a sense of what it's like doing contracts in the civvy world. No one really gives a damn until it all goes to ratshit, and then they turn to guys like me to save the day.

I posit the next what-if: What do we do if our car is followed? I suggest we should have a back-up vehicle, whenever we take the rocks anywhere out of the hotel.

I explain that at present we have no measures in place to guarantee security whilst the rocks are in transit across the city. I keep pushing it, but the more I do the more I sense that Sebastian and Irani are starting to actively resent me.

Well, I'm not here to be their mate. I'm here to keep them and the diamonds safe. Trouble is, I'm not writing the cheques. I need Sebastian to rubber-stamp and bankroll any security measures I want put in place here.

As I argue for why such things are absolutely vital, I can see the two of them drifting away into thoughts of another Pimm's, and the possibility of a sumptuous dinner in the sheikh's palace.

Plus the juicy promise of making some seriously big diamond deals.

CHAPTER 8

For several hours the sheikh fails to show. Finally, Omer, his right-hand man, puts in an appearance at the hotel that evening.

'There is nothing today,' he tells us, waving his hand dismissively. 'The sheikh will be able to see you tomorrow, I am sure. For now we go eat.'

En route to Omer's favourite restaurant he makes it clear that the sheikh wouldn't be seen dead in the Hilton. To him, the three of us are just grovelling tradesmen, and we should expect to be treated as such. We have to go to his palace if we want to sell him some bling.

We arrive at what Omer assures us is the finest restaurant in Abu Dhabi. It's a fish house, and I notice that there's a VIP area. I ask Omer if that's where the important people sit, and he immediately demands that the four of us be seated there. I know now that I can play him.

It's clear that we've fallen into the strange embrace of the sheikh's schizoid hospitality. Whilst we may be despised tradesmen, we're to be treated to the very best. One hint to the sheikh that Omer's given us anything less than a splendid time, and that'll be it – curtains for Omer.

Once I've understood this, I know how to work Omer, and I let him know that I know. Pretty quickly, I figure I can shift my security demands onto him. I'll make it the sheikh's responsibility to ensure the security of the rocks, at least whilst we are the 'honoured guests' in his sheikhdom.

Over the following days the sheikh continues to fail to meet us, and I continue working my demands into Omer. A back-up car for when we shift the rocks; an armed guard force from the sheikh's personal bodyguard, as escort; a series of actions-on that I get the guard force to train for: all if it is 'no problem' for Omer.

I even come close to getting my hands on a weapon. But at the last moment Omer bottles out of handing an AK47 to a 'round-eye', as he calls us whiteys.

Five weeks pass like this, waiting for the sheikh. We keep getting stood-to, to go visit his palace, and he keeps calling it off at the last minute. There's only so much time you can kill lounging by the pool, and it's driving me stir-crazy. Finally, we're given the green light: *he is going to see us today.*

I can't resist letting Sebastian go and dress in his local garb. He emerges into the hotel lobby looking one hundred per cent like a fish out of water. Standing still he might just pass as an unusually tall, stooping Arab, but as soon as he starts walking the cover's blown. He has the stiff-legged, English-gentleman glide to him. Impossible to hide.

I let him know now that there's no need to make like a local. We've got Omer, the back-up car, plus the sheikh's bodyguard team. It's fine being overt, if you've got the firepower and back-up to support it. We're as safe as we're ever going to be running diamonds across Abu Dhabi, and Sebastian can dispense with the local disguise.

Sebastian hurries upstairs. Five minutes later he's back, dapper and beaming in pinstripe and pink. We mount up the lead car, and

I give the green light to proceed. As we set off across the city, I'm wondering what exactly to expect of the sheikh.

We pitch up at the gates to this glistening palace, and we're waved through without stopping, just as I'd drilled them. I gaze around me, and its flunky central here. There are tiny figures mowing the grass, sweeping driveways, and trimming verges every which way I look. I have to admit it's impressive. Very.

But instead of taking the long, sweeping drive that leads to this wedding cake of layered white steps at the front of the palace, we turn left and are whisked around to the rear. It's worse than using the tradesmen's entrance: we're ushered into the servants' quarters.

The first hint of the sheikh's arrival is the influx of a retinue of lackeys. They start grovelling around and dropping pink rose petals along what I guess must be the path he's going to take. Those not dropping petals are spraying the air with incense.

It strikes me the sheikh must have a serious body odour problem to require all of this. And then I realize that maybe it's the other way around. Maybe the sheikh doesn't want to have to sniff the unclean air where the servants live, and where tradesmen come to hawk their wares.

In he comes. He's overweight, his bulk enveloped in the flowing folds of his robes. Plus he's glacially distant and supercilious.

Sebastian's spent the best part of an hour getting the goods displayed as best he can on one of the tables in the servants' quarters. The sheikh bends to inspect a diamond-encrusted bracelet.

He picks it up in his chubby fingers, turns it over a couple of times while it glints magically in the sunlight, then flings it across the table at us.

'This is not what I want to see.'

At this point I'd like nothing more that to chin the fat, arrogant son-of-a-bitch. Five weeks of tension and boredom, only to have two million quid's worth of jewellery thrown back in our faces.

He turns around to leave. He flicks a hand over his shoulder. 'I don't wish to see any more. But perhaps the sheikh-her will.'

With that he waddles away, and he's gone.

We do a reverse journey back across the city to the hotel. En route I'm fuming. All that work, all that preparation and planning, plus the five weeks we've been kept waiting – and we get barely ten seconds of the arrogant prick's time. *Fucking unbelievable.*

But Sebastian seems to have taken it all in his stride. 'I'm afraid that's just how these types do business.' He shrugs. 'Needs must, old boy.'

He explains that the 'sheikh-her' is the big man's fiancée. Sebastian's only chance of making a sale now rests with her wanting to see the diamonds. Trouble is, as males and infidels we're not allowed to even speak to the sheikh-her, let alone to meet her.

I sense it's going to be a tricky business getting her together with the diamonds with any remote degree of security.

Omer is our go-between. The day after our abortive meeting with the sheikh, he pitches up at the hotel in white jeans and pink flip-flops. Up until now he's worn either local garb, or a smart Western-style suit. I can't help doing a double-take. He looks gayer even than Sebastian.

Omer explains that it's a Friday, the start of the weekend in the Gulf, and so he's in his 'weekend attire'. Fair enough. He confirms that he's spoken with the sheikh-her, and she does want to see our wares. The challenge is, how to get this sorted.

'You see, you must not even look at this magnificent women,' Omer explains. He waggles his finger at us. 'Not even the windows of her car.'

Omer suggests we rendezvous with the sheikh-her's driver in a

McDonald's car park, in downtown Abu Dhabi. Oh, and we're not allowed to look at the driver, either. We're to keep our eyes shielded as she collects the diamonds, and drives them to an undisclosed location at which the sheikh-her will examine them.

I'm flabbergasted at this so-called plan. It's got more holes in it than a leaky sieve. But Sebastian seems to think it all perfectly fine. Either he's desperate to make a deal, or the sun's fried his brain. Once Omer's departed, I make my feelings known to him.

'Sebastian, mate, are you seriously suggesting you want me to hand over the goods to some woman we can't even get a look at to ID her, and she's going to drive off with them to some place we have no idea where it is . . .? Mate, if you're happy with this I'll let it go down. But if you listen to my advice, I wouldn't bloody go there.'

Sebastian shrugs. 'I'm afraid that's just how they do business around here, old boy.' He gives me a weak grin. 'Needs must and all that.'

The following afternoon we pitch up in the McDonald's car park, just as planned. We wait an hour in the baking heat, and finally this big black sedan pulls up next to us. I hand over the two precious bags to Omer, feeling like a total wanker as I do so.

'Remember to please keep your eyes shielded,' he remarks, as he takes them.

I'm doing nothing of the bloody sort. The glass of our vehicle is tinted, and no way can either Omer or the driver see in. I'm going to get as good a look as I can at the bloody sheikh-her's driver.

The window hisses down, and there she is sitting in her seat wearing full-on black robes from head to toe, but with these massive, gold-plated Gucci shades perched on her nose. Omer's grovelling and practically bowing onto the tarmac as he hands over our precious bags – and that's to the sheikh-her's *driver*.

The window hisses up again and the sedan's gone. I get a good look at the licence plate, and make a mental note of it. It's all probably entirely futile – we've just willingly handed over £50 million worth of diamonds to complete strangers – but I haven't completely given up on the job that I'm here to do.

We have no option but to file into the McDonald's, where we sit in uncomfortable silence drinking brews. Three hours later the sedan returns. Driver-lady hands the bags back to Omer, who hands them back to us. In our car and well out of sight, Sebastian begins to count and catalogue the rocks a tad nervously.

Back at the Hilton I check the bags into the safe, and I'm glad to be done with the bloody things.

Omer takes a call on his mobile. From his expression, I can tell it must be the Great Lady herself – the sheikh-her. He finishes the call, and informs Sebastian about which pieces she may be interested in.

The problem now is the price. And so the haggling begins.

But as for me, I'm sick to death by now of the bloody rocks.

CHAPTER 9

We're out of Abu Dhabi a couple of days later, and not a moment too soon as far as I'm concerned. I've had more than a bellyful of the place. Sebastian's tried to keep it quiet, but he's failed to make a single sale. After messing us around for six weeks or more, the sheikh and his fiancée have haggled so hard that Sebastian has had to decline to do business with them.

As we go through the airport, I make sure that we give Bubba and his boys the widest berth possible. And joy of joys, the flight back is heavenly empty, even in cattle class. I get four seats to myself, and discover that two bags of diamonds make a passable, if lumpy, pillow.

Kelvin is there to meet us at the airport, and he ferries me back to the NCP car park to collect my wagon. It's been sat there for approaching seven weeks, and the bill is horrendous. Not that it's my concern: Hemley's are paying.

I head for home looking blacker than a witch's tit, from all the time spent lounging around the hotel pool. And I've got a bank account with a very healthy balance, thanks to sixty-four days on Hemley's payroll.

I figure the costs to Hemley's of the trip must be well in excess of £100,000, and all for no sale. But as far as I'm concerned, it's

Mission One on the circuit accomplished. In spite of the abysmal security arrangements, the goods are back in Hemley's vault without a single rock missing.

Job done.

At times the buzz of doing that £50 million diamond run almost came close to being in a good firefight with The Regiment. *Almost.* But the sheer arrogance and greed of that pampered sheikh really stuck in my craw.

I could have retired on the proceeds of selling just the one piece of jewellery he so contemptuously threw across the table. My past life couldn't have been further removed from Hemley's London diamond-dealing halls, or the glittering Abu Dhabi palace of that Arab sheikh.

I was born Wayne Smith to an unmarried couple who already had the one son. My mother and father, Della and Martin, had something of an on–off relationship. Martin was a painter and decorator, and money was always tight. Once I came along, Martin left Della pretty much for good.

Della found herself having to juggle single parenthood, work, and the pressures of looking after a baby boy. She couldn't cope. I was put up for adoption aged six months. I was a sickly baby, and by the time my adoptive parents came to visit me I was in the intensive care unit at the local hospital, with severe intestinal problems.

Alan and Audrey Campion already had the one adopted child, a little girl called Anne. Audrey had given up work to look after Anne, and Alan had recently been suspended from his job. He worked shunting trains on the Southampton docks, but he'd been accused of running a cigarette-smuggling racket along with the ships' crews.

With neither of them working, Audrey and Alan had fallen upon hard times. Even so, they reckoned they still needed a son to 'round off' the family. They came to visit me at the hospital in a motorcycle and sidecar, and when I was finally well enough to travel back to Southampton with them, that was how I went – bundled in blankets and stuffed onto Audrey's lap in the sidecar.

Alan and Audrey lived in a small semi on Southampton's Harefield Estate, a sprawl of council housing in a pretty rough part of town. They had pretensions to being upstanding, churchgoing middle-class folks, without the means of being so.

They renamed me Philip Lewis Alexander Campion, and severed all contact with my blood parents. On the outside we appeared to be a good, respectable family, and Audrey did all she could to hide our penury from outsiders. But behind closed doors my adopted father started taking out his frustrations regarding work, and money, on me.

From my earliest memories Alan was beating me, and for no apparent reason. The beatings got steadily worse, and my nose was repeatedly punched in by my sadistic 'father'.

I can remember getting ready for school one day, and taking an early morning punch in the face from Alan. The blood from my flattened nose was splattered red across my white shirt. Audrey changed it with a cold, rough detachment, as if it was my fault that I'd been punched in the face.

I never would be able to forgive Audrey for not standing up for me. I never could understand why she acted as if it was my fault that I was getting beaten. I was never once taken to a doctor, and so it wasn't until years later that the repeated fractures of my infant nose were diagnosed – and all at the hands of my so-called father.

As time went on the money worries worsened, and Alan started to beat Audrey too. Finally she decided she'd had enough. Audrey divorced Alan, and took little Anne and myself with her. She had recently received a lump of cash – her inheritance from her parents – and part of the court settlement was that she buy the three of us a home.

For a while life seemed to brighten, but then Audrey started suffering from these dark depressions. She'd go missing for days on end, only to be discovered wandering around in a wood where she'd tried to commit suicide. I remember my big sister Anne walking me to primary school, and watching as the police chased my 'mother' across an open field. She was shrieking hysterically, and I was dying with embarrassment inside.

When she wasn't running off and going loopy, Audrey took over from Alan on the violence front. She beat Anne mercilessly, but when she figured she'd try the same on me, I decided to give it back to her.

I was six years old by now, and big for my age. I wasn't going to let my adoptive mother get away with all that Alan had. It was the first time in my life that I'd really stood up for myself, and fought back. It felt good.

But still Audrey did her best to make life hell for me. She dressed me like an upper-class twit, in tweedy jackets and paisley shirts buttoned to the neck. She never bought me anything remotely fashionable, and she cut my hair in a floppy posh-boy fringe that tumbled over my eyes.

I was attending a state school populated largely by working-class kids, and it was hardly surprising that they started picking on me. When I told Audrey about the bullying, all she had to say to me was this: 'He who doesn't fight but runs away, lives to fight another day.'

I figured I had three options: run, fight or go under. I tried running, but that just made me seem like a coward, and that in turn goaded the bullies into trying to get me all the more. I'd taken repeated punches in the face from Alan, so I wasn't unused to a beating. Alan's fists, and the power behind them, were far worse than anything those school kids could throw at me physically.

I decided to stand and fight. At first I took some beatings, but gradually I started to give as good as I got. And I learned that the only way to stop the bullies was to fight them fearlessly. It didn't mean I didn't feel fear: I just couldn't ever show it.

Show fear and you're finished. That was the lesson of those first playground brawls.

As a result of all the fighting, I was referred to an educational psychologist for being 'disruptive'. As far as I was concerned, I was fighting for my survival, and that's exactly what I told her.

After Alan's abusive behaviour, Audrey seemed to turn against men in general. In spite of my youth I became her number one target. She never fed me enough, but she did boil choice fillets of fish for the cat. I began stealing them from the cat's bowl, whenever Audrey's back was turned, and ideally before the cat had slobbered all over it.

Still I was permanently hungry. I was never given any pocket money, like all my schoolmates were. That prevented me from going down to the shops, to buy sweets or toys. Again, it was something that marked me out as a misfit.

I resolved to deal with the lack of food and money in the only way I could – by thieving. I was seven years old when the church poor box in town started taking a hammering. I viewed the thieving as a necessity of survival. I used the money to buy fish and chips to fatten myself up a little.

I took on a paper round to earn some legal money. Eventually, I was accused of stealing £5.36 of my takings. Had I stolen the cash? Of course I had. I'd spent it on food. Again, it was all about survival. The owner of the newsagents took me to court, and I decided to plead not guilty.

Whilst the court case was pending, Audrey and I started to fight as never before. She accused me of being an embarrassment to the family. I told her she was a useless, cruel, spiteful mother. I meant every word of it, too. Eventually, the inevitable happened: the Social Services took me away from Audrey and put me into a children's reception centre called Willow Lodge.

Willow Lodge was basically somewhere they sent troubled kids, while they tried to decide exactly what to do with them. Normally, having a court case pending would give you some credibility in a kids' home, but not when you were accused of stealing your paper-round money.

The fact that I was pleading not guilty did redeem me to a certain extent, for it meant I was trying to beat the system. The trial of the century got under way. I dressed for it in my finest Audrey nobby gear, in an effort to impress the judge, and stuck to my not guilty plea.

I guess it must have worked, for I was acquitted. I'd beaten 'the system', thrown off the charges of stealing £5.36, which in turn earned me some 'respect' with my peers in the kids' home. Even the staff at Willow Lodge seemed to hold me in a little more esteem. But a few weeks after winning the case I absconded from Willow Lodge. I did so because of the boredom, and because I hated being locked up. I spent days living rough in the woods, sleeping wild and scavenging whatever I could find to eat.

Running away became a regular thing with me. I teamed up with Mick, another lad from the kids' home. We would head for a deserted railway siding and sleep out in one of the railcars. The police would be alerted whenever we went missing, but it was too much of a pain to go chasing after us.

We'd shoplift whatever we needed to eat. One of us would keep watch and cause a distraction, whilst the other stuffed his waistband full of food. We'd head for our camp deep in the woods, and feast on our ill-gotten gains. We always had a fallback plan if it all went wrong, and an emergency place to meet if we were split up.

Years later, I'd find myself putting such survival skills to good use in the SAS, and on the lawless world of the circuit.

CHAPTER 10

In the spring of 2002 I get the shout for the big one in terms of private security work: Afghanistan. I've been out of The Regiment for over a year now, and I'm craving some real action. It's some six months after 9/11, and the Afghan capital, Kabul, has been liberated from the Taliban by US and British forces.

Again, I take a call from my ex-SAS mate who runs the private security firm Omega One – 'Double Zero' it's called in the trade. Hemley's had few complaints about my Abu Dhabi job, and I've started to build a reputation as a private operator.

I say yes to the job over the phone, although I've got few details of where I'm going or what it will entail. In truth, I'm desperate for the cash. It's got so bad that for the first time in my life I've signed on the dole, and been into the local job centre looking for work.

I'd spent an entire afternoon doing a job seeker's interview with a woman I guess was trying to be helpful. She asked me what I expected to earn in terms of an annual salary. I told her £50,000 a year, which was a fair wage at that time working the circuit.

She'd consulted her computer, and told me the only thing she had vaguely suiting the security-sector profile was a vacancy for a lollipop lady/person in nearby Ramsgate. She checked out the wage the local council was offering. From the way she was laughing, I guessed that a Kent lollipop person would earn marginally more than a Jordanian goat-herder.

By contrast, the Afghan security job is offering to pay top dollar. Basically, it entails setting up a team from scratch to look after a pan-European embassy that's going to be based in Kabul. It comes with full diplomatic privileges and immunity, weapons passes, plus a large weekly paycheck.

We're going to be a four-man team of 'white-eyes' – foreign contractors – with a far larger Afghan security staff under us. It's a set-up job, which means we can run the operation just as we want to.

I head for London to meet the rest of the Afghan team. Tommo is the team leader, and I'm his second-in-command. Like me he's ex-Regiment, but from a generation above. He'd got out once, hated civvy street, and gone back in again. He's just come out for a second try. Tommo is tall, balding, craggy and clean-shaven. He's pushing fifty, very capable, and he's got bags of operational experience. He's a cracking bloke, and I can think of no one better to lead our team into Afghanistan.

Next in the team is Chris, a tall, lean, well-spoken ex-RAF door-gunner. Having flown in on countless operations with the RAF, I've got nothing but admiration for the bravery and ability of their aircrew. But being skilled in Chinook or Lynx operations doesn't necessarily mean you can survive on the streets of Kabul. It's a risky time to be going in, directly in the aftermath of the Taliban's fall. Kabul is a total security vacuum. There's little infrastructure, security, food or whatever. At times the locals are still queuing on the streets for UN rations, the supply lines into the city are so strung out and chaotic.

I sense that Chris is a good bloke, but I'm worried about his experience under fire – for sure as eggs is eggs we'll be getting into some shit fights on this one.

Lastly, there's Micky, or 'Micky Mouser the Scouser', as he's know to his mates. Micky's ex-French Foreign Legion. He's a thickset, dumpy, squat bloke, with a diamond tattoo on his left ear.

I've never worked with an ex-Legionnaire before, so Dave's a complete unknown. He looks tough and capable, and I figure Omega One wouldn't have hired him if he didn't know his onions.

We get a final briefing on the job from the Johnno, the head of Omega One.

'You're going in to look after the embassy's Ambassador and staff. He's already there in Kabul, plus there's one armoured vehicle available to you. Unfortunately, it's a $200,000 Mercedes G-Wagon, so it's too good for the job at hand. It can't take dirty fuel, or handle the worst of the roads in Afghanistan.

'The Ambassador's ordered a weapons package for you – one that we drew up – but it'll take time to reach you. In the meantime, you may have to source weapons locally. Expect no military back-up to be around or available. At present, there's no compound security, no cooking facilities, no bedding and no beds. You'll be taking sleeping bags and kipping in the empty shell of a building.

'That's the bad news, and that's why the money's good,' Johnno continues. 'The good news is the contract's open-ended, so for those of you who want it there's as much work as you like. We can keep you guys contracted for as long as you've got the appetite for it.'

That last bit is music to my ears. Broke Ramsgate lollipop person, or gun-for-hire in Kabul on an open-ended, juicy contract? As far as I'm concerned it's a no-brainer.

Before leaving for Afghanistan, I go down to the job centre to sign off, as you have to. Some bloke is free, but I wait until I can see the same woman as before. I tell her I need her to sign me off, as I've landed myself a job.

She snatches the paperwork. 'Show me,' she demands.

'There you go, love,' I tell her. 'Now that's a security contract.'

She seems hugely miffed. Her attitude is like: *How can this man possibly earn this kind of money?* As I leave her dingy office, I vow that from that day onwards I am never going into a job centre again.

Tommo and I travel out first, taking Prayers-In-the-Air (Pakistan International Airways – PIA) to Islamabad. There we transit onto a light aircraft operated by the UN, which is full of UN do-gooder types. It flies into Kabul International Airport, set on the outskirts of Kabul.

As we come in to land I can appreciate the challenges of fighting any wars here. Kabul is surrounded by towering hills, and all roads out wind through horrendous mountain passes. The only vaguely safe way to travel across the country is by air.

We touch down in a cloud of dust, wrecked aircraft and old anti-aircraft posts scattered all around. As with the Abu Dhabi diamond run, we're going in unarmed and unsupported. Our apprehension levels are high. We don't know what will happen on the ground here at the airport. We've been told we'll be picked up by a driver, but there are no guarantees. And in contrast to Abu Dhabi, Afghan is a full-on conflict zone. Going in unarmed and unsupported and with naff-all intelligence isn't ideal. But as Sebastian would say: *Needs must, old boy.*

Tommo and I make it to the door of the aircraft, only to be confronted by two shaven-headed guys in plain combat-style clothes, plus shades. They have badly concealed lumps in their clothing, and they are clearly US intelligence types. As we climb down the steps, I can feel their eyes following us. It's as if they've been awaiting our arrival.

They follow us into the terminal, which is more of a ruined old shed. They're shadowing our every move. Every time we stop, they stop. Every time we move, they move. They have the surveillance skills of a clown on a unicycle. Tommo and I are torn between finding it hilarious and hugely annoying.

There are fifty pages of passport stamps to get before we're finally allowed through. The two CIA dickheads are still on our heels. We exit the terminal, and Tommo sets off as if heading for the car park.

Suddenly he stops dead, and the lead follower cannons into the back of him.

'Can I help you, mate?' Tommo demands. 'You make a habit of walking into people?'

The lead CIA dude is glowing with embarrassment, like we've suddenly blown his cover. As for me, I'm cracking up with laughter.

'Erm, jeez, you talking to me . . .' he stutters.

Tommo lets him know we've pinged the both of them, and they scuttle off back into the terminal. Idiots.

There's a 4×4 with diplomatic plates waiting in the car park. The driver leans out and waves at us, grinning ear to ear.

'Mr Tommo? Mr Phil? Welcome to Afghanistan,' he calls over. 'Come put your big bags in my vehicle.'

The driver introduces himself to us as Dilaka. He's about as big and as sweaty as Bubba was in the Abu Dhabi customs hall, but that's where the similarity ends. He's clearly totally barking, but in an entirely likeable kind of way.

He weaves the car into the traffic headed for Kabul, and he's talking nineteen-to-the-dozen as he does so. He explains that he taught himself to speak English, which isn't half bad.

He's clearly only recently graduated from the donkey cart, the way he drives the 4×4. It's a brand-new Mitsubishi Pajero, and he's pleased as punch at being behind the wheel with a couple of white-eyes as his passengers.

Dilaka keeps leaning out the window and giving the fist to anyone who gets remotely in our way. He seems to know everyone this side of Jalalabad. He keeps honking at his mates, so he can show the wagon off. Then he takes us on a quick circle three times around his house, so he can show us off to his family.

Still, I can't help but like Dilaka, and I sense that he's going to be very useful to us here.

'Dilaka, you're the Ali Baba of Kabul, mate,' I tell him.

'I no Ali Baba,' he laughs, taking both hands from the wheel and slapping his forehead. 'I no Ali Baba.'

'Yes you friggin are, mate. Now hands back on the wheel!'

It's not my first time in Afghanistan, but it is in Kabul. Tommo's too. One side of the city is a scene of utter devastation, like nothing we've ever seen before. It's a grey, grainy flattened moonscape. The tumbled, blasted ruins remind me of a scene from the Blitz – whole neighbourhoods pulverized, ripped apart as far as the eye can see. It's a testament to the decades of brutal fighting that have ground this city into hopeless ruin.

Once I'm done gawping at the destruction, the next thing I notice is the packs of stray dogs. A sure fucked-up combat and death-count indicator that is, especially bearing in mind how well fed these mutts look – grotesquely fat in some cases.

That can only mean one thing: a sudden glut of fresh meat on the streets. Animals adapt to a combat situation as quickly as humans do. Often quicker. They have no conscience like humans, no taboos never to be broken. In war, with bodies left lying on the streets, packs of stray dogs do the obvious and eat them.

Looks like they've been having a right feast of it here in Kabul.

CHAPTER 11

This sort of stuff doesn't exactly faze me. I'm expecting Kabul to be a chaotic, war-torn wasteland. I've seen the UN tree-huggers get off the plane at Bagram, and go all frosty-eyed at how beautiful and magical the scenery is.

Well, the mountains are awesome. That's true. I can't wait to get in amongst them, that's if I get the chance. But Kabul most definitely isn't. It's a tinpot shithole of a place. I've been in enough of them to know how to recognize one, and know what to expect.

The city is crawling with people, and the next thing I notice is the lack of womanly flesh on the streets. The tree-huggers will be going ape at every burka they see, that's for sure. *Look at that! How terrible! We need to liberate them!* But as far as I'm concerned it isn't terrible. It's just their way of doing things out here, and who are we to say otherwise? Best to let them get on with it.

Dilaka announces that we're nearing the embassy compound. We're whizzing through Wazir Akbar Khan district, one of the least-blasted areas in the city. This is the upmarket, former diplomatic part of town, and already it's reverting to type. Post-Taliban, new embassies are springing up everywhere.

Big steel gates are thrown back and in we go to the embassy

compound. It consists of a run-down-looking villa for the Ambassador, surrounded by an immaculately tended lawn. There's a guard hut to one side of the front gates, and some low hut-like buildings to the rear.

The Ambo's out, so we go for a poke around the residence. Apart from the one bed upstairs, which we presume is the Ambo's, there's not a stick of furniture anywhere. At one time this must have been a seriously plush residence. The cool, marble-tiled floors are testimony to that. But right now, it feels as if someone has died in here and left their ghost to haunt an empty, echoing shell of a building.

Up until now, the Ambo's been kipping over at the US embassy, one of the few secure buildings in town. We dump our kit in the deserted villa, and Dilaka suggests we drive over to meet him. It's a five-minute journey in good traffic, Dilaka adds, a half-hour when Kabul's gridlocked. Right now the traffic is light and we should be fine.

Dilaka drives up to the end of our street, hangs a left at a junction with a tiny roadside kiosk on it, threads the wagon around the back of the US embassy, and there's the office of the European embassy, right next to the Iraqi embassy. He takes us in so we can meet the boss.

The Ambo's a Swede, name of Steen Erickson. Strictly speaking he's 'His Excellency Steen Erickson', but he's not one to stand on ceremony. He's mid-fifties, tall, lean and craggy-looking, and he's dressed in a woolly cardigan covered in bobbles. There's something of your grandfather about him, but I don't doubt there's hard steel beneath the hand-knitted exterior. He's clearly pleased as punch to have the two of us hooligans pitch up, which doesn't go unnoticed or unappreciated.

He asks us if we've eaten. When we say we haven't, he announces a trip to the Herat Café. I have visions of Kabul's version of the

Abu Dhabi fish house that Omer took us to. Surely, one or two choice eateries must have survived the chaos and the war. We pile into Dilaka's wagon and head for downtown Kabul.

The Herat Café turns out to be a little short of what I had imagined. The Ambo strides in, and he's ushered to his usual table. It's a chipped formica affair, with some plastic chairs to park our arses on.

The first thing I notice is that you can't see the other side of the place for the flies. The second thing I notice is the brevity of the menu. It's a verbal one, delivered by the scruffiest waiter I've ever seen in barely comprehensible English.

'Kebab, or kebab and chips, sirs?'

Spoilt for choice as we are, Tommo and I follow the Ambo's lead and go for kebab and chips.

The Herat Café turns out to have no refrigerator, and the owners keep the meat under the carpet. *Literally.* They don't even try and hide it. It isn't done behind our back or anything.

Having taken our order the waiter grabs a corner of a nearby rug, hoicks it back, peels a handful of kebab sticks out from under it and throws them on the grill pit.

Nice.

The Ambo's watched him do it, and appears to be completely unfazed. I guess we have to act likewise. He is the client after all, and the client is always right, especially one who pays as well as this one.

The Ambo tells us how he had a British security team in Nigeria, his previous post, and what superlative operators those guys were. He loves the fact that we're here, and for that I figure I can forgive him even the Herat Café. But it doesn't stop me from tootling off to have a nose around the kitchen. In short, Gordon Ramsey would have piled in if he'd taken a look at the place. He's experienced fuck-all compared with the sight and smell of the kitchen at the Herat.

Surprisingly, the chips turn out to be okay, as long as you put enough salt and pepper on them. After feasting at the Herat, the Ambo whisks us back to the office, to meet the rest of his staff.

Hercule, the chargé d'affaires, turns out to be this big fat French guy who speaks like the lead actor in 'Allo 'Allo! I've always believed that France is a lovely place ruined by the French: this guy is the living proof of that. He can't conceal his displeasure that we're Brits, can't understand why there isn't a French security detail, and why the language of the embassy isn't French for that matter. In short, he's a typical look-down-his-nose-at-you Froggie twat.

There's another Frenchman there – Hercule's assistant – who is even more of a wanker. Pepe is his name, and he is a complete tree-hugging idiot. He makes it abundantly clear that having a security detail is an unnecessary extravagance as far as he's concerned, and more of a danger than a safeguard.

Pepe and Hercule seem to be running a who-can-be-the-most-condescending-twat competition, especially when dealing with the local Afghans. Their offices are stuffed with Afghan servants, whom they seem to think they should treat like their pets.

Fortunately, we answer to the Ambo only, so it's all good. And it's clear as day that he shares our lack of enthusiasm for the French contingent. Could I imagine portly Hercule or nobby Pepe eating at the Herat? Could I fuck. Maybe that's why the Ambo insists on eating there: It's the only way to shake off the Froggies.

The niceties over, it's time to get down to business. We ask the Ambo what gear he has for us. He shows us a pile of comms kit, helmets and body armour. The latter looks like he's procured it from Mothercare: it's like a baby-changing mat with a head hole at one end.

Tommo and I explain how the weight of the body armour alone makes it unusable. All it'll serve to do is keep your torso intact as your arms and legs get blown off. Plus we show him how the rear plate will ride up when sitting in a vehicle, snapping your neck in the process. I can see me putting in a call to Francis at Guartel to order us half-a-dozen of his Kevlar beauties.

But our real problem isn't the Ambo's poor taste in body armour. It's our lack of weaponry. He shows us the shipment he's asked for, and there's some choice gear on order, but he has little idea when it might actually arrive in Kabul. And Hercule's supposed to be on the case, which probably means it will never get here. Hercule's a typical tree-hugger type. He'd rather use Myra Hindley as a babysitter than have a properly armed security detail.

There's little to be done about it today. Evening's already upon us, and there's a curfew been imposed on Kabul during the hours of darkness. The only way to pass through the Afghan Army road-blocks at night is to know the right password. They're issued daily in Farsi, and more often than not they're utterly unpronounceable. Dilaka whisks us back to the Ambo's residence before night swamps the streets.

During my years serving in the military I'd learned to appreciate the value of local knowledge, and the intelligence it can yield. You can have all the advantages of satellite imagery, surveillance drones and communications intercepts, but nothing beats the intel you can glean from a local person on the ground.

It can come from any number of sources: taxi drivers, shop-keepers, waiters and just everyday folks you meet on the streets. Local knowledge from a trusted source is gold dust. Of course, you have to make the call on how much you can rely on an individual. And even then you stick to the TNF – Trust No Fucker – rule.

But here in Kabul, I reckon Dilaka's going to be our local source diamond class. On the drive back to the embassy residence I raise the issue with him that's foremost in my mind: scoring some 'toofangchai', Farsi slang for pistols. Plus a couple of AK47s would be nice, and anything else that he can get for us.

Dilaka makes a big act of umming and aaahing, which I guess is to drive up the price. It's a fine show of this-is-going-to-be-a-hard-one-lads. He tells us he'll make some inquiries, and we should speak about it the following day. But he stresses that it won't be easy.

We reach the residence, and in time-honoured fashion Tommo and I sling our hammocks in one of the huts to the rear of the main building. It's got an earthen floor, and no electricity, but we've both slept in worse.

We're unarmed. The two Afghan gate guards are armed only with wooden batons like broomsticks, and they look about as much use as an ashtray on a motorbike. But Tommo and I stick to the first rule of proper soldiering: never refuse a good feed or a kip.

We take to our hammocks and zone out.

CHAPTER 12

Over the years spent soldiering in far-flung parts of the world, I'd come to believe firmly in the adage that 'Experience is the knowledge that endures'. By immersing yourself in a foreign culture you can acquire a depth of knowledge that enables you to make the right judgements at the right time. You can be 'streetwise' in their world. Whatever you like to call it. And it can prove a lifesaver.

Here in 'Afghan' – no 'white-eye' operator calls the country anything other than Afghan for long – the first priority is to learn the local lingo. Ever since setting foot in his vehicle I've been working on Dilaka brushing up my basic Farsi.

The day after I asked him about scoring some 'toofangchai', Dilaka tells me he's come up trumps. He's found a bloke who has the weapons for us, both pistols and longs. The only question is, where do we make the rendezvous to inspect the goods?

We insist on doing so at a time and place of our choosing. We pick a stretch of the Airport Road, which we know has a US military checkpoint at either end. That gives us some sense of security. We also plan to get a back-up vehicle into position early, where it can get eyes on the meeting point.

We've got line-of-sight radios provided by the Ambo. We figure one of us can be in the watching car, radioing details of what they see to those in the embassy's one armoured vehicle, the Mercedes G-Wagon. That way, we'll be forewarned about the arms dealer's arrival, and how many blokes he's got with him.

For all his apparent bravado, Dilaka refuses point-blank to come with us. He's shitting himself. Already he can sense the rubber hosepipes being used on the soles of his feet if we get caught.

By now Chris, the ex-RAF door-gunner, has joined us, so we're three. Tommo has to stay with the Ambo, our High Value Target (HVT), for the team leader has overall responsible for the HVT's security. It's down to Chris and me to score the guns.

I volunteer to make the rendezvous, whilst Chris will drive the back-up watcher car. It strikes me as being somewhat fucking insane as I head down the Airport Road at dusk, and alone in the armoured G-Wagon. But fuck it: *Needs must, old boy.*

I pull up behind this yellow taxi, the vehicle I've been told to meet. This fat, well-fed local guy gets out and walks to the door of my vehicle. He doesn't seem pleased to see me on my own, minus the driver.

One white-eye; no Dilaka. He's clearly pissed as hell. He refuses to get into the G-Wagon. Instead, he gestures for me to follow him.

In the military I was taught the subtleties of learning to read body language. We learned how to detect when someone was actually posturing for trouble. People often telegraph their intent, and as so much of what we used to do was about dealing with local warlords, militias and other volatile groups, being able to read the trouble signs was invaluable tradecraft.

People who are easy in their mindset demonstrate it in their appearance: there's no need to stand up and make themselves appear bigger, or thrust out their chest. They move slower, and are not always searching for back-up or an exit point. And the guy who removes his watch, or has a hand behind his back gripping an ashtray or pistol, is unlikely to be your best friend. In a sense, a lot of this is second nature. But making the process conscious and overt by learning it serves to sharpen it.

Right now, as I watch the Kabul arms dealer stomping off back to his vehicle, I know I'm dealing with someone who's looking for trouble big time. Or at least, he's acting that way.

I figure I don't have much choice but to follow him. I'm out on foot heading towards the yellow taxi. As I move, I bluff checking for a pistol in my belt. And I bluff a glance to the heavens, as if I'm checking for some top cover. It's all a little desperate, but what the hell else am I to do?

Finally, I do a quick exchange on the radio with Chris, over in the watcher vehicle, making sure the gun dealer's seen me make the call. Then I slide into the seat beside him, in the rear of the yellow taxi.

Up front there's another bloke, but he's not saying a word. You can cut the tension with a knife.

'*Mushkila?*' I ask. *Do we have a problem?*

In answer, the fat arms dealer pulls out a pistol from his pocket. I recognize it immediately. It's a Makarov, a Soviet-manufactured 9mm short handgun. About as reliable as a cheap Chinese watch.

Still, it's an okay killing weapon at close range in the rear of a yellow taxi. I'm poised to go for the guy's throat, whilst knocking the pistol arm away so he can't get a clear shot, when he waves the gun at me and says: 'Four hundred dollars.'

With the other hand he reaches under the driver's seat and pulls out an AK47, only it's plain to see that the assault rifle is missing a stock, which makes it next to bloody useless.

'Six hundred dollars,' says the fat bloke, waving the AK about.

I take it from him. There's no magazine, the stock's been snapped off, and there's just a few 7.62mm short rounds – the calibre used by an AK – taped to the side of the weapon.

'What's this?' I ask, in my broken Farsi. I gesture at the broken stock, and laugh. 'What can I do with this?'

He smiles an oily, menacing smile. 'Very fine weapon,' he declares. His English is about as good as my Farsi. 'AK47. Very best. You fix stock. No problem.'

'*Khalas*,' I tell him. It's finished. Bollocksed. Useless. '*Khalas*.'

He's not looking happy.

I reach for the Makarov and check the mag: there's two rounds in there and that's it. I try working the mechanism, but it feels rusty and gummed up to fuck. I can hardly test-fire the pistol to see if it works in the back of a yellow taxi, but I'd be amazed if I could hit a barn door at twenty paces with the thing, that's if it'll fire at all.

The only possible way I can think of killing anyone with either weapon is if they die laughing at the things. I tell the arms dealer as much. He's getting increasingly angry now, and blokey in the front is looking itchy and restless, like he's waiting for a signal.

I decide it's time to get the hell out. I tell him '*Tashacour*' – many thanks, but no thanks – then scootle out the door. I walk at a steady pace towards the G-Wagon, feeling murderous eyes on my back as I do so. And I wonder if one of those two Makarov rounds is about to plant itself between my shoulder blades.

I tell myself that we're on the Airport Road, and the arms dealer knows from the radio chat that I've got back-up. I don't feel as safe as houses exactly, but as clandestine arms dealing goes on the streets of Kabul, we've run this operation by the book.

I reach the G-Wagon and dive inside. Unless they've got an armour-piercing weapon like an RPG in their yellow taxi, I'm safe now. I gun the engine, burn some rubber and head down the road to where Chris picks me up and tails me back to the embassy compound.

I go find Dilaka. I tell him nice try, but I was looking for an arms dealer, not a scrap metal merchant. Maybe something got lost in translation. To be fair, Dilaka does find it quite funny. And he promises to find me some real weaponry, 'Very soon, Mr Phil, very soon.'

Unfortunately, the Ambo has other intentions. The day after my abortive arms deal, he announces that he – which means 'we' – has to undertake a 'little journey'. I'm imagining a drive to the outskirts of Kabul, to liaise with one of the aid agencies, or the military bases located there.

But no. The Ambo's got it into his head that we should drive to Jalalabad, on the eastern border of the country.

The European embassy's role here in Afghanistan is funding development and reconstruction work. Basically, it's helping the people and the country get back on their feet. The embassy finances the work of the European Commission Humanitarian Organisation (ECHO), which will do the rebuilding here on the ground. The Ambo's job is to manage all of that, and he's a great believer in what ECHO can achieve.

So am I. It's admirable stuff, and I'm all for it. But not when it entails driving to Jalalabad with no weapons, no spares for the vehicles – not even jerrycans for extra fuel – no back-up, and no reliable communications system. Our radios are short-range only, cellphones don't work out of Kabul, and the signal on our sat-phones gets blocked by the mountains.

Jalalabad is over 200 kilometres to the east of Kabul, on the borders of Pakistan's lawless North West Frontier Province, and the Tribal Areas. Just to be clear, that's the territory where Osama

Bin Laden and his Al Qaeda cronies are believed to be hiding out, now they've been kicked out of Afghanistan.

In short, the road to Jalalabad is one of the most lawless and dangerous in the world.

Tommo does his best to talk the Ambo out of it, but to no avail. The Ambo's adamant that he's going. Apparently, it's vital that he meets some local Afghan bigwig in Jalalabad, to discuss plans to rebuild the Kabul–Jalalabad road.

Tommo and me are doubtful the G-Wagon will even make it. It's fine around town, but the very weight of the thing on the ruin of the road to Jalalabad may destroy it. I go ask Dilaka for his take on the drive to Jalalabad. Is it really as bad as we've heard?

Dilaka takes one long look at me, then lets out this wail. 'Oh my God! Mr Phil, no Jalalabad! No the road through Sarobi! This is bandit central in Afghanistan.'

That more or less confirms what we've heard. Sarobi sits halfway along the route to Jalalabad. During the war between the Taliban and the Afghan Mujahideen, Sarobi was the territory of the notorious Afghan warlord Gulbudin Hekmatyar, and his bloodthirsty henchman, 'The Dog'.

It's the one place in Afghan that everyone has warned us about. The road from Kabul to Sarobi is known as 'Sniper Alley', the chances of getting shot up there are so high. And if you reach Sarobi itself, that's where you get ambushed, robbed, kidnapped and worse, by Hekmatyar and his band of merry lunatics.

'God be with you,' Dilaka says, throwing up his hands, 'but Sarobi is the one place where no one is spared.'

'You mean God be with *us*, don't you?' I counter. ''Cause you'll be driving the G-Wagon, won't you, Dilaka?'

Dilaka says he'll be honoured to drive us, but somehow I doubt he's going to make it.

Sure enough, when the day of our departure dawns Dilaka phones in sick. Supposedly, he's got food poisoning. Tommo and I joke that he probably ate at the Herat Café. Serves the fucker right if he snuffs it.

We're taking two vehicles: the armoured G-Wagon with the Ambo in it, as the best we can do security-wise, plus Dilaka's Pajero that he's 'too ill' to drive. We load up a couple of crates of bottled water, our personal first-aid kits, plus the useless UN body armour and helmets.

And we're off.

We're less than a week into our time in Kabul, and we're acutely aware of how foolhardy this trip is. But the Ambo's not for turning. He seems convinced that his diplomatic immunity will protect him on the death run to Jalalabad.

We exit Kabul at the crack of dawn, determined to do the journey in one day. We're heading out into the boondocks on a road that the British Army have got seriously whacked on several times during the long history of our wars in Afghan.

As we head east into the mountains, I've got this horrible, sinking feeling. We know there are no Western security forces whatsoever on this route. All there is are a few motley Afghan Army checkpoints. Most of the Afghan Army lads are indistinguishable from the bandits and the Taliban, or they're working for both sides.

In short, the road we are now embarked upon is the Trust No Fucker highway.

If I had put up this plan to my CO in the SAS – three unarmed security dudes driving a High Value Target (HVT) like the Ambo from Kabul to Sarobi in such conditions – I'd have been laughed out of the camp. It's as if Kelvin has been parachuted in from Hemley's to draft the orders.

Yet I guess this is the world of private military operations. As a civvy contractor, you have to bend to the needs of the client. We've got no option but to man up.

Needs must, old boy.

CHAPTER 13

Tommo is in the armoured G-Wagon along with the Ambo, taking up the rear. Chris and I are in the unarmoured Pajero, making up the vanguard. We're taking it unusually slowly, as we don't want to knacker the G-Wagon's suspension. We're following this long, deserted ribbon of a road that stretches to the jagged horizon, climbing across high knife-edge ridges and plunging into dark valleys. The Pajero's going up and down like a whore's knickers on payday.

I hate to think how the G-Wagon's faring. I figure there's more chance of Nelson getting his eye back than the G-Wagon making it all the way to Jalalabad. But at least the Ambo can't say we didn't warn him.

After several hours at a painfully slow pace, we make it onto the bottom road that cuts through the valley of Sarobi. Already it's pushing past midday, and the one thing that's absolutely vital is that we make it to Jalalabad in daylight. Come nightfall, the journey will be suicide.

Sarobi sits in a sweeping valley, with a dam set between high mountains. There's a jewel of a lake, which during peacetime used to be dotted with tiny fishing boats. Pomegranate orchards on the lakeside produced delicious fruit, and before the decades of war here this was a playground for Afghans day-tripping out of Kabul.

But that was then and this is now. Sarobi sits in the valley of death, and we're deep in the heart of its shadow.

The first sign that we're approaching Sarobi town proper is a checkpoint that looms in the distance. There's a scruffy crew gathered around a couple of white pickups, each with a heavy machine gun mounted in the rear.

I slow the Pajero and scrutinize their positions, but there's no telling who they are. They could be Afghan Army, could be Taliban, could be Hekmatyar's murderous bandits. Or it could be Mullah Omer and Osama himself for all I know.

I radio through a warning to Tommo, in the rear. But it's not as if I can say what I want to say: 'Ready your weapons, mate.' All I can manage is a pathetic: 'Keep your eyes peeled.'

We roll to a halt at the checkpoint, and a row of muzzles are levelled at us. Whoever these gunmen are, they're staring at us in complete amazement, their eyes out on stalks.

I wind down the window. I try a winning smile, and a greeting in the local lingo. '*Assalam alaikum*' – *Peace be unto you.*

The nearest bloke rubs his eyes, like he can't believe what he's seeing. It's as if we've just fallen to earth from Mars. He even forgets to do the traditional Muslim reply: '*Alaikum assalam*' – *And unto you, peace.*

I'm cursing Dilaka and his cowardly food poisoning, for we don't have any effective way to communicate with these gunmen now. I try explaining in the few words of Farsi I have that we're making for Jalalabad.

There's a load of gesticulating and questions, but none of us has much of a clue what they're saying. I figure it's along the lines of: *Who the hell are you guys, and where the hell have you just appeared from, and where the hell d'you think you're going?*

Eventually, the boys with the guns must realize they've got limited choices: either they open the roadblock and let us through, shoot us up, or turn us back to Kabul. For some reason – and shaking their heads with incredulity – they decide to wave us on.

Trouble is, the G-Wagon's barely able to move now. Its suspension is totally wrecked. It's down to a few miles an hour.

We crawl onwards to Sarobi town, then pull up for a Chinese parliament on the roadside. The Ambo still appears determined to make it to Jalalabad, even if he has to continue on foot.

We point out the obvious – that the G-Wagon's slower than the second coming of Christ. We can't all cross-deck into the Pajero, 'cause with all the kit the Ambo's bringing there isn't the room. Plus the Ambo insists that the wrecked G-Wagon has to be taken back to Kabul.

That means one of us lot has to try to drive it alone and unarmed, back along the way we've just come. Not surprisingly, no one wants to volunteer.

Tommo argues he can't do it, 'cause the Ambo's security is his personal responsibility. Chris doesn't look too keen to volunteer. In fact he's chewing his lip and glancing around himself, as if ghosts are about to jump out of the mountain walls.

For a moment I consider drawing straws for it, but if Chris gets the short straw I figure he may just refuse to go. And then we'll look like a right bunch of amateurs in front of our client.

So I guess it's muggins has to do it. 'Fuck it,' I shrug. 'I'll go.'

There are smiles all round now that I've volunteered. I get given a satphone, a couple of bottles of water and a medical kit. The goodbyes are short and sweet, and then the Pajero sets off east, and I mount up the G-Wagon. I do a clunking, kangarooing three-point turn, and point the bonnet west for Kabul.

I set off down the road we've just driven, my arse going fifty pence a pound. As the crippled G-Wagon lurches from puddle to puddle, I am cursing the day that I took this Afghan contract. I'm angry that the Ambo's refused to listen to all of our advice. Plus I'm furious that Chris put on a puppydog face, and I somehow fell for it and volunteered to do this lone drive.

But once I'd volunteered to take the G-Wagon, I had no choice. I'd said I was going to do it, so I had to. No turning back. I'm in the car with the doors locked, alone and unarmed, and I'm shitting myself. *What the fuck have I done?*

I'm making five to ten miles an hour, depending upon the terrain. It's like I'm driving a ticker-tape parade all on my own. I have to cross back through Sarobi, where every Afghan and their dog are staring at me.

I tell myself that at least it is a straight route through to Kabul, so I can't get lost. Then I hit the same roadblock that we passed through not an hour before, on the Kabul side of town.

I roll to a halt and the same guy who tried to question us is staring right at me. He walks over and peers through the window. Rolls his eyes in total disbelief, and offers up a few prayers to Allah. Then he raises the chain and waves me through.

So it's back into the valley of death I go. The road ahead is utterly deserted. I don't see another vehicle for the next three hours. I am acutely aware that last light is little more than a couple of hours away, and I'm driving the slowest, most buggered vehicle that's ever ventured on this journey.

No doubt about it, this is hideous. My mouth feels sandpaper dry, I am so fucking scared. I keep swearing to myself and cursing out loud: 'You fucking idiot, Campion! You fucking, fucking idiot!'

I spot figures on the road up ahead, plus a couple of vehicles arranged in a makeshift roadblock. Whoever these guys are, they weren't here a few hours back when we made the drive out.

I run the anti-ambush drills I did in the military through my mind at lightning speed. Standard operating procedure is to keep driving when you hit an ambush. You do so because in the time it takes you to stop and turn around, you are a far easier target than that presented by a speeding vehicle.

But that's all predicated on a Land Rover or similar barrelling through at 70 miles an hour, not a crippled G-Wagon hobbling through at five. Plus the gunmen's pickup-type trucks are mostly blocking the road, and I've not got the momentum to blast a way through.

My one consolation is that no way am I getting out of the G-Wagon. They'll have to open the thing up like a can of beans if they want to get at me.

The armour's pretty much impervious to small-arms fire. They'll have to mallet me with a couple of RPGs, stitch me with some armour-piercing heavy machine-gun rounds, or roll some grenades beneath me to crack the G-Wagon open.

As the roadblock approaches, I count a dozen figures. I've got plenty of time to do my head count as the G-Wagon chuffs and lurches its way forward. They certainly don't look like Afghan National Army, which I figure were the boys back at the Sarobi checkpoint.

So who the fuck are this lot then?

They're got AK47s held at the ready, but I don't see anything big: maybe they don't have the firepower to split me open. I feel like some giant tortoise as I near them; slow and ponderous and hiding beneath my shell. And I am absolutely shitting myself with fear.

Then I have an idea. They obviously think I'm a lunatic already, a white-eye driving at walking pace alone from Sarobi to Kabul. It can't make matters any worse what I'm about to try.

There's a magnetic flashing light that goes on the roof of the G-Wagon – the kind of thing you'd use when leading a diplomatic cavalcade through the city. I break it out of the dash and slap it on the roof, and get it flashing away blue in the late afternoon sunlight. Then I fire up the siren that goes with it, and get that warbling away.

And so, in a flash of blue light and with an earsplitting wail, I pull to a halt at the checkpoint.

CHAPTER 14

The leader of the gang stands at my 3 o'clock – so to the right-front of my windscreen – his AK muzzle levelled at my head. Whatever impression the flashing lights and siren may have made, it doesn't seem to have got me waved through.

He starts screaming at me to get out of the vehicle, or something similar. He's gesturing wildly with the muzzle for me to dismount, and the dark, hate-filled eyes behind the thick beard leave me in no doubt on this one.

In his mind I'm a white-eye infidel pig, and I'm going to get some.

I start shouting back at him, gesturing at the doors and windows of the vehicle. '*Mushkila!* Armour! Armour! *Mushkila!*'

I'm trying to tell him that if he opens fire, he'll get the rounds right back at him, as they ricochet off the armour and the inch-thick reinforced glass.

I am trying to appear as if I'm the one in a position of strength here, but truth be told I'm shitting my load. I have visions of being whisked off into the mountains, thrown into an orange jumpsuit, and with my beheading broadcast live over the internet.

He comes around to my driver's window and uses his gun butt to club the flashing blue light off of the roof. Then he slams the muzzle hard into my driver's window.

I can see his lips moving, mouthing words of violence and death at me. I've got a good idea what he's saying: 'GET OUT OF THE VEHICLE, YOU INFIDEL PIG, OR YOU DIE!!!'

His buddies move in closer. I'm surrounded by gun muzzles. My mind's racing at one thousand miles an hour as I consider my options. But there are none: I don't have the speed or power to blast a way through; I can't go back; I don't have the weapons to fight.

But of one thing I am certain: *I am not getting out of the vehicle.*

Then I have an idea. I grab the satphone, whip up the antennae, and start to make a call.

'Yankee Six Zero, this is Fucked G-Wagon, d'you copy?' I shout into the mouthpiece. 'I'm a blue G-Wagon with fucked suspension 20 kilometres east of Kabul on the Jalalabad road. I'm halted at a hostile checkpoint made up of two white pickup trucks and gunmen. I need immediate drops danger close around my position, your choice ordnance. Coordinates are: 89567345. Repeat: 89567345.'

Special forces soldiers are taught a good deal about air controls, the craft of calling in warplanes to target. It's one of our key weapons assets when on operations. I'm doing the act of the JTAC – the Joint Terminal Attack Controller – as if I've got a fleet of American warplanes circling overhead, providing top cover.

All the while I'm gesticulating wildly at the sky above me, and yelling out '*Mushkila!*' – problem – and trying to mime an American F15 jet pounding them from the air.

Matey at the window has got a trigger finger whiter than bone by now, as he cranks up the pressure on the AK's firing mechanism. He's yelling at me to get out, and I'm yelling to him that he's about to be pulverized by an F15's cannon fire and bombs.

Then he steps back and opens fire. The muzzle spits flame, not five yards away from me, and a bullet slams into the G-Wagon's side panel. The noise of the impact is deafening, like I'm inside a massive steel drum being pounded by a sledgehammer

But by the way matey leaps back in fear and surprise, I figure the ricochet near took the fucker's head off.

Nice one, Fucked G-Wagon. I'm warming to you.

I start screaming my final attack instructions into the satphone. 'Yankee Six Zero, this is Fucked G-Wagon. Broken Arrow! Repeat, Broken Arrow! You're clear hot.'

Broken Arrow is one of the codewords used by a JTAC. It means: 'Position surrounded and about to be overrun by the enemy.' It clears a pilot to drop bombs at danger-close distances to his own men – lower than the blast range of the ordnance – and to do strafes on top of their own position if necessary.

The fact that the G-Wagon has spat his own bullet back at him seems to have matey spooked. I can sense we're at a tipping point now – the moment where either I continue chugging onwards towards Kabul, or I get my head sawn off.

Matey starts searching the skies above. His brothers do likewise. One starts pointing into the air. I don't know what the fuck he's spotted, but I hope and pray they mistake it for an avenging F15.

A second later matey gives some kind of signal, and in an instant he and his brothers melt away into the bush to the side of the road.

I presume they're taking cover from what they imagine is an impending airstrike. Either way, I am not hanging around. I edge the vehicle ahead, nose between the two pickup trucks, and – joy of joys – the road to Kabul opens before me.

It is approaching dusk by the time I reach the long climb that leads into the mountain pass before Kabul. Whoever the guys were at the roadblock, they must have swallowed the airstrike charade, for no vehicle has pursued me, and no rounds have been fired in my wake.

I'm almost home.

But as I start the long drive into the pass, I catch sight of a line of red lights blinking in the semi-darkness. It's a queue of vehicle tail lights, stretching far into the distance.

The road behind me is deserted, and I have no idea from where all this traffic has appeared, or what the hold-up is ahead. I come to a halt behind the rearmost vehicle. Before me stretches a queue of the sick, lazy and lame of the Afghan highway. There are scores of beat-up Afghan buses each with a hundred locals, plus their chickens and their goats, crammed into them. There are broken-down taxis and ancient jingly trucks back to back with rickety old donkey carts.

And then there's me. I couldn't look more out of place. I'm like a pork chop at a Jewish wedding.

A crowd gathers. I've still got the siren wailing, and I've managed to retrieve the flashing blue light and place it back on the roof. Matey's swipe with the AK knocked it clean off, but it didn't break the lead that connects it to the vehicle.

The locals keep grinning and smiling at me, and waving me onwards. They're signalling me to move on down the line. One part of me is thinking that this is it: I'm being set up for the final kill. The other part is telling me that I can't stay here and I can't go back, so best drive forward.

I start moving ahead at the G-Wagon's snail-like crawl. I get to the front of the queue, which ends at the start of a steep incline. There is nothing to indicate what they've stopped for here, or why they are queuing. I get waved past the last vehicle, and I'm on my own again, heading into God only knows what.

The road begins climbing ever more steeply. The pass into Kabul is a never-ending series of blind hairpin bends snaking further and further into the hills. There are hundreds of these switchbacks, around each of which I'm expecting to discover the reason for the hold-up, and to get either captured, or to have my head blown off.

I'm down to a couple of miles an hour on the steepest inclines. At this speed I'm incapable of ramming an eggshell out of the way. I figure the Afghans either waved me through to be genuinely nice to me, or to see me get shot to pieces and have a good laugh.

I decide on a course of action if I do run into the bad guys. I'll drive the G-Wagon off the edge of the road, and see where I end up. Every corner I'm readying myself to point the wagon into the abyss, and to drive over.

I don't see a single vehicle coming down, and nothing is following me up. This is spooky as fuck. I have never felt so scared. I'm approaching the very top, and I figure I'm just a few miles short of the city limits. Maybe I'm getting there.

I round one of the final bends, and my heart practically stops beating. Up ahead in the gloom is a figure on the road. I can see the silhouette of a gun, plus webbing and some kind of headgear.

I glance to the side of the road, and just my fucking luck – this final section of highway has concrete barriers to either side. No going over the edge then. I've got no choice but to keep plodding onwards towards whatever lies in wait.

I start cursing to myself in frustrated, fearful anger.

Momentarily, my headlights illuminate the figure up ahead. In that moment, I catch a glint of metal reflecting off the gun that he's carrying. It is definitely not an AK47.

In fact, it looks like a French FAMAS – a bullpup-style assault rifle, with an unmistakable thick carriage handle running half the length of the weapon.

No Afghan gunman carries a FAMAS.

I catch a hint of a recognition flash on the guy's sleeve.

It looks for all the world like an ISAF flash.

I slam on the anchors, wrench open the door and start sprinting towards the figure up ahead, yelling 'Bonjour! Bonjour!' in my best schoolboy French.

The poor fucker hasn't got a clue what's hit him, as 18 stones of shaven-headed Englishman cannon into him, and gives him a very French-style man-hug.

He seems as shocked to see me as I am him, maybe more so.

'*Mon Dieu! Mais qui êtes-vous?*' he starts yelling. *My God! Who the hell are you?*

I pull out my embassy ID card and wave it in his face: 'European embassy! European embassy!'

He pulls out a torch, shines it on the card, into my face for a second, then back to the card. He's got this look of utter disbelief on his features. A crowd of French soldiers starts milling around. They're staring at me like I've just beamed down to earth.

They go and fetch their officer. He asks me where I've come from. I tell him Sarobi. He asks me where my 'companions' are. I tell him that I have none, I'm alone. He asks me where my weapons are. I tell him that I have none.

He seems utterly lost for words. Then, shaking his head in disbelief: 'But you are crazy. You are zee fuckin' crazy Henglishman.'

I couldn't agree more. Yep, I'm zee fuckin' crazy Henglishman, and I have never been so happy to see a Frenchman in all my life.

I explain that I'm based in Kabul, and just need to get my

vehicle back to Wazir Akbar Khan district. He glances at it doubt-fully, then back at me.

'But your car is, 'ow do you say – fucked?'

'Yeah, mate. Completely fucked. It's been like that all the way from Sarobi.'

He stares at me for an instant, then turns and barks some orders at the guys behind him. They fall out, heading for two French military vehicles to the rear of the checkpoint.

'You are zee crazy, crazy Englishman. So, we provide you zee escort into Kabul.'

With a French military escort I proceed at a dead crawl to the ISAF base on the city's outskirts. There, the French officer com-manding insists on giving me a lift to the embassy residence in a functioning vehicle. Not only that, but he offers to repair the fucked G-Wagon in the ISAF workshop.

On the drive into town, the French Colonel gets me to retell the entire story of my journey to and from Sarobi. He's staring at me like I've got horns growing out of my head, and he keeps slapping his thigh and laughing uproariously.

He drops me at the embassy compound, and shakes me warmly by the hand: 'Monsieur,' he says, 'you could not pay me enough money to do what you 'ave just done . . .'

I shrug. What can I say? I thank him again, and promise to drop by to pick up the G-Wagon in a couple of days' time.

That night, I'm lying in my hammock alone in the compound, reflecting on the day that's just gone.

I'm barely a year out of the military, and that Sarobi drive was like being on escape and evasion for real. It's the scariest thing that I've ever done in a life spent soldiering, and fighting in the shadows. I was completely on my own; I don't speak the lan-guage; I had no local knowledge or intel; and I was unarmed in a vehicle that was completely fucked . . . in one of the most law-less parts of the world. I had no map, three bottles of water and a smile.

It's the old adage: you get dealt a shit sandwich, you've got to put some ketchup on it and get the fucker down you.

But no doubt about it: it's a miracle that I'm still at liberty, and breathing.

CHAPTER 15

A couple of days later, I take the French ISAF commander a bottle of malt whisky, a dozen Montecristo cigars, plus some seriously smelly French cheese, to say a big and heart-felt '*Merci*'. And I vow to myself that I will never again slag off the French rugby team. Well, at least until the next time they play England.

By now the story of my Sarobi drive has done the rounds of the ISAF base. In spite of the gifts that I bear, and my bonhomie towards them, it's clear the French soldiers think that I am totally mad.

A couple of days later the Ambo returns, together with Tommo and Chris. The Ambo's got a look on his face like he's a puppy next to a pile of shit. He knows he's done wrong ignoring our advice, and pushing ahead with the trip to Jalalabad. But he's the client, and I'm not about to make a big deal out of it. All I say to Tommo is that my lone drive in the G-Wagon was 'a real epic'. But I do wind it in to Chris a bit: 'Missed out on a good trip there, mate.'

Of one thing we're all certain now. After the drive from hell to Jalalabad, none of us is ever leaving Kabul again without being seriously tooled up.

I go find Dilaka and give him some serious stick for bottling out of the Jalalabad mission. Then I tell him that whatever else, we've got to score some 'toofangchai'.

93

Dilaka reckons he's hit pay dirt on the weapons front. He's found some guys out near Bagram Airbase who've got the best supply of weapons this side of Sarobi. They're happy to meet, and sell us whatever we're after.

Only trouble is, we've got to do it on their turf, or not at all.

The arms dealers are based in a large compound to the east of Bagram Airbase. I tell Dilaka we'll go do the deal there, but only if he agrees to drive us. I've got an extra hold over Dilaka by now, and I figure this is the time to use it.

It's becoming increasingly obvious that the Ambo doesn't actually like Dilaka very much. And it's clear why. Dilaka's forever cleaning his beloved Pajero, in an effort to impress the Ambo. We've even nicknamed him 'Mr Grovel' as a result.

But all the cleaning and polishing has had quite the reverse effect on the Ambo. It means that Dilaka's never without a rag in one hand, plus these enormous sweat patches under each arm. The Ambo hasn't exactly warmed to Dilaka's appearance, or his body odour.

There's a second embassy driver called Sayed. He's tall, rake-thin, and has this massive black Taliban-style beard. He's quiet and reserved, but he's got this one massive advantage over Dilaka: no sweat patches. The Ambo's taken to using Sayed as his main driver.

At the end of our road is this tiny roadside kiosk that sells everything you could wish for. It's open all hours, and as a result I've nicknamed the shopkeeper 'Ronnie Barker'. And I've asked Ronnie Barker to get me something in short supply in Kabul: a can of deodorant.

Ronnie Barker's just come up trumps with a can of Gillette underarm spray. I show it to Dilaka and outline the deal. If he drives us to the arms dealers' place, he gets to keep his job. I explain to a bemused Dilaka that the Ambo doesn't appreciate his body odour.

Dilaka still doesn't get it, so I point out the sweat stains. Time to get brutal: 'Mate, you sweat like a pig and it stinks.'

I explain that either he does something about it, or the Ambo's going to fire him. You can't have a diplomat's driver looking – and smelling – like Dilaka. I offer him the answer, the can of Gillette. But he only gets it if he does the drive to the arms dealers' place.

As a bonus, I've also brought him a new T-shirt so he can wash the one he seems to be permanently wearing. I guess Dilaka's getting the message by now. He takes the Gillette, and the knock-off 'Levi's T-shirt, and agrees to do the drive. But he refuses point-blank to leave his car, or go into the arms dealers' place. That, he figures, is my job.

Chris, Dilaka and I make the drive out towards Bagram. We pull to a halt outside of this massive, mud-walled compound. It's more like some medieval fortress than it is your average Afghan home.

Dilaka and Chris are staying with the vehicle, so I'm off into the building on my own. I get ushered through this massive wooden gate by a couple of guards. They look like they're expecting me. I'm taken to a staircase, and led into the fortress's cellar.

It's thick with smoke and chatter down there, but the room falls silent as soon as yours truly enters. No wonder Dilaka refused to come. There are all sorts of seriously menacing fuckers down here. This is the proverbial Afghan den of thieves.

Anyone could be Taliban or worse, and I know I risk getting kidnapped or killed. But fuck it, after the Sarobi experience I know how dearly we need some firepower. It's another case of needs must, old boy.

My 'situational awareness' radar has cranked into overtime now. At it's simplest, if the Afghan arms dealer who's offering me my first cup of sweet mint tea starts to distance himself from me at any moment, I'll be instantly on my guard.

Those in the know move away from an individual when they realize something bad is about to happen to him or her. It's very often a simple process of clearing the field of fire, or isolating that person in preparation to seize, overpower and kidnap them.

If this happens, my only possible response – my 'what-if' – is to run. I'll be back up the stairs like a rat up a drainpipe, clubbing any of the guards who try to stop me with the 'Big Hampshire Hammer', as my right fist became known on the streets where I grew up.

There's only one thing for it: act relaxed, but be ready to run, run, run.

There's nothing wrong with running. Elite soldiering isn't about being bulletproof, or superhuman. It's more often about getting yourself and your mates out alive, and knowing when to stand and fight and when to make yourself scarce.

We do the 'Assalam alaikum' thing, and I take a sip of my thimble-sized glass of tea. A lumpy sack gets dragged out of the shadows. Eyes stare out at me from the curtain of smoke that hangs in the room: quiet, watching, filled with a catlike curiosity.

I don't sense overt threat yet. But I am on the verge of deciding this was a bad idea, and making a rapid exit.

I'm reminded of a time back in the UK, when I drove onto a travellers' site to buy a second-hand car. Without thinking, I asked for 'Pikey Bob', as the guy selling the motor was known down our local pub. It was the ultimate in having zero situational awareness.

'Pikey Bob' may have been the nickname he answered to down the boozer, but not on the gypsies' site. There everyone was a 'Pikey', which is an insulting term for gypsies or travellers. I realized as much just as soon as the words were out of my mouth.

I made an excuse and rapidly left, before it could kick off. I called Pikey Bob on his mobile, and arranged to meet him on neutral ground to do the deal. I chose somewhere I knew was covered by CCTV, and I had a couple of guys watching in the background. That way, I got the car without having to go to war with a whole tribe of Pikeys.

But right now in this Kabul cellar there's no CCTV, no watchers, and I'm hardly on neutral ground. This is the arms dealers' domain, and I'm completely on my own. My only option is to keep my situational awareness cranked up to max, and to do a runner at the first hint of trouble.

There's an ancient-looking Afghan geezer with this massive grey beard leading the proceedings. He takes the bulging sack, opens the neck of it, and pulls out this AK47. He passes it to me to examine.

Amazingly, the weapon is fresh out of the factory, and still packed in greaseproof paper and gun oil. It's clearly never been used, and it comes complete with several mags of ammo.

I ask him how many he has, and he indicates two. I tell him I'd like them both. We're communicating in a mix of broken English and Farsi. Then I ask him the crucial question: *How much?*

He pulls a calculator out of his robes and punches in a figure. Shows it to me. 'Thousand.'

'Dollar or Afghani?' I ask him.

For a moment there's silence, then everyone cracks up laughing. There are hoots of merriment, and cries of 'US dollar! US dollar!' from around the room.

Good one Phil. It's broken the ice. The Afghani's the local currency, and right now it's about as worthless as bog paper.

I say: 'Thousand dollar?! No, no, no!'

I take the calculator and acting all jovial I punch in a rival figure.

The old man takes it, laughs a chesty ho-ho-ho, then punches in a new figure and gives it back to me. And so the process goes.

I'd far rather have pitched up at the Kabul Gun Store downtown, and purchased what we needed on the open market. Trouble is, there isn't one. And somehow, with the Afghans I sense that if you man it out and show them respect, combined with firmness and a lack of fear, they in turn will respect that.

Finally, we settle on a price of 200 dollars apiece for the AK47s, which I figure isn't half bad. Plus I purchase a great big unopened tin of 7.62mm short ammo to go with the guns.

I'm about to start the long process of saying an Afghan goodbye, when I have a thought. Hang on, how do I know the weapons actually work? They may be brand-new, but perhaps the very reason they are unused is that they're part of a dodgy shipment.

I turn to the old man, who's offering me a final cup of tea. '*Tashacour*,' I thank him. I take a sip. Ahhh – lovely. Then: 'But Baba, how do I know the guns work?'

Baba's like an Afghan expression for 'respected elder.' He smiles. He points to a window set high in the cellar wall behind him. He motions for me to fire off a few shots through there.

No time like the present. I lean out, and fire off a few rounds with each weapon towards the deserted hills at the rear of the compound. No doubt about it, the AKs are as sweet as a nut.

The deal's done, and I'm just saying my goodbyes, when there's a commotion outside. The guards have seen a column of US Amtraks – armoured personnel carriers – snarling out of Bagram Airbase, and heading fast in our direction.

There's a squad of US Marines in support, and it's soon obvious what has happened. The US military are coming out to investigate the gunfire that came from our cellar window!

I'm forced to remain in the cellar and lie low – which means countless more cups of tea – whilst the Marines complete their search for the 'insurgents'. It's hours before I'm able to rendezvous with Dilaka and Chris, and head for home.

But by the time I do so we're up two brand-new AK47s, which means the team's got some firepower at last.

Now all we need to do is get them properly zeroed in, and we're ready for business.

CHAPTER 16

By the time we manage to get onto the British Army shooting range, at Camp Sutah on the outskirts of Kabul, I've managed to score us a shotgun as well.

Tommo, Chris and me have started doing regular orientation drives around Kabul, to familiarize ourselves with the city. During one of those I spotted what looked like a sawn-off shotgun on one of the street-side stalls. I got Chris to stop the car so I could check.

Sure enough the weapon was a Gucci-looking seven-round pump-action sawn-off, short enough to slot beneath a vehicle's front seat. In the military we used to call the sawn-off the 'Barclay Card', for you could buy anything you want with one. This was supposedly a Remington, but on closer inspection I noticed that whoever had manufactured it had also made a spelling mistake.

Apparently, this was a 'Rimmington'.

It was fucking hilarious and I had to have it. Twenty minutes haggling later, and it was mine for fifty dollars. A snip.

We've been given access to the British ranges at Sutah, because we're forging links with the Army based upon what we can offer them in Afghan. First off, they've asked us to train the lads on local weaponry.

Back in the UK they'd done months of pre-deployment training, but all with SA80s, LSWs, GPMGs, plus Milan and LAW antitank missiles. All standard British Army and NATO kit, but not exactly very widely used in Afghan.

Now, they're in a situation where they could easily have to pick up any number of unfamiliar weapons, and fight with them. Plus, they'll likely be taking prisoners, and they need to know how to make their weapons safe. Otherwise, a captured enemy fighter might turn his AK on them, and open fire.

During my years in the military I've trained with just about every weapon ever used in modern warfare, so I'm familiar with most of them. I've started teaching the young lads at Camp Sutah how to operate and make safe AK47s, AKMs, rocket-propelled grenades (RPGs) and pistols like the Makarov.

There are any number of AK variants sloshing around Afghan, and they all have their unique peculiarities. The ones made in China are welded together from several plates of metal, and are prone to blowing up in your face. By contrast, the Russian-made AKs are machined from one chunk of metal, and they're bulletproof.

I'm also training the young British soldiers on the Minimi, a drum-fed light machine gun that's just being introduced into the regular Army. The Minimi was my weapon of choice when on combat operations, and it's the absolute dog's bollocks of a weapon.

Pity the same can't be said of the Rimmington.

When we get out onto the ranges I can't wait to try out the pump-action shotgun. I hold it over the far side of a sandbag barrier, and chamber the first round. As I pull the trigger it blows up, the barrel disintegrating violently.

As I stagger about, a little disorientated, I am aware that the days of the Rimmington are well and truly over. It's a shame, as the sawn-off would have been good fun, not to mention useful. It's a fine weapon to keep close in a car, as a crowd disperser.

It's then that Chris points out that I'm bleeding profusely from the front. Looks like a chunk of blown-up Rimmington has somehow got through the sandbag barrier, and embedded itself in my chest.

I make sure I get a photograph with Chris, and some of the squaddies, before heading for Camp Sutah's field hospital. Sure enough, I'm diagnosed as having a piece of gun barrel embedded in my chest cavity. The Army surgeons haven't had anyone to operate on since their arrival in Kabul, and they get all excited pulling the lump out of me, and stitching up the wound. This is the start of an excellent working relationship with the British Army lot at Sutah.

As private operators we have freedoms that the regular squaddies do not, and they in turn have things that we lust after. They have racks of gleaming ammo, which we find very useful. They have warehouses stacked full of British Army ration packs, which offer as good a way as any to evade an invitation from the Ambo to the Herat Café.

Plus they've got great scoff on the go in the base canteen. In return we do weapons training for the lads, and score them any Afghan rugs or semi-precious stones they may want from the Kabul markets. We've also started picking up good snippets of intel on the city streets, stuff that the ops room at Camp Sutah finds very useful.

But all work and no play makes Phil a dull boy. The stress of the Sarobi job, plus the arms deals on top of it, means we're all on edge. We're approaching four weeks into the job by now, and we're in dire need of some down time. There's a no-alcohol rule at the embassy compound, and little chance of finding a drink in and around Kabul.

It's now that the Ambo gets to head home for a week's leave, as he's served over a month in-country. Whilst he's away we get invited to a piss-up at the Dutch embassy by their security detail, and you bet your fucking hat we're up for it. We've been drier than the Sahara. Tally-ho! Up and at 'em!

We drive over there in the afternoon, and there's shedloads of free booze. Typical of the Dutch, they've shipped out crates of fine Dutch lager. By evening we're truly minging, and we've eaten nothing more than several plateloads of nibbles.

There are tiny sausages adorned with cocktail sticks, each of which is flying a miniature paper version of the Dutch flag. For some reason Chris decides to stick one of the Dutch flags into the side of my shaven head. This strikes me as being a fine idea, so I ram one into the other side to even it up a little.

The Dutch embassy's security team are all serving special forces types. They can't quite seem to decide if this is funny, or if Chris, Tommo and I are just a bunch of horrible lunatic British beer monsters taking the rise out of their national flag.

It's then that the Dutch Ambassador heads over to see what all the fuss is about. She catches sight of my shaven head bearing two of her national flags, points at it and cracks up laughing. She makes a beeline for me, and does a closer inspection.

'But this is simply fantastic,' she enthuses. 'So patriotic, and you I think are not even Dutch? You know, I think I need one too!'

I grab a sausage, eat it and indicate that I am ready and willing with the flag. But as I go to impale it in her head, she keeps flinching. I can see her protection detail are torn between protecting their client from this insane Englishman, or letting her get what she's asked for.

I'm killing myself laughing, as is the Dutch Ambo. I try again, and again she flinches. I decide it's time to get serious. I grab her in a headlock, and drive the flag into her scalp. She comes up for air looking a little flustered, but with the flag seriously embedded, and flying as patriotically as you could wish for.

Result.

There's a moment's silence wherein no one knows whether she's going to find it funny, or whether Big Phil Campion's just caused a serious international incident. Her security team don't know whether to laugh or to cry, or if they're all about to face the sack. Chris is staring at me like he can't believe what I have just done.

She glances in the wall mirror, touches the flag, then starts laughing her tits off. Next, she grabs me by the waist as the music cranks up, and pushes me towards the doorway of the embassy ballroom.

'Come on, you crazy Englishman,' she cries. 'We fly the flag, and you show me how to do your conga!'

It's past midnight by the time we decide we either have to leave now, or we're going to fall over. We're hours into the curfew, of course, but we've never seen any checkpoints on the back streets. We decide to avoid the main thoroughfares, and leg it.

We're fine until we reach the main road junction that leads into ours. As we stand in the shadows surveying the roundabout, there are the lights of Ronnie Barker's off to one side. Glad to see it, I tell myself. I'd have been bitterly disappointed not to find him open at such an hour.

Trouble is, we can see uniformed figures illuminated in the halo of light thrown out by his store. Afghan National Army or Police. Not easy to tell which from here. We start walking as nonchalantly as we can towards the roundabout.

We're halfway across when the challenge rings out in Farsi. 'Halt! Who goes there? Password!'

There's no way that Chris, Tommo or I are stopping. Instead, we sprint for the small side road that leads to our compound. We've only got about fifty yards to make before we can disappear into the tree-lined gloom of our street.

A weapon opens up on us, but it's hard to hit a group of men running at speed at night. Plus we have to hope he's not zeroed in his weapon properly, which is often the case with Afghan conscripts.

We dodge the fire, which is massively off target, and make it home safely. We crash out in the hammocks, and sleep the sleep of the dead.

The next morning I head down to Ronnie Barker's to buy a packet of fags, my skull feeling like a jackhammer's pounding away inside it. Ronnie's face lights up just as soon as he sees me. He starts wagging his finger at me. He knows full well it was us doing the runner the night before, and he seems to find it hilarious.

With all the narrow shaves we've had to date, I guess we're getting a little blasé about the security threat in Kabul. And as always is the case, it's then that it really comes back to bite you on the arse.

CHAPTER 17

The Ambo returns, and we get warned off for the embassy's first big diplomatic shindig. To Hercule and Pepe's bitter regret, it's a British visitor that we're receiving. Chris Patten, at that time the European Commissioner for External Relations, is coming to visit Afghan President-in-waiting Hamid Karzai, plus the European and the British embassies.

It's a full-on schedule, and we still don't have enough weapons to arm up our team. By now our fourth member, Micky the ex-Legionnaire, has arrived, and we've only got the two AK47s.

Not a bother, we think. As Patten is a Brit visiting the British embassy, and we are fellow Brits, we figure their security detail will assist us.

Tommo and me put on our suits, and head up to Her Majesty's Embassy to seek help. The British Embassy Close Protection (CP) team are all serving Royal Military Police (RMPs), never my favourite types. These guys just cannot seem to get their heads around civvies doing what we are doing here in Kabul.

Regardless, Tommo explains to them that we need an armoured back-up car for Patten's visit, plus back-up from them, as we have too few weapons to fully secure him. Their team leader is a bloke called Derek, and it's clear that he wants to be in charge of the entire operation.

I'd rather have boiled my own head than use Derek as a team leader on this one. Tommo clearly feels the same. Eventually, we reach a compromise: Tommo, Chris and Micky will drive the Ambo and Patten up front in the armoured G-Wagon. I will take the British embassy's armoured Land Rover as back-up, with Derek and some of his RMP buddies riding shotgun.

In spite of the spirit of cooperation and teamwork fostered by this plan, Derek stubbornly refuses to help us out on the weapons front. Fortunately, there's a German heading up the European Union office in Kabul. He's become a number-one fan of ours, after seeing how we're looking after the Ambo. He's got a two-man German GSG9 team – the Grenzschutzgruppe-9, their counter-terrorist Special Forces unit – providing his security.

Over the weeks we've got to know the GSG9 guys well, and they're sound as a pound. One's the spitting image of David Beckham, so we've given him the wholly unoriginal nickname of 'Becks'. The other's a German skinhead that we've nicknamed 'Gonzo'.

We go see Gonzo and Becks, and ask them if they can help us out on the weapons front. The GSG9 are so well resourced by the German government that they have two full sets of combat gear, one tailored for day ops and one for night missions.

Gonzo and Becks are happy to loan us two complete sets for the day, including MP5 sub-machine gun, ammo, grenades, webbing, body armour, the works. They know they could get into huge trouble if they get found out, but they can see the need and are eager to help.

So, while the Brit RMPs have refused to give us the steam off their shit, the Germans GSG9 boys have given us the world. How fucked up is that?

There we are the morning of Patten's tour kitted out in full-on Gonzo and Becks gear. Derek and his RMP blokes pitch up, and their eyes are out on stalks. Derek keeps demanding to know where we got all the kit from, and it's clear as day that he hates it.

'Vorsprung durch Technik, mate,' is the only response that I'll give him.

They're the only words of German that I know, and I've learned them from the Audi adverts. Means 'progress through technology,' or something similar. Every time that I say it Derek gets more and more wound up, which is a bonus.

Derek's problem with us boils down to this. RMPs are a bunch of pretend soldiers and failed coppers. I've had dozens of run-ins with them in the past, and I have never met a good one. They've got massive chips on their shoulders to start with, and now Derek sees the likes of us earning more in a month than he does in six.

I take the wheel of the back-up vehicle. I place Gonzo's MP5 in the door rack next to me, where it's just a hand's length away. It's a lovely, stubby, compact killing machine, and just right for vehicle security.

Derek and two of his RMP buddies are in the rear, their long, unwieldy SA80s sitting awkwardly in their laps. We head for the airport, collect Patten, and drive him back to the embassy without dramas. Then we're onto the main leg of the visit.

Patten is off to tour the Afghan ministries and to meet Karzai. All the roads that we'll be using are sealed to traffic and pedestrians, so that our cavalcade can sweep through uninterrupted. This is standard procedure for ministers and the like transiting through Kabul.

We emerge from Wazir Akbar Khan district, and the G-Wagon is motoring along in front of us with the two High Value Targets (HVTs) – Patten and the Ambo – chatting away in the rear.

All of a sudden, there's a commotion to the side of the road, and a figure breaks through the cordon. This Afghan bloke emerges, pedalling frantically on his pushbike, and he's headed right towards us.

On this trajectory he'll pass directly between the G-Wagon and our Land Rover, which will be prime time to detonate any bomb belt he may be packing.

We've already had suicide bombings in Afghanistan. As he barrels towards us, I can see his one hand fiddling beneath his robes, whilst the other grips the handlebars.

That's it, I tell myself. *Enough fucking around.* I aim the Land Rover at him, and put pedal to the metal. I smash into him, the bull bars throwing him up over the bonnet and down into the road behind.

The armoured Land Rover crunches and kangaroos heavily over the pushbike, and then we're powering through. I see the white faces of the Ambo and Patten staring out the rear window of the G-Wagon, and I know they've seen the whole thing.

Then I hear this voice from the rear. 'What the hell d'you think you're doing?' It's Derek, and he's got the mother of all flaps on. 'You could have killed the guy. You probably have . . .'

I eye him in the mirror. 'I wasn't about to have that fucker ride into our convoy, and blow his suicide belt and us all to fuck.'

'But you just smashed into him! What d'you do that for? You could have swerved . . . That's your bloody act-now-ask-questions-later-attitude . . .'

'Listen, pal, I'd rather be judged by twelve than carried by six,' I cut him off. 'And so I reckon would our HVT. So best you do your job, and shut the fuck up.'

We reach our destination without further mishap. I get out of the Land Rover and Tommo motions me over. He asks me what happened back on the road. I explain the exact chain of events.

He looks me in the eye. 'Phil,' he says steadily, 'there's no worries, mate. You did exactly the right thing back there.'

Nearby is a contingent of Afghan police, providing security for the ministry. I know Derek is gunning for me, and wants to have my blood. I need to head him off at the pass. I grab our interpreter ('terp'), and go have a word with the nearest Afghan copper.

I ask to speak to their officer. A guy comes forward. I explain via the terp what just happened. The Afghan police officer starts laughing uproariously. He tells me via the terp that the bloke on the pushbike got exactly what he deserved.

'Here in Afghanistan, there is big threat to VIPs,' he continues. 'Assassination. Suicide attack. Kidnap. Always we move VIPs by convoy, and close off all streets. All Afghans know this. Anyone breaking through cordon is up to dodgy business. Well done for stopping him.'

By now Derek's steaming. He's livid that I've not been arrested and thrown into some torrid Afghan jail, preferably without trial. He and I are developing this burning hatred for each other, and we won't speak a further word for the entire remainder of Patten's visit.

I know I've made a real enemy here, and I can sense trouble. Derek's not going to forgive or forget, and neither for that matter am I.

Later that day I'm back at the embassy residence, chipping a golf ball into a bucket on the lawn. I've had my golfing gear shipped out from the UK, so I can get in some practice during my down time. Chris Patten wanders over.

'D'you mind if I have a swipe?' he asks.

I gesture at the spare clubs. 'You're more than welcome, mate.'

Patten and I are chipping away, taking it in turns. After a while he pauses.

'Hope you don't mind my asking, but what was all the commotion on the drive to the ministry?'

I glance at him. 'An Afghan on a pushbike came barrelling through the cordon, and was making for the vehicles. Could have been a suicide bomber. I knocked him off his bike.'

I explain to Patten how the Afghans cordon off the roads, and no one – *but no one* – is allowed through. I explain how I couldn't have shot the bloke, for we were travelling in an armoured vehicle, which stops bullets going out, as well as coming in. I had no option but to knock him out of the way.

Patten wrinkles his brow and lines up for his chip: 'That seems fair enough to me.'

The incident with the pushbike took place in full view of Ronnie Barker's. The next morning I go to buy my packet of fags, and Ronnie's seen it all.

He makes a steering-wheel gesture, then mimes a guy pedalling his bike madly. He's grinning ear-to-ear as he does so. Then he mimes me knocking the guy off his bike, and gives a thumbs-up.

Finally, he mimes the cyclist pressing a button on his belt and mouths 'Boom!'

I'm left in no doubt that I did the right thing by smashing that cyclist out of the way.

CHAPTER 18

I've got the embassy staff doing their grocery shopping at Ronnie Barker's by now, and business for Ronnie is booming. In turn, he's started giving me the odd packet of fags for free, as a thank you.

Everyone is calling him 'Ronnie' now, first and foremost the Afghans. The kids who run his errands don't have a clue who Ronnie Barker is, but that doesn't stop them yelling out 'Rony Braker! Rony Braker!'

Ronnie seems to love it more than anyone, and he even refers to himself as 'Rony' now. It strikes me that as far as the local Afghans are concerned, Ronnie Barker is this little Afghan bloke who runs the corner shop in Wazir Akbar Khan district.

It's a funny old world.

After the Patten job, we hand back our Gucci kit to Becks and Gonzo. We're clearly in need of some extra firepower, and I go have another chat with Dilaka. This time he finds us a source who can sell us a couple of well worn, but well maintained, AKs, plus a couple of Makarovs.

Finally, our team is properly gunned up, which means we can devote some much-needed time to recceing the city, and mapping out our escape routes should things go tits-up at the embassy. Which sure as eggs is eggs they will do. It's just a matter of time.

We start driving recces throughout Kabul, mapping and spot-coding junctions. Junction one east on a certain road will be 'Red One', junction two is Red Two, and so on and so forth. Plus we get to recce possible escape routes from both the embassy buildings, and spot-code those.

We rehearse driving those escape routes day and night, over and over and over. It's not rocket science, but this is the bread and butter of what I've learned during my years in the military. And it means that we have a good chance of evacuating the Ambo, and getting him out of Kabul in one piece, whilst not relying on any other fucker for assistance.

Tommo, Chris, Micky and I have been working on–off shifts in rotation for pushing two months now, and we're knackered. It's clear we need an Afghan team trained up to stand in for us, at least some of the time.

We talk through our recruitment priorities with the Ambo. His one key concern is that we take blokes from across the board in terms of tribal groups: Tajiks, Hazaras, Pashtuns, whatever. We know this goes against the grain in terms of how things work in Afghan, but the Ambo is adamant. A European embassy such as his can't be seen to show any bias.

We start from scratch, getting Dilaka and the Ambo's chef to use their networks and bring blokes in. All claim to have prior military experience – to have fought with the Afghan Mujahideen against the Soviet Red Army, or the Taliban.

We make the decision from day one that we won't have them gunned up. We don't want anyone other than the white-eye team carrying weapons in the compound. Plus we aren't about to teach the Afghan guard force to be underwater knife fighters. They'll have nightsticks – wooden batons – and Maglites, but no shooters.

We drill them in a series of responses they're to make to any emergency. If it all goes noisy, they're to use the radio to fetch us lot, and we'll take it from there.

We give them basic 'first responder' training in first aid, in which you make sure any casualty is stabilized, before going to fetch help. We sort a visitor tag and booking system, to keep tabs on those coming to visit the embassy. Slowly, we're getting there.

Tommo completes his three-month contract, and decides it's enough for him. He's moving on to pastures new. As for me, I can't get enough of Kabul. I'm loving it. I'm getting seriously into this country, and the freewheeling, wheeler-dealer nature of how things get done here.

Martie, another ex-Hereford guy, gets parachuted in to take Tommo's place as team leader. We nickname him 'Martie the Prince of Mince'. He's a well decent bloke, but he's got this unfortunate camp air about him. In fact, he comes across as being bent as an Arab's dagger.

The Ambo takes an instant dislike to the man. He doesn't like having the Prince of Mince as his CP team leader. He tells me as much, and that Martie has to go. I contact Double Zero and tell them that Martie's not working out.

The Ambo's made it clear that he'd be happy with me as team leader, 'cause what you see is what you get. I do what it says on the tin.

The client is everything in this line of work. Double Zero have got their teeth into a juicy fat contract, and apart from Martie, the team's working well. The Ambo likes us, 'cause we get stuff done. We don't see problems: we look for solutions. The Ambo digs that.

Double Zero dispenses with Martie's services, and I take over as team leader. But just as I do so we lose a key member of the Kabul lineup, one that I've feared we're going to lose for some weeks now.

In spite of Dilaka's protestation that he smells like a rose garden now that he's started using the Gillette, the Ambo finally decides that he's had enough. Dilaka gets the chop, and a new driver, Faisal, comes on board.

Faisal is young, clean and smart, and he speaks excellent English. I liked Dilaka a lot, but Faisal's a breath of fresh air – literally. There's only the one problem: there's several Faisals on the embassy's staff already, so to avoid confusion I rename him 'Brian'.

Faisal is in love with everything Western, and he goes around telling anyone who'll listen his new name: 'I'm Brian.' The Ambo doesn't even get to know that his real name is Faisal. Brian is exactly what the Ambo wants in terms of a driver, yet little do we know what a tonne of shit this guy is going to bring down upon us.

But first, I've got to deal with recruiting the local guard force. We've signed up some three dozen Afghans by now, and every day there's more coming on board. They're running an outer cordon of security for both the embassy office and the Ambo's residence. If that gets breached, then the four of us white-eyes move in either to plug the security gap or to evacuate the Ambo and his key staff.

We've adopted a new set of operating procedures. Once we've 'housed' the Ambo – got him safely into the residence from wherever he's been working that day – we stand down the white-eye team. That gives each of us an evening off. We've been working 24/7 for approaching four months now, and without some down time we'll go mad.

By stepping down the intensity of our duties, we're stepping up that of the Afghan guard force. Trouble is, they start to take the piss almost immediately. They are constantly falling asleep on duty, or sneaking off to watch movies in the guardhouse. Worse still, they don't seem to think there's anything particularly remiss in such dereliction of duty.

I left the Army as a Staff Sergeant, and in the British Army you'd first try speaking reason to any bloke caught taking the piss on duty. As part of our recruitment filter each of our Afghan guards has to speak a little English, and my Farsi is getting reasonable by now.

I try having words with the guards, and explaining exactly why sleeping on duty is not fucking acceptable. I try explaining that in Kabul, it could lead to horrendous casualties. I try shaming them by pointing out how they're letting their fellow Afghan guards down, not to mention us.

It has zero effect. I still keep finding guards who've dragged their beds outside and are having a nice kip. I try upping the ante. I fine the offenders; I dock their pay; I suspend one of the worst blokes from work. But the rest don't seem to pay it any heed.

Finally, I'm doing my midnight guard inspection and I come across one of the guards flat-out asleep. He's even had the gall to pull two of the plastic mess tables outside, and push them together so as to make himself a bed. I grab him by the lapels, and as I pull him to his feet he goes as if to attack me.

In a flash, the Big Hampshire Hammer has clocked him one on the jaw, and he's laid out flat on the ground. I check him over for a pulse, and he's fine. He'll come to with a headache and a bruised jaw is all. I decide to complete the rest of his stag, as he's not capable, and I make it clear to the other guards that the gloves are off now.

I catch any other fucker sleeping on duty, they'll get more of the same.

The transformation in our guard force is immediate, and close to miraculous. The jungle drums start beating, and word goes around like wildfire: if you're caught sleeping on duty, Big Mr Phil will knock you out, and that's just for starters.

But I keep the wielding of the Hampshire Hammer quiet from

the Ambo. I know secretly he'd approve, yet publicly whacking the local staff is not the kind of thing he can endorse. But whilst it may not be politically correct, it fucking delivers.

This is the only kind of discipline these guys have ever had from the Mujahideen and the Taliban, and it's all they understand. It's not right, maybe. It's not a shining example of equal opportunities in action. But effective it is. Highly so.

At its simplest, these blokes are used to doing what they're told, and getting a boot in the head if they step out of line. And it's going to take time – a great deal of time in some cases – for them to adapt to the Western, democratic, politically correct way of doing things. In fact, I doubt if they'll ever get there.

So, the choice for the guard force boils down to doing their duty, or saying hello to the Hampshire Hammer. And it seems to be working a treat.

Trouble is, I've not factored Brian – our new driver – into the equation.

CHAPTER 19

Brian is scrupulously clean, tidy and punctual. For the Ambo, he's the perfect driver who can do no wrong. But he has one major weakness that I become aware of. Whilst he swears he is a good, fine, upstanding Muslim, he is obsessed by women. Or, more accurately, by sex.

Brian is forever trying to get his hands on our soft porn magazines. Even *FHM* gets him all hot under the collar. He seems torn between the strictures of Afghan Islam, and the more relaxed, easy-going ways of the West. From only ever having had burka-clad women in his life, he's now seeing girls in the mags getting their tits out. Pretty quickly, he's talking as if every Western woman is like the ones he's seen in *FHM*. Truth be told, some of the female visitors we're getting in Kabul aren't helping much, either.

We get a lot of women passing through due to ECHO's humanitarian and development work. I don't mind tree-huggers per se, as long as they screw the nut. Some do: they dress sensibly and appropriately, which means wearing long pants and tops, to keep their flesh covered.

But then we get these female visitors who are to Brian like a walking wet dream. They pitch up in their tight, figure-hugging clothes, with acres of luscious blonde hair on show, and the Afghan males are staring at them as if they're lumps of meat, and available. And Brian's always at the forefront of the leering.

I try briefing these visitor types, most of whom are young, starry-eyed and determined to single-handedly rebuild Afghanistan and liberate the downtrodden Afghan women. I try telling them to screw the nut; to show no flesh, and keep their hair tied back or covered.

Predictably, I'm told that I'm just as bad as the Taliban. I take a deep breath and try really hard to be patient and polite.

'No,' I tell them, 'far as I'm concerned nothing would make me happier than you getting your tits out. But this is just the reality of life here in Afghan. And if you don't accept it, either someone will get very angry and pan you in the face, or you'll get raped.'

In the back of my mind, it's Brian who I fear might just be the first in line to assault them.

Whilst access to porn is pretty much a given for your average British soldier, it is very much a no-no for your average Afghan male. Under the Taliban, women who showed even the barest flash of ankle under their burka were beaten by the fanatical Virtue And Vice Squads. The Virtue And Vice goons – part of the Taliban's Ministry for the Promotion of Virtue And Prevention of Vice – toured Kabul scouring the streets for a flash of bare female flesh. Plus any woman out and about without her obligatory male escort would be equally savagely beaten. That male escort – her *maran* – either had to be the woman's husband, or a member of her close family. Any woman caught on the streets without a *maran* was in big trouble.

Under the Taliban even music was banned. And it goes without saying that being in possession of pornography would be a massive no-no. It would result in a public flogging, a stoning to death, or a beheading in Kabul's 'chop-chop square'.

Afghanistan is a deeply conservative Islamic country, and the Taliban had simply been the most extreme expression of that. That was the bigger picture within which Brian's desperate attempts to get his hands on some porn worried me. If I, or any other white-eye, got suckered into providing him some, where would it end? It wasn't the same as lending your porn magazine to a mate, who generally could find ways to satisfy his carnal needs via wives, girl-friends, or a brothel on an Amsterdam stopover.

Brian hailed from Jalalabad, so he was billeted in the embassy compound whilst working in Kabul. He lived in a converted garage on the compound. He was engaged to be married to some woman back home, but of course no sex before marriage in Afghan. So with Brian, there was no immediate outlet for his desires.

One night I'm relaxing in my hammock, when I get the call on the radio.

'Mr Phil! Mr Phil! Emergency!' It's one of the Afghan guards up at the embassy office, and he's panicking big time. 'We are overrun! Gunmen everywhere! People have been taken . . .'

I'm the team leader, this is my show, and the shit's hit the fan. I can hear my three fellow white-eyes making their weapons ready. They've obviously been scanning the radio net in their sleep, and they're on it.

I fetch the guys, and we're locked and loaded and ready for action. As per our standard operating procedures, one bloke will stay with the Ambo to secure him, whilst the rest pile into the vehicles to go investigate.

By now we've got a Land Rover Discovery, as well as the G-Wagon. It's faster, so I take that, with the other blokes following in the armoured beast. I scream down the road, tyres screeching on the roundabout at Ronnie Barker's, and up past the US embassy going like a bat out of hell.

I reach the embassy office, only to find the front gates have been rammed by some kind of vehicle, and are smashed to fuck. I can't drive in, as there's a body flat on the deck in the middle of the entranceway.

I slam on the anchors and come to an abrupt stop in the gateway. I see the G-Wagon skid to a halt behind me, and in seconds the three of us are on the deck in all-round defence.

I'm expecting gunfire, but there is none. In fact, it's spookily, ominously silent. My mind's racing. *What the fuck is going on? Who the fuck has hit the office? And where the fuck are the bad guys?*

One of our Afghan guards pokes his head out of the shattered gateway, and starts screaming. He's pointing down the road, and yelling hysterically at me in Farsi. I can't understand a word of what he's saying, 'cause he's so out of control.

I look where he's pointing.

Some three hundred metres down the street, there's a group of Afghans with guns. As I look towards them they start yelling aggressively, and taking up fire positions. We reciprocate, taking cover behind the armoured G-Wagon. It's about to kick off big time.

We three are outnumbered ten to one, but I've got two of the best on my shoulder, and we'll give as good as we get. My main worry is who the hell is attacking us and why, and who they might have hurt or seized from within the office.

I figure maybe it's a kidnapping. Nothing else seems to make any sense here.

For several seconds it's frozen in a stand-off, with us menacing them with our weapons, and them menacing us back. Something has to give. I make the decision to break the stalemate.

I yell at my blokes: 'Fucking cover me. I'm moving forward to find out what the fuck's going on.'

I sling my AK over my shoulder. I put my hands down at my sides, where the gunmen can see them, in a non-aggressive posture. Whoever these guys are, I need them to know I'm coming forward to talk – to parley – not to launch some Jedi use-the-Force elite warrior assault.

I start walking.

I'm halfway towards the gunmen when they yell at me to drop my weapon. Instead, I turn around and retrace my steps. I hand my AK and my Makarov to the lads, and I drop my webbing kit with them.

I turn around and start the walk again.

I'm the boy from the kids' home who made it into The Regiment, and now I'm running a private security job with a staff of fifty under me. No way am I letting it all go tits-up on my watch. So it's once more into the valley of death, alone and unarmed.

Needs must, old boy.

I make two hundred and fifty yards, and with each step I'm expecting to feel a bullet in the guts. We've taken delivery of our space-age Kevlar body armour by now, but in the scramble to get here I've forgotten to slip it on. I'm a soft-skinned, unarmed target.

A voice rings out, yelling at me to halt. I do as instructed.

A figure comes forward. He's a burly, rough-looking Afghan, dressed in traditional garb, and he's not looking entirely friendly. He pats me down, to make sure I've got no hidden weapons.

Then he spins me around, places a hand on my shoulder, and points me towards the group of gunmen.

I reach them, and still no one's being overly aggressive or threatening. I'm pushed onwards, towards a gate in a nearby compound wall. But once I'm through it, and away from the cover of my team, the mood turns.

I get punched in the head from behind, and there are muzzles shoved in my face. There's a mob of gunmen around me screaming abuse in Farsi. I know I've got to react fast, or I'm going under.

The first guy who tries to shove me from the front, I knock his weapon aside with one hand, and palm him hard in the chest with the other. He practically takes off.

At the same time I'm yelling: 'FUCK RIGHT OFF OUT OF MY FACE, YOU CUNTS!'

I repeat the performance with the next two blokes who try it, and they start to back off. I've shown them that I'm not afraid, and that I'm willing to stand and fight. Either they put a bullet in me, or they're going to have to say hello to the Hampshire Hammer.

Respect.

'Where's your fucking boss man?' I demand of them, in Farsi. 'Show me your big man if you want to talk.'

I'm telling them that I'm not negotiating with the organ-grinder's monkeys. Either it's the organ-grinder himself, or nothing.

They lead me further into the building. We cross this open courtyard, and there's a lumpy, indistinct figure lying on the floor. For a moment I fear it's one of the embassy staff, hostage number one in whatever game is being played here.

Then I realize that the figure is dressed in a burka, and there's a hysterical crying coming from deep within the folds of the material. I look closer. The sieve-like holes at the front of the burka are splattered in blood.

Whoever the figure is, she's clearly taken a savage beating to her face.

She won't look up from the ground as I pass. I've got this ominous feeling now. Whatever shit has gone down here, it seems pretty certain that a local woman is involved.

I step into a room. It's thick with smoke, ill-lit and brooding. All noise ceases as I enter. All eyes turn on me. It takes a second or so for my vision to adjust to the gloom. Then I see two figures kneeling in one corner. Each has his hands on his head, and is facing the wall.

I recognize one straight away. It's the Ambo's driver, Brian.

CHAPTER 20

Brian's a total mess. He's pissed and probably shit himself with fear, as the stain around his crotch evidences.

One of the gunmen tries shoving me into the room, in a show of bravado.

I turn on him, and palm him in the chest. '*BURRA! BURRA!*' I'm yelling, which means 'hands off' in the local lingo

It's instantly clear who the big man is in here. He's sat astride a sofa, with these flunky-type gunmen to either side of him. All are glaring at me.

The boss man stares at me for a few seconds. 'So, I see you not afraid,' he finally remarks, speaking passable English.

I look him in the eye: '*Mushkila?*'

Do we have a problem?

He looks a little taken aback: 'You speak Farsi?'

'No Farsi. Inglesi.'

Let's do this in English.

He's unsure what languages I speak now, which gives me a tiny bit of an edge. And he's getting the message that I'm not willing to take the back seat here.

I ask him again, in Farsi: '*Mushkila?*'

He replies in broken English. 'We had the information your driver had the womens in the rooms. They are not married to this womens. But they are having the sex with this womens. So we check. We find this man,' he gestures at Brian, 'how do you say . . .'

He gestures a man masturbating.

'Wanking,' I offer, helpfully. 'That's called wanking.'

'As you say – wankling – over this women, and this man,' he indicates the other kneeling figure, 'having the sex with this same women.'

He shakes his head in disapproval. 'Two men having the sex with this one womens . . .' Then he adds, somewhat unnecessarily: 'All this strictly the forbidden things in Islam.'

I nod. 'I understand why you are upset. But you've broken the law by going onto embassy property. That is European territory, and you shouldn't be there.'

He says: 'Yes, maybe, but these mens need the punishment. The how-do-you say – the justice. I take them to Afghan police so they can justice them.'

I say: 'Fair enough, they should face justice. But I don't want them dealt with unfairly. I don't want them dealt with tonight, not whilst tempers are running high.'

If Brian and the guard get their 'justice' tonight, they'll be beaten to within an inch of their lives, that's if they're lucky. More likely, these guys will kill them.

Brian's been an idiot, that's for sure. But I like him. And in our rulebook, for what he's been caught doing he'd likely get a 'well done' from the lads. A bit pervy, maybe, but fair enough in a time of war.

'You've clearly given them a good beating.' I motion towards Brian and the guard, both of whom have black eyes and bloodied, puffy faces. 'Let's make that enough for tonight, okay?'

The big man gives me this look. 'These two mens put up big fight. My mens had to control them.'

I know this is bullshit. Brian couldn't beat the skin off a rice pudding, let alone give anything to the kind of hairy-arsed Afghan troopers this guy's surrounded himself with. But I let it go.

'These mens are Afghan,' the big man continues. 'They need to be dealt with by Afghan. Who are you, anyway?'

I flash him my ID card. 'I'm the European embassy's Security Representative,' I tell him. I'm trying to bluff it that I'm a diplomat somehow.

'I want see your Ambassador,' he declares.

'The Ambassador isn't in-country,' I counter. 'But if you can wait until the morning, I will bring full diplomatic representation to speak with you.'

It's a ploy to try to buy Brian some time, to get him through this night. I can see him glancing at me out of the corner of his eye, desperately. He's hanging on my every word.

'If you guarantee their security, you can keep them until the morning,' I continue. 'Then, I will bring the diplomats. But I don't want to return here to find them smashed to pieces, or dead. And there's still the issue of you entering European property illegally.'

He shrugs. Smiles this nicotine-stained smile. 'Agreed. They not die tonight.' Then, bizarrely, he gestures at the low table in front of him. 'You and I will drink the tea?'

I accept, largely for Brian and the guard's sake. Anything to try to build some rapport with this guy; to keep them both alive. Tea is poured, then the big man offers me a ciggie. I light up and he's asking me where I come from. I tell him London, 'cause it's easy. We chat about football, which is the one thing that we have in common.

In the process of talking, I manage to throw in a few big names, President-in-waiting Karzai's amongst them. In return, I find out exactly who this guy is. He's a political leader for this district of Kabul, the equivalent, if we have one, of a county councillor.

Which means he's not that far up the food chain, but far enough to get away with topping Brian.

I leave, promising to be back in the morning with 'the diplomats'. As I exit the compound his apes are still eyeballing me. I give them a good long stare, and a winning smile.

I walk back to the wagon, give the lads a quick heads-up, and we do a quick DIY job to block up the smashed-in gate. Chris, who is a superlative medic, starts dealing with the wounded, whilst I do a damage assessment. The compound's been shot up a little, as the gunmen seized Brian and his fuck-buddy, but there's no serious damage done.

A couple of hours later we stand down. We drive back to base and gather in the *salle à manger*, the embassy residence's kitchen-cum-canteen.

And there we have a good laugh about how close everyone came to shooting everyone, and what a total liability Brian's proven to be. It's a case of come back Dilaka, all is forgiven, even the sweat patches.

The next morning I go see the big man again, but by now I feel about as welcome as a turd in a punchbowl. Brian's fate is already sealed, no matter what our diplomatic delegation may argue. Someone high up in the Afghan police has been tipped off, and it's gone way above the big man's pay grade, or mine for that matter.

The last I see of Brian is his face in the back of a prison bus, being carted off to somewhere worse than hell. He looks as if he's just been diagnosed with terminal brain cancer, the poor bastard.

Brian was a decent bloke, and I feel for him. He was due to get married in two weeks' time, and now his life is over. And all because he was trying to rehearse a bit of what he wanted to do to his wife when they finally tied the knot.

Following the Brian incident, we have a massive shakedown of security. My biggest worry is how the gunmen breached the office perimeter, and snatched people seemingly at will. We rig up CCTV covering all angles of approach, and get some nasty coils of razor wire strung around the walls.

The Ambo wants one of us white-eyes on duty at the office now at all times. I argue that won't work. If one of us lot had been present during the Brian incident, we'd have had no choice but to brass up the attackers big time. On seeing the front gate being rushed, we'd have started double-tapping the Afghan gunmen.

A lone operator is highly vulnerable. He's got no back-up, no partner to watch his back. His only option is to use instant, lethal force and aggression. If that had happened during the Brian incident, it would have turned into a total bloodbath. It's far better to keep the four of us together at the residence, as a Quick Reaction Force (QRF). It was only because I had serious back-up that I managed to defuse the situation without anyone getting killed.

The Ambo sees the logic of my argument, and that's how we decide to configure things from now on.

In spite of the Brian incident – or maybe because of it – I'm starting to build a great rapport with the Ambo. I guess he recognizes I put my life on the line walking into that gang-fuck alone and unarmed, in an effort to rescue the situation. It's the lone G-Wagon drive from Sarobi mark two.

A few days later, the Ambo has to present himself to President-in-waiting Hamid Karzai on some important European business. It's the first time they'll have met, and I'm determined to stick with the Ambo as his security at all times.

Recently, Karzai's security team saved him from an assassination attempt down in Kandahar, to the south of the country. It's evidence enough that suicide bombers can strike anywhere, anytime,

and conceivably inside Karzai's palace. That's why I'm staying with
the Ambo wherever he goes, and even if I have to do so kind of
undercover.

Karzai lives in this grand, palatial building, surrounded by plush
gardens in which there's a VIP parking area. The Close Protection
(CP) teams of visiting dignitaries all managed their visits in the
same way: they drop their VIP at the entrance to the palace, then
gather with the other CP teams in the VIP car park, awaiting his
or her return.

I decide to run things differently.

The private security teams out here have an informal uniform:
it's desert-boot footgear, 5/11 cargo pants, MP5s or AKs slung on
a chest sling, and CIA-style shades. For the visit to Karzai's palace
I don my suit, tie and shiny shoes. This means that in the eyes of
everyone – my fellow CP operators included – I must be a diplomat.

I have a Makarov tucked in my waistband, but it's well hidden.

We pitch up at the palace, park the G-Wagon in the VIP area,
and the Ambo and I head inside. There's a group of diplomats
waiting to meet Karzai, and the Ambo falls into conversation with
them. I can't stay on his shoulder, for then I'm obviously security.
I take up my own position where I can keep eyes on him, but where
it's not obvious who I'm with.

The Afghan President-in-waiting comes down the staircase, works
the room a little and comes over to me. He shakes me by the hand.
We do the introductions and he asks me where I'm from. I tell him
the European embassy, and it's clear he just presumes that I'm the
Ambo.

We fall into this easy conversation. Meanwhile Karzai's CP team
have got their eyes out on stalks. These guys are all Americans, and
they know me well enough already from around town. They're
dressed in their smart, pressed uniforms and they're tooled up to

the nines with body armour, webbing kit, thigh-mounted pistol holsters and shades. They're staring at me like: *What the hell is this necky Limey doing wandering around in a swanky suit, and talking to the Afghan President-to-be?*

They're at a loss as to what to do. They can hardly interrupt Karzai's and my conversation, to tell him that actually I'm not the Ambassador, I'm his security bloke.

'So how are you finding Afghanistan?' Karzai asks me.

'Very nice,' I tell him. 'Lovely. We're planning a trip up the Panjshir Valley shortly, and isn't the weather pleasant this time of year?'

'Where are you from?' Karzai asks.

'I'm from Southampton.'

'How long have you been here, and how are you settling in?'

By now the Ambo's hovering on my shoulder, waiting to break in. It's like a role reversal, but the Ambo doesn't elbow me in the ribs or kick me in the shin. He's incredibly laid back, and anyway I reckon he appreciates the crack of the thing. Plus he likes having me there as his unshakable shadow.

Eventually, I step back and the Ambo steps forward and it's all good. We retire to this meeting room. There's a large, oval polished table with nametags set around it on seats. I remove the one next to the Ambo's seat, and take it.

There's this big kerfuffle when finally they realize there's not enough seats for everyone in the room. I sit there tutting under my breath, as the palace lackeys run around trying to sort it out. The Ambo's totally aware that it's me who's messed things up, but he's not breathing a word. In fact, he loves it.

It's the Herat Café factor again. The Ambo's got this wild, unorthodox streak which runs real deep, and that's why he and I get on so well. Come to think of it, he's the kind of maverick, lateral thinker we could have used well in The Regiment.

But maverick though he may be, the Ambo's still hamstrung by political correctness. And it's our policy of recruiting an Afghan security team regardless of tribe that is proving our biggest liability, now that Brian's gone. The embassy is trying to enforce a policy of 'equal opportunities' in a country that's been segregated along tribal lines for millennia. I've warned the Ambo that this is a recipe for disaster. He knows it. And so it proves.

It doesn't take long before our Afghan guard force has started segregating themselves. We've ended up with Pashtuns in one building and Tajiks in another – two tribes who just months ago were at each other's throats, fighting a murderous civil war.

At the residence, the Afghan chef has built her own personal empire in the kitchens and *salle à manger*, where every staff member comes from her tribe, the Hazara. It's reached a stalemate that is a triumph of Western political correctness over Afghan reality.

And I know that it's not working, and that soon it's going to blow.

CHAPTER 21

I figure we need more razor wire, both to keep our tribal ghettos firmly segregated and for our own security reasons. That stuff is nasty, and a real deterrent to troublemakers, both inside and outside your operation.

Piled up to shoulder height, it forms a tangled mesh of wire coils, each sprouting mini razorblades like talons. You touch that stuff it snares you. The more you struggle, the deeper the fang-like blades bite, snagging clothes and slicing deep into soft body parts. It's lethal.

Trouble is, there's been a rush on razor wire recently in Kabul. It's in precious short supply. I try all the usual sources, but can't seem to get hold of any. Then I get a call from this Aussie guy called Bruce, who works for a defence stores procurement company in Kabul.

He's heard I need razor wire and he can get me some. He claims to be ex-Aussie SAS – a Regiment with as fine a reputation as Hereford, or so the Aussies would have it. I figure a bloke like that isn't going to fuck us around. Bruce comes to see me, we shake on the deal, and he promises to get us our razor wire 'within days'.

Two weeks go by and there's not a sniff of it. The Ambo's on my back, as he knows we need it bad. Otherwise we might suffer a second Brian incident, only this one on a massive scale, and fuelled by age-old tribal enmities. I beg some razor wire off the British Army base at Sutah, but it's nowhere near enough to go around.

I keep calling Bruce, but he's not answering his cellphone. I'm fucking fuming. I do some digging, working the network. It turns out that Bruce isn't ex-Aussie SAS at all. He was a nightclub bouncer back in Sydney, before heading for the rough and tumble of Kabul.

A few weeks later I'm at a UN party downtown. I'm on duty and I'm not drinking, so as to allow the rest of my team to let their hair down proper. Halfway through the evening, a familiar figure walks into the room. It's Bruce.

He's a big guy. Bigger than me, in fact. And it looks as if he spends a lot of time working out in the gym. It strikes me he was probably primping himself in the gym when he should have been procuring us our razor wire.

He can hardly avoid me here, so he strides over. Tries a man-hug. 'Phil, mate! How you doin'? Long time no see, mate.'

I tell him he should come outside to see the new tyres we've got on our vehicles. I tell him they're these new run-flat models, which can take any amount of gunfire and keep rolling.

We step around the back of the UN building, and as soon as we're out of sight of the revellers, I let him have the Big Hampshire Hammer. Once only, with all the pent-up rage and anger that's accumulated over the razor-wire incident, right on the point of the chin. He lifts slightly, then goes down like a sack of shit.

He's not quite out cold, so I lean over him to have words. 'You made me look like a total twat in front of the Ambo. You lied to me, repeatedly, and put lives at risk on my operation. You got what was coming. Cross me again, mate, and you're dead.'

I know Bruce is the kind of wannabe wanker who'll try to get me in the shit for what I've just done. The next morning I'm up mega-early, so I can go have words with the Ambo. I catch him in the *salle à manger*, getting an early breakfast.

'Steen, you know the bloke supplying the razor wire who fucked us around?'

He nods. 'Yeah. Useless Bruce.'

'I knocked him out last night.'

The Ambo pauses, then laughs. 'Well, it is a good job they do not have the same legal system here as we have in Sweden.'

That's it – enough said. A little later Bruce's boss puts a call through to the Ambo. Sure enough, Bruce has reported me for assault, but the Ambo's having none of it.

'There is nothing to discuss,' he tells him.

In fact, the Ambo thinks it only right that his security team take no shit off anyone. That's what he wants in a team, and that's what he's got in us lot.

The next time I run into Bruce, he asks me why I hit him. I figure maybe he was too out of it to have heard the words I told him on the night. So I tell him again: he'd lied about the razor wire, and put the lives of my clients in danger. Plus his story of a life of derring-do in the Australian military elite is a crock of shit.

I never have been able to abide the bullshitters of this world. Bruce was an insult to the rest of us – lads like me who'd made their way in the world the only way, the hard way. I'd made my way out of the kids' homes and into The Regiment by sheer guts and stubborn determination, and because no one was going to stop me. And when you've fought so hard to attain your elite warrior status, the very idea of someone stealing it for free is infuriating.

Plus it cheapens the pedigree of those of us who dare.

*   *   *

I'd never been given the slightest break in my life, and I'd learned not to expect any. I'd never been given a leg-up, and I'd never been given any quarter. And in some ways maybe it was those years of bitter struggle that had given me the hunger to make it in the world.

Back in the kids' homes, my best mate Mick had a brother who lived in a squat. We were pushing eleven years old when Mick and I started acting as watch, whilst the older boys went thieving from the dockyard. Mick and I got cigarettes and drink in return for our efforts, plus a little money.

I was amazed at how brazen Mick's older brother and his gang were. They started nicking cars and taking them for 'joy rides' on the gravel tracks around the New Forest. Mick and I joined them. On a couple of occasions we were caught red-handed by the police, but we just shrugged it off. We told the police that we'd been hitch-hiking, and the guy who had picked us up had run off, leaving us with the car. The police would deliver a lecture about the dangers of young boys being picked up by 'weirdos', and that was that.

One day Mick and I were spotted by an off-duty member of the kids' home staff. He phoned the police, and they chased us along the seafront at Southsea. I was caught and chained to the railings, as the police went after Mick. A group of elderly ladies seized the initiative and surrounded me, giving me a good lashing with their umbrellas.

With each blow they were telling me exactly what they thought of me. When the police returned and saw what was happening they cracked up laughing. Once back at the police station I proceeded to give my arresting Sergeant a proper mouthful, and in return I got a good thrashing.

When the staff from Willow Lodge came to pick me up, the coppers told them that I'd resisted arrest, and that's how I'd got hurt.

I wasn't about to say otherwise. To snitch on anyone – even the 'coppers' – was unacceptable in the kids' home.

Eventually, I was moved from Willow Lodge to Lakeside Lodge, a 'secure' facility. The move was designed to stop me from absconding, but I wasn't about to allow anyone to get in the way of my freedom. All I'd ever experienced from those who curtailed my freedom – my adoptive parents first and foremost – was violence and abuse.

Freedom, and the freedom from adult abusers, was the oxygen of my life. Living rough in the woods I could be free from those in authority, and free of the abuse that came with it. Nothing was going to curb my quest for freedom, least of all Lakeside Lodge. I viewed the place as a challenge, and made sure I escaped even more often. I went over fences, through roofs and out of windows. Any remotely feasible escape route was good enough for me. On one occasion I was caught whilst lowering Mick from a third-floor window, on a rope made of lashed-together bed sheets.

The staff grabbed me and dragged me back inside, not realizing that I had hold of the 'rope'. Mick fell, hit the deck and broke both his ankles. I didn't know that he was hurt, and hoped he'd got away. As a result Mick had to crawl all the way around the care home perimeter to get help.

As time went by, my quest for freedom became driven by darker priorities. The vetting system for kids' home staff was almost non-existent, and those running Lakeside Lodge were dodgy as hell. The night staff consisted of two older blokes, and from the very first they gave me the creeps.

My bad feelings were confirmed when I saw them dealing with the bed-wetters. They'd arrive on the scene, and force whichever boy had wet himself to succumb to a groping. There were younger kids than me at the place, and the night staff would check down the boys' pyjamas to 'make sure you've taken your pants off before bed'. They pretended to be doing so to protect the young boys' manhood, claiming it 'wouldn't grow properly' if they kept their pants on. But all the while they'd be having a good long feel. I knew what was going on, but it was everyone for himself in that kids' home.

From the very start I warned those two night staff to 'fuck off and leave me alone'. I threatened to alert the day staff to what they were doing with the younger boys if they tried anything with me. They must have thought I was bluffing. Late one night the two of them came to my bed for a 'pants check'. Before they'd even touched me, I grabbed the wooden bed leg that I kept hidden beneath my pillow, and started smashing the nearest guy over the head.

The other bloke had to haul me off, but not before I'd given the Groper a damn good malleting. The day staff were told that the Groper's head injuries had been caused by an accident. But after that the night staff left me well alone, so much so that I could come and go in the dark pretty much as I pleased.

It was fight and survive in those homes, as it had been with my adoptive family. And in a way, it was learning to survive in that brutal school of life that set me up for the life of a soldier.

My education was non-existent; my qualifications and life skills were bordering on zero.

All I did know was how to fight and survive.

CHAPTER 22

By now I'm onto my third three-month contract in Kabul, and I've got some eighty Afghan staff under me. It's grown into a big operation, and it's a far larger force than I ever had any degree of control over during my time in the military. It's a serious level of responsibility, and there are the stresses and strains that go with that.

Thankfully, the Ambo's hugely supportive, and he's also game for a laugh. Whenever there's a chance of some down time, he grabs it with both hands. As a kid I was big into fishing. It wasn't so much the sport I enjoyed, it was more being out alone in the wilds, with the chance of something tasty to eat at the end of it.

We take a trip across to Bamian, 'cause the Ambo wants to see the site of what were once the world's largest Buddhas. These Buddha figures had been carved out of the sheer, rock cliffs, hundreds of feet high. They must have been an awesome sight when intact. More's the pity, then, when the mindless Taliban fanatics decided to blow them up.

Demolitions were actually my key specialism in the military. I like blowing stuff up and destroying things. I was a bit of vandal when a kid, so it was all the better getting paid to do it. But whatever brainless lunatics decided to blow up the Bamian Buddhas needed a belt of C4 strapped around their waists on a short fuse. The wankers.

There's a stunning river that runs through the Bamian valley, one lined by weeping willow trees. I suggest a spot of fishing to the Ambo, to cheer us up after seeing the ruins of the blasted Buddhas. He's not a big fisherman, but he mans up and wades in regardless.

I've read somewhere that you can find 'snow trout' in Afghanistan's cold, high-altitude streams, and some weird ray-finned fish called a Common Miranka in the warmer, lowland waters. I figure the Bamian river might be right for containing the latter, but we don't catch a thing. Still, I figure I'm on my way to a world record for fishing the world's most dangerous rivers, which is a consolation.

By now the Ambo's got a new right-hand man at the embassy office, a Brit called Julian. Julian's become one of the key fixtures in our efforts to have some serious fun. He wasn't that appreciative of my team at first, not until one of us lot had to drag him out of a shitfight on the streets of Kabul.

Julian had driven to the UN Club, to have a game of squash. One of the new blokes on my team, a superlative operator called Jase, was riding shotgun for the day. As Julian had gone to play his game, he'd made the usual dismissive remark: *What was the point in Jase sitting in the vehicle for the next hour?*

Halfway through the game, a suicide bomber had driven a truck packed with explosives into the gate of the UN compound. There was the world's most almighty explosion, and the UN base was burning.

Jase went in, dragged Julian out of the squash hall where he'd been cowering and shaking like a dog having a shit, and bundled him into the vehicle. Jase used the armoured G-Wagon to get him out of there pronto and back to the embassy residence. After that, Julian becomes our biggest fan ever, second only to the Ambo.

The four of us – Jase, Julian, the Ambo and me – strike up an unusual golfing partnership. Every month I have to go on a run to Pakistan by air, to pick up cash so the Ambo can pay the local staff. Whilst in Islamabad, I've taken to purchasing the city's supply of golf balls.

Hidden amongst the mountainous outskirts of Kabul I've discovered a huge, deserted lake that makes the ideal driving range. Every Friday when Kabul shuts down for the weekend, we take the golf bags and head up there for a spot of sport. We drive the balls into the lake, taking turns to see who can cause the biggest splash at the greatest distance.

Then I discover that there's a golfing green nearby, one that's been turned into a minefield. Not a bother, we decide. We start this competition to see who can drive a ball from the edge of the green to a nominated hole.

It's all good at first. But each time we go there to play, we're surrounded by a growing crowd of Afghan kids. Finally, they start running onto the green to grab the balls. It's not quite what we had intended.

One day Jase, Julian and I head up to the lake. We're driving some balls into the water when the first shots ring out. Jase and I hit the deck, dragging Julian down with us, and there's a sustained burst of fifteen rounds hammering over our heads.

I get my eyes up for long enough to see the gunman, who's legging it across the rocky shore of the reservoir. Whoever or whatever he was shooting at, he seems to be bugging out, which means we can break cover and get Julian the hell out of there. We bundle him into the vehicle, burn some rubber and we're gone.

Julian tells us he finds it all very 'warry'. Later that evening, over dinner he regales the Ambo with the story. The Ambo seems miffed to have missed out on some fun, and makes us promise to count him in the next time.

Beneath all this tongue-in-cheek bravado, we know it's hotting up for real in Kabul. Not a week goes by without an explosion or a gun battle, and we've been caught in a good few ourselves. We've been up around the US embassy twice now, and had a gunfight kick off big time.

One time we were passing by the embassy gate, and some lunatic in the car behind let off a shot in the Yanks' general direction. In response, the gate guards loosed off a whole series of mags at the vehicle to our rear, smashing it apart.

Luckily, due to our prearranged escape routes, we got to drive the hell out of there. The real danger these days is to get caught in the crossfire of a terrorist attack, a US Army response, or a bout of tribal infighting.

Suicide bombings; car bombings; truck bombings; swarm attacks against installations by groups of fast-moving insurgents: all of the above are on the up. Plus there's been a spike in kidnappings, the victims held for multi-million-dollar ransoms.

Any white-eye is a target for the Taliban and their kind. And a VIP like the Ambo is an extra-juicy prize. The Ambo's acutely aware of this, and that's why he wants a team around him who pull no punches, and who aren't about to fuck around when the bullets start to fly. The Ambo gets it. He gets what we're about. Some of the other dips don't, and I don't rate their chances of survival that highly out here.

I decide that our vehicles are becoming the proverbial bullet magnets. The G-Wagon may be armoured, but it screams out a mile off: *White-eye – come and get me.* Instead, I want a means of transport like the locals use. And I want something that can take me anywhere in the city totally unnoticed, and where no white-eye ever goes.

Chiefly, I've got in mind the vast slum that lies to the rear of Wazir Akbar Khan district. We've nicknamed it Brookside, and it's a vast cesspit of tiny one-roomed mud hovels populated by Afghan refugees. Two decades of war have produced millions of homeless, and I figure there's a million or more of them in Brookside.

I head for one of the main markets in downtown Kabul, and find just what I'm looking for. It's a battered old Kawasaki KDX 175cc off-road bike, in clay blue and orange. Nice colour scheme, and the typical choice of your average Afghan: honking.

I haggle for hours on end, and finally we settle on five hundred bucks. The seller agrees to throw in a battered blue full-face helmet, complete with go-faster stripes, and it's a deal.

The motorbike's a personal acquisition of mine, as opposed to an embassy purchase. I've tried explaining to the Ambo what I need it for, but he just doesn't seem to be with me on this one. He can't get his head around why I'd spurn a $200,000 armoured G-Wagon for a crappy little zip-around-in-thin-air trials bike.

Well, he's about to find out.

I score myself a blue dishdash to match the bike's paintwork and a pair of flip-flops, and with the helmet on and an AK slung across my chest I am totally indistinguishable from the locals. Or so I reckon.

I start riding the city streets alone on the KDX. The visor's scratched to buggery, but if it's this hard for me to see out, I figure no one's getting a look at my face to ID me as a white-eye. After a few short runs, I decide it's time to man-test it.

I drive out of Kabul heading for the British base at Sutah. I roar through the gates, only to find the squaddies in the midst of a spot of square bashing. I proceed to pull a wheelie all across the parade ground, scattering squaddies in every direction.

The Sergeant Major, who's a good mate of mine from my Green Army days, goes completely apeshit. He's screaming at his men: 'GET THAT FUCKIN' JUNDIE OFF MY FUCKIN' PARADE GROUND!'

I figure that's proof positive. No one who sees me on the KDX thinks of me as anything other than a local. I come to a halt on the bike, as this wall of British squaddies comes rushing towards me.

I pull off the helmet. They stop dead in their tracks. I smile my biggest smile, and an instant later they're roaring with laughter. I've been up here training most of these lads on local weapons, plus the Minimi squad assault weapon, so they recognize me.

Even the Sergeant Major can't help but laugh his rocks off. I get a bit of an ear-bashing from some of the older officers, who seem to seriously question my sanity, but the young lads think it's great. And if I'm honest, so do I.

Next, I start using the KDX on jobs with the Ambo. With the roads closed off for diplomatic cavalcades, we've always been prevented from sending anyone on ahead of our convoy. But not now we're not.

I take to zipping down the backstreets, and it's like being in a Bond movie. The secret is to head for whatever gap you can find, and just keep moving. I'm zooming up and down stairs, along pavements and across roundabouts, and driving the KDX as if I've just stolen it.

Any number of times I hit a roadblock, zip the thing around with one leg planted in the dirt, and scoot off in the opposite direction. There's a very good reason for this. If I get stopped and challenged I have to speak, and then my cover will be blown. People will know that I'm a white-eye, so it's crucial never to stop riding.

It's a ride to live, live to ride kind of thing.

At first the Ambo can't understand how I'm always there ahead of him, getting his security and shit sorted at whatever destination he's headed. Plus the other CP teams are spitting blood that I'm keeping one step ahead of them.

I start taking the KDX up into the hills around Kabul, for some more golfing fun. It's a perfect icebreaker with the Afghan soldiers who man the anti-aircraft guns and isolated checkpoints up here on the high ground. I take them small gifts of batteries for their radio sets, and British Army ration packs, to lighten up their day.

Plus I give them a quick spin on the KDX.

There's a method to my madness here, a chaotic, evolving, random-motion kind of logic that's working its weird magic. We're in the midst of mapping some seriously off-road escape routes for getting the Ambo out of Kabul, for when it all goes tits-up big time. We'll need friends on these mountaintops to make those routes workable. And as the days go by, the Afghan soldiers up here are all getting to be good mates with motorbiking 'Big Mr Phil'.

I go out on a money-run to Pakistan, and I'm determined to purchase a pair of Rupert Bear golfing trousers. Unfortunately it's a Friday, and I've overlooked the fact that it's the start of their weekend. All the shops, even the top-notch golfing ones, are closed. Lesson learned: take good note of local daily and weekly rhythms and timings.

In fact, getting in tune with the daily pulse of a place is a key to survival. In Kabul, it enables me to work out when parts of the city should or shouldn't be busy. If a normally crowded street falls silent during rush hour, I know it's not a good moment for me to be there. Time to spin the KDX around and burn some rubber.

I do a second Pakistan money-run, and manage to score a pair of classic tartan pants. They're green, black and red, just like Rupert Bear trousers should be. I ride the KDX up to my favourite mountaintop guard post proud in my new threads. By the time I've reached their bleak position, the Afghan soldiers are hooting with laughter.

I do a couple of circuits around their gun emplacement, just so they can really admire the tartans, then I pull over for a brew. We're shooting the shit, and I'm handing out British Army brew kits, and all the while I'm taking a good look at the surrounding terrain.

These guys sit slap bang on the favoured escape route that we've scoped out – one that gets us out of the city without using any of the main roads. Trouble is, it passes by a couple of key Afghan Army communications facilities, which is why the guard post is here.

Civvies aren't really allowed up here. But by now the Afghan soldiers are getting used to Big Mr Phil, the mad Englishman. I reckon the tartan pants are the clincher, for who amongst them is ever going to forget me pitching up here in my Rupert Bear costume?

The next time I'm up here – or maybe the time after that – and I've got the team with me, plus the Ambo, and we're running for our lives, I reckon they'll know it's just Big Mr Phil, and they'll laugh and point and wave me on through.

It's not rocket science this. It's what we called 'hearts-and-minds operations' back in the military.

And I figure it's hearts and minds that might just save our skins here in the cauldron of Kabul.

CHAPTER 23

By now I know Kabul city better than I do London or Southampton. I know all the backstreets, alleyways, short cuts and rat runs. I know what times of day they're clogged up and what time of day they're clear. I know where the checkpoints are if they want to close the city down, and how to avoid them.

The KDX has been the key to all of this.

I figure I'm ready for the ultimate test: to ride Brookside. The shantytown stretches like a vast globule of vomit running down from the hillsides to the city limits. It's the ultimate in covert escape routes: off-limits, unmapped, labyrinthine, chaotic, and closed to outsiders.

No one is even going to dream of us trying to escape that way. And no one is ever going to try to follow us through there. If I can find a way through, the slum will take us into the hills, from where we've already mapped a route through to the far side.

I do the first drive in daylight, alone on the KDX. It goes like a dream. No one pays me any heed, and whilst I hit a good few dead ends, and stinking alleyways too steep to navigate, I stick to the golden rule: *keep riding*.

I map the route through by memory. Once back at base, I draw a sketch from what I've fixed in my head. Now we have to move on to part two of testing the escape route: will it take a vehicle like the Pajero or the G-Wagon?

We do the first drive during broad daylight, but dressed like locals. We take the Pajero, for it's less obviously a white-eye wagon. We get some weird looks as we barrel through, but the route works like clockwork. We drive it by day again, then by night, and finally by night showing no lights and using Night Vision Goggles (NVG).

We've now got our escape route sorted. I write up the standard operating procedures we'll use to evacuate the Ambo, and leave them on file at the base. If I'm away or I've been shot or captured, any one of the lads – even a new guy – can pick up the file and follow the escape route out of there.

It's a peach. If and when it all goes horribly wrong in Kabul, every CP team will be bogged down on the main highway trying to get out. As for us, we'll be heading east via Brookside, avoiding the city completely. We'll be long gone into the hills, from where we've mapped routes to the airport, to the British camp at Sutah, and even to the Jalalabad road.

We had a popular saying in the military units I served with: *Presumption is the mother of all fuck-ups.* It's rule number one of elite soldiering: never presume or surmise. You have to prove you can do what you say you can do, ideally by using dry runs before attempting the mission for real.

We do the same here in Kabul. One night we get the Ambo into the G-Wagon, the lads in the Pajero as back-up, and we make like we're on the run for real. We head into Brookside driving on no lights and with NVG, and we're going like a couple of bats out of hell. The Ambo loves it, but more importantly we rehearse what has to be done.

Then we take the Ambo out onto the ranges, at Camp Sutah, and we rehearse our fire drills when evacuating a vehicle. We carry him down the ranges in pairs, doing fire-and-manoeuvre drills with live ammo, the rounds buzzing around the Ambo's head like angry bees.

The only people doing such drills to the level we are in Afghan are the lads from The Regiment. But I figure the Ambo has to experience what it's like to be under fire, and to be in an ambush, so that he doesn't freeze and fuck up our escape procedures when it happens for real.

The Ambo's so lit up by what we've done that he demands the rest of the senior diplomatic staff get similar training. I've never had so much fun as when we get Hercule and Pepe down the ranges, and practically shoot their Frenchie balls off.

Money couldn't buy such entertainment. Priceless.

Then the Ambo decides all new dips who arrive in-country have to do a weekend course with us, before being allowed into Kabul. No problemo. Why should they fly in and presume they know how to operate in the world's most dangerous city? Better they experience a little lead flying around their heads, before they get anywhere near Kabul.

There isn't another dip in Afghanistan better protected or prepared than ours, and the Ambo knows it. He wants to say a big thank you to me for all that I've done for the mission to date.

He blags me an invite to one of the swankiest diplomat parties this side of Paris. There's the finest alcohol available in bucketloads, along with tray after tray of caviar and foie gras and the like. I've rarely, if ever, seen such a feast of fine booze and fine food. The place is swimming with slick dinner jackets and bow ties, and shapely women in high heels and slinky Prada dresses. It's hard to believe that all of this is actually taking place in downtown Kabul.

I glance around the ballroom, as I take another glass of Moët and neck it, and lunge for my umpteenth helping of caviar. I reflect upon my life. I can't help but wonder how it's gone from shit sandwich – my upbringing – to caviar canapé, the kind of setting that I now find myself in.

A fine-looking woman sidles over to me. 'Hello,' she purrs. 'I've not seen you around before. Which of the embassies are you with?'

I smile that winning Big Phil smile. 'I'm not. I'm an uneducated, ill-mannered, gun-toting rough-as-fuck ex-soldier who shouldn't even be here. I'm a wolf amongst sheep, love. A gun-for-hire. But if you stick by my side, you'll have more crack tonight than you'll get with any of the dips in a month of bloody Sundays. Champers?'

I can see that she's intrigued. A little shocked even. But she accepts the glass of bubbly, and can't pull away.

I have never tried to hide my past from anyone, no matter who they are, or what venue I find myself in. I have never pretended to be anything other than I am – the boy from the shitty kids' home who somehow made good.

I learned my lesson the hard way that there's no use pretending to be someone you're not.

I was aged twelve and a serial absconder feeding from rubbish bins and sleeping rough, when the state decided to give me a second chance. I was offered a way out of the kids' homes – a government-sponsored place at Kingham Hill, a posh, fee-paying boarding school for the children of the privileged.

I had a social worker, Dianne Ferry, who used to visit me regularly. For some reason she saw this great potential in me, in spite of my feral ways. It was Dianne who had talked the authorities into offering me the chance of a place at Kingham Hill.

Dianne had carried out these various tests on my IQ, and I had scored astoundingly well. She knew I was intelligent, quick-witted and sharp, if a little wild. I guess she recognized that all I needed was to be given the one break in life.

Dianne was the one adult who I actually trusted. I felt closer to her than I ever had done to Audrey, or my beat-me-up 'father'. I knew that Dianne had my best interests at heart. Now she'd won me a place at a top-notch private school, which even back then charged thousands of pounds a term for boarding pupils.

I promised Dianne that I'd give Kingham Hill my best shot, and that I'd try to make good.

Of course, nothing could have contrasted more with my previous life than Kingham Hill. Set in the leafy green rolling hills of the Cotswolds, this was about as far away from my previous schooling, and my upbringing, as ever you could get.

Founded in the 1800s by a Christian philanthropist, Kingham Hill has its own chapel, swimming pool, drama theatre, cricket pitch and pavilion, plus riding stables of course.

My arrival there – sweeping down the long gravel driveway, through acre upon acre of manicured lawns – set my heart racing. As the grand stone buildings of the school drew closer, I wondered how on earth was I – the boy from the kids' home who was happiest living rough in the woods – going to fit in here?

During term times I was scheduled to board at Kingham Hill. During holidays I would return to Lakeside Lodge, whereas all the other pupils would be going to their homely houses, and their ever-so-nice parents.

Living such a split life was hardly going to be easy, but I was determined to make it work. At first I tried to hide my background from the other kids, desperate as I was to fit in. But I had just about zero chance of doing so. From the very start it was obvious that I wasn't their kind.

I didn't particularly struggle with the academic side of things, but the social side was a nightmare. I didn't speak like the other pupils. I hadn't been through the same 'prep-school' system that they had. I didn't know the mores and social etiquette that was expected of me.

And all of that singled me out as a misfit.

Within the first week I'd earned the nickname 'Kevin', a withering reference to my social class. The pupils had found out pretty quickly that the state was paying for me to be there, and in their eyes that made me common as muck.

The school chaplain, a Reverend Shepton, could see what I was going through. He made a real effort to talk to me about it, and to help. I confessed to him how hard it was for me being there, and how lonely and isolated I felt.

But it wasn't good to be seen with the Reverend too often. The older boys taunted me remorselessly, accusing me of being a 'teacher's pet'.

Knowing what a golden chance I'd been given, I was desperate not to lose it. I tried to keep my head down, but the constant mockery and low-level bullying was really getting to me.

But worse even than that was the way that everyone excluded me – the outsider, the lowlife misfit – from their group.

I had never felt so alone. It was clear that it couldn't last.

CHAPTER 24

When my first Christmas came around, the headmaster invited me to spend the festive break with him and his family. I was pretty much estranged from Audrey by now, and he knew I had nowhere else to go but the kids' home.

I was sorely tempted to take him up on his offer, but I turned him down for fear of being bullied. Plus there was a part of me that wanted to be loyal to my friends at Lakeside Lodge. I knew Mick and the other kids wouldn't be having a very merry Christmas of it themselves, and I wanted to stand by them. In reality, they were the only friends that I had. They accepted me for who I was, as one of their tribe. So I spent Christmas at Lakeside Lodge, and returned to Kingham Hill for the start of the spring term.

There was a mixed-race pupil in my year whose name was Cornelius. His parents were super-wealthy, and he had everything a kid could wish for. Cornelius spoke with a plum in his mouth, and he'd clearly been spoiled rotten in life. He and I had been at loggerheads from the very start of my time at Kingham Hill. Cornelius loved nothing more than to point out how I was different, and how those differences betrayed how I should never have been allowed into Kingham Hill.

He pointed out that I wore a standard-issue school uniform,

whereas all of the other kids had tailor-made suits. He was forever imitating my Southampton council estate accent, and tormenting me over where I went 'home' to during the holidays. He was never happier than when he had me isolated, and the other pupils ganging up on me. I tried to roll with the punches. I knew I couldn't resort to using my fists, for that would be the end of me at Kingham Hill. But I couldn't keep turning the other cheek for ever.

It all came to a head one evening during prep. Cornelius started taking the piss, because I couldn't afford the money to pay for a forthcoming school trip. He was taunting me by saying to the other kids that they should do a whip-round, so 'poor council estate Kevin' could come.

I couldn't take any more. Inside, I snapped.

Calm as can be I walked out into the boot room – the place where the pupils kept their outside shoes – picked up the heavy metal floor buffer, walked back in and without a word I slammed it down onto Cornelius's skull.

Cornelius collapsed onto his desk, bloodied and out cold.

I knew right away that it was all over for me at Kingham Hill.

I turned around and hurled the floor buffer through the study window, shattering it into a thousand pieces. In the shocked silence that followed, I started screaming at the other boys, challenging any one of them to have the guts to come forward and fight me.

All the months of teasing and torture had exploded inside me, and I was raging, the fight monster clawing at my soul. I had that message from my first fights at junior school running through my mind: *Show fear and you're finished.*

Anyone steps forward to take me on, I'm going to fucking kill him.

The standoff ended when a group of prefects intervened, and managed to talk me down. They took me to the school sanatorium. There I stayed for three days, whilst the school authorities deliberated what to do with me.

Sure enough, I was expelled. I was returned to Southampton and placed in George Buildings, a top-security assessment centre reserved for the truly bad boys.

I felt as if I'd let myself down savagely. I'd let my temper and aggression get the better of me. My one big chance had been blown, and I reckoned the state would have no time for me now.

Almost as soon as I got to George Buildings I ran away. I slept rough and broke into derelict buildings. I got a change of clothes by stealing off washing lines. I fed from bins. I knew I'd reached a new low in life, but I just wanted some time alone to sort my head out, and to deal with all the shit that had been dumped on me at Kingham Hill.

In those bitter, angry moments I asked myself if I regretted flooring Cornelius. Yes I did. But only because I'd blown my chances of getting the education of my dreams. Did I believe he deserved it? Yes, I bloody did. He was a bully and a snob who used his status to hurt others.

He'd been born with a silver spoon in his mouth, and all that had done was make him a total shit to those less fortunate. Maybe he didn't quite deserve the level of violence that I'd unleashed on him, but I'd been tortured for six months and finally I'd cracked.

After a couple of weeks living rough I found my way back to George Buildings, but even my social worker had washed her hands of me now. Dianne had been so proud of how I was doing at Kingham Hill. She'd felt her faith in me had been vindicated. But not any more. I'd betrayed the confidence that she had put in me – or at least, that's how she saw things – and it was the end of the road for her with me.

Eventually, I was transferred from George Buildings to a more permanent establishment. Hawk's Lease was a Church of England-sponsored kids' home, near Lyndhurst, which was run by the Church's Children's Society.

On my very first night I did a runner. I went AWOL for several days, living rough in the New Forest. Luckily for me, those running the home let me come back again, for it turned out to be a totally fantastic establishment. The staff were unlike anything I had ever experienced before: they were dedicated, humane and understanding.

There was an education centre, but you only had to attend if you felt like it. At weekends I was allowed to disappear into the New Forest, where I'd sleep rough, fish for trout, and live off the land. That satisfied my urge for solitude, freedom and the outdoors, so there was little need to run away any more.

At nearby Calshot there was an Activities Centre, with a dry ski slope, a climbing wall and water sports facilities. I began to spend a lot of time there, and it was the combination of the freedoms of this new home, plus the opportunities I found at Calshot, that reignited my enthusiasm for life.

One member of staff at the activities centre, Dave, took me under his wing. Dave was rumoured to have been in the SAS, which was hugely mysterious and exciting for a teenage lad like me. He taught me all these survival skills, which sharpened my ability to live rough in the wild.

Towards the end of my first year at Hawk's Lease, Audrey drove up to see me. She hadn't visited for years, and I refused point-blank to see her. She sat in her car, screaming and crying hysterically, until the staff persuaded her to leave.

They could understand now why I didn't want to spend any time with her.

I was approaching my sixteenth birthday when I did my course to qualify as a ski instructor. The Calshot Centre agreed to take me on, under a Youth Training Scheme (YTS). I left the home, got my own digs, had my rent paid by the council and earned £25 a week on top. Life was on the up.

Martin Dewey, a guy working at the Centre, was my guiding influence by now. I did extra, volunteer work at weekends, helping with boat repairs and painting. I learned how to sail, got myself a girlfriend, and being big for my age I managed to get served in most of the local pubs.

That Christmas I carried out the beery threat that I'd made in jest to the landlord of my local, the Turf Cutters – to stuff his Christmas tree down his chimney. Once I was sober I apologized, and spent three hours getting it down from the roof and resurrecting it.

After another night at the Turf Cutters I tried to rugby-tackle a New Forest pony. Another time I tried to ride a huge cow with a thick, furry coat. It was all a bit of harmless fun, and I was determined to avoid the pitfalls that most of the kids from the care homes fell into – drifting into a life of crime.

But with the period of my YTS fast running out, I had to consider my options. I had zero qualifications. The only exam I had passed was my cycling proficiency, and I had to do that twice – the second time getting a good mate to do the slow ride part of the test. The Army seemed about the one route left open to me.

It was Martin, plus his boss, Griff, who pushed me into joining up. Just before my seventeenth birthday they told me they'd have to let me go from the Calshot Centre. It was the best thing they could have done for me. I wanted to join the Paras, but my local Army centre was recruiting for the Royal Hampshires. So I signed up with them.

Back in Calshot I had a quick leaving do, and everyone wished me the best. My girlfriend told me she'd wait for me, and the next thing I knew I was getting on the back of an Army four-tonner at Lichfield train station.

Every platoon of the training depot had been named after a battle honour earned by the Regiment. I was joining Meeanee Platoon.

As we drove through the gates of the base I noticed how spotless and clean everything was. In no time, it became my responsibility to keep it so. Haircuts, kit issue, kit inspection, marching like an idiot, clean, clean and more cleaning whilst all the time being yelled at – the first few days flew by. All the time that I'd spent living rough in the woods served me well now. I proved to be the fittest recruit, and the more kit I had to carry the happier I was. The only thing that let me down was my total failure ever to look smart.

One morning the officer on inspection stopped in front of me, and accused me of not having shaved. I argued that I had. He argued that I had not. I decided to shut up and take it.

When the officer went around the back of me he barked: 'Soldier, you have shaving foam in your ears!'

'Can't have, sir,' I replied. 'I didn't shave this morning.'

The parade ground erupted in laughter. Even the NCOs couldn't keep a straight face. But it was straight to the punishment block for me, and a good beasting (being made to do endless press-ups, runs, and other exercises). I didn't mind. It was another opportunity to keep fit, and it got me out of litter duty.

The six weeks flew by, and soon it was time to pass off the square. I was seventeen years old and I felt enormously proud as I was given my Royal Hampshires beret.

Finally, I had achieved something in my life. I'd stayed the course.

That weekend was free time, the first since we'd arrived in camp. I spent it exactly where I was, for I had nowhere else to go. As I lay on my camp bed in the empty quarters, I knew that however long I spent in the Army it was going to be a good time.

And finally, I felt as if I belonged. I'd never had a real home or a family. Now I'd found one.

I'd still only completed basic training, so I knew there was a lot of shit ahead of me. But no worries, I told myself. I'd taken this sort of crap and more in the kids' homes. For the first twelve months in the Army you were a nobody – a 'crow' as the veterans called it – and everyone knew it. Well, I'd been a nobody for years, so it was no big drama.

But it was one hell of a journey from there to leading an eighty-man security detail in Afghanistan.

CHAPTER 25

The constant tension of our Afghan operation is getting to my team of white-eyes, so I decide to relax the strict no-alcohol policy. I introduce the 'two-can' rule for our one day off a week – that's a few cans of beer, and no one getting so shit-faced he can't walk.

We've had a couple of the team secretly drinking in their rooms – the mud-floored huts – so I figure I've got to relax the rules a little. The 'two-can' rule is just an extension of 'big boys rules': you're allowed to let your hair down, as long as you can make it for parade the following morning.

My team knows the rules, or at least they should do. They've each spent a great deal of time in the military. I know that if I don't let the guys have some down time, they'll go nuts after a few months out here. The two-can rule is the answer, as far as I see things.

Micky, our ex-Foreign Legion guy, is one of the first to have his day off after the two-can rule comes into force. It's late at night, and I'm sat in my room doing some last-minute paperwork for the Ambo. I've managed to score myself a nice Afghan rug to go on the dirt floor of my hovel of a hut. It makes it a fraction more homely.

Micky comes wandering over from his hut, which is similar to mine but set on the opposite side of the Ambo's villa. He starts banging on about his time in the Legion, telling all these stories of derring-do. I can tell he's had a few, but he's not fallen over yet, so I decide to cut him some slack.

Then he hocks up this big greenie and proceeds to spit it onto my rug.

I stare at him for a second. 'Mate, did you or did you not just gob on my rug?'

He shrugs, like he doesn't give a shit, and sways about unsteadily.

'Listen, mate, it's the two-can rule, not the bloody two-hundred-can rule. I'll let it go this time, but I suggest you get your arse into bed and sleep it off. And don't ever gob on my rug again.'

He slurs this half-apology, then proceeds to spit on my rug for a second time. I can't believe it. I figure he's so pissed that he doesn't actually know what he's doing, but that doesn't stop me from hauling his arse to the door, and shoving him in the direction of his hut.

'Get to fucking bed,' I tell him. 'Bed! Now!'

He stumbles off, then half turns. 'I'm gronna fuckshin kills yous,' he slurs. 'Yous dead.'

'Get to fucking bed, you twat,' I tell him. 'And best hope I've forgotten all this by morning.'

He weaves off across the lawn, and I figure I'd better follow him. Last thing I want him doing is gate-crashing the villa, where the Ambo will be fast asleep by now. I see Micky go into his hut, and hear him stumbling about, and crashing into furniture.

I figure he's home and dry, and I'm just heading back to my hut when I hear a distinctive 'clack-clack'. It's the unmistakable sound of a weapon being made ready.

I sprint for my room, and grab my HK MP5 sub-machine gun. Next door to me I can hear Chris making ready his own MP5. He's clearly heard the whole thing. The two of us emerge, just as the roar of a gunshot comes echoing out of the thin walls of Micky's hut.

Micky has opened fire, and it doesn't escape my notice that the Ambo's villa sits pretty much bang in between his hut and ours. Chris and I dive for some cover behind the brick wall that cordons off our quarters from the villa.

I tell Chris we're going to have to disarm the pissed-up fucker. I tell him to cover me as I go forward. Then I'll cover Chris as he moves forward, at which point one of us will have to go through a door or a window. And I want it all done before the gunfire wakes the Ambo.

I move ahead through the darkness as Chris covers me. There's no further fire from Micky's hut, and I get up close against the wall. I decide to risk a peek inside. I wriggle up to windowsill level, and peer over. There's Micky lying face-down on his bed, with a pistol still gripped in his hand. His finger's no longer on the trigger, and he's splayed out as if he's shot himself. I get the HK trained on his head, as Chris appears on my right-hand side.

'I reckon the stupid fuckin' twat's shot himself,' I hiss at Chris. 'I'm trained on his head, mate, so go open the door and see if you can see any blood.'

Chris moves around the front of the hut. I see the door open a crack, and then Chris is in the room, prising the pistol out of Micky's fingers. Micky doesn't move a muscle or even flinch as he does so.

I move around to join Chris. 'There's no blood,' Chris whispers. 'He stinks like a brewery, and he's out cold.'

I collect Micky's other weapons, and as I do so I notice a bullet hole in the side of his hut closest to our quarters. Rather than putting a bullet in his brain, he's taken a potshot in Chris's and my direction. Lastly, I gather up his passport and any cash that I can find.

'We'll let him sleep it off,' I tell Chris, as we close the door. 'That's unless the stupid twat causes any more trouble . . .'

Chris and I head for the *salle à manger*. It's late now, but I figure with the time difference there should still be someone from Double Zero reachable on the satphone. I get hold of Johnno and brief him on what's happened. Then I tell him that Micky has to go. I say we need a replacement bloke urgently, or the Ambo's going to wonder why we're down to a three-man team.

It's a miracle the shot hasn't wakened the Ambo, and I want to keep it that way. He will not be impressed if he learns that his security team have just had to deal with one of their own getting paralytic, and brassing up the compound. I know the Afghan gate guards have seen it all, but for an Afghan it's fairly normal behaviour.

Johnno tells me I need to get Micky on the first flight out of Kabul. Meanwhile, they've got a Double Zero employee in Kabul working on some other security contract. Johnno will call that guy, and get him to fill the hole left by Micky, at least until they can get me a proper replacement.

Chris and I sit up all night, drinking brews and shooting the shit in the *salle à manger*. We've got one ear each on Micky's hut, scanning for any trouble. It turns out that Chris was an RAF boxing champion in his day, and we've both got the same idea regarding Micky. If he wakes up and tries to cause any more shit, he'll be saying hello to the Big Hampshire Hammer, not to mention Chris's fists, and we'll knock the fucker clean out.

It's six in the morning when Micky stumbles into the *salle à manger*. He looks like death warmed up. He glances over at Chris and me. 'Eh, what the fook's going on?' he mumbles. 'Where's me weapons and shit?'

Chris stares at him in disbelief.

I say: 'So, you don't remember what you did last night?'

He shrugs. 'No, mate.'

I say: 'Micky, you are lying like a hairy egg, you wanker.'

He says: 'Like a hairy egg? What's one of them?'

I say: 'Yeah, like a hairy egg. Ever seen one? No. Must be a lie then.'

Micky proceeds to come clean. He admits that he drank more than a skinful, and let loose with his pistol. He ends with: 'Look, I didn't mean it, guys. I was pissed-up, like, wasn't I?'

I say: 'Listen, mate, you haven't just crossed the line – you've wiped your arse on it as you went over.'

'What are you gonna do?' he asks. 'You haven't told Double Zero . . .'

'Of course I've told them,' I cut in. 'What d'you expect me to do?'

He looks worried. 'What did they say?'

'You're going home, mate. I'll get you on a flight, or you're on the bus to Jalalabad, but either way you're out of here.'

Micky tries to protest. He tries telling me I can't do this to him. I tell him I'm team leader, and it's a done deal. He's out of here. Best he goes pack.

He disappears, and he's back a minute later complaining that he can't find his passport, wallet and shit. I tell him I have it all. I go to my room and work the phones, trying to get him booked on a plane out of Kabul. There's not a seat free on any flight that day.

We mount up the Land Rover Discovery, and I drive him into downtown Kabul. I head for the central bus depot, which is a chaotic pit of a place, full of beaten-up old jingly trucks, wrecked buses, and a motley assortment of vans converted into makeshift minibuses.

I find the bus to Jalalabad, and get Micky a seat on it. I ask the driver when it's leaving. He tells me in an hour's time.

I tell Micky that the bus driver's got his passport, and he'll get it back when – *if* – he reaches Pakistan.

CHAPTER 26

I put a call through to Double Zero and tell them what's what. They ask me please not to send Micky out on a bus via Jalalabad, and the Khyber Pass. Anything but that. I relent. I agree to fly him out instead. But only on one condition: he's not staying with us. I go find the worst flea-ridden shack of a downtown hotel, and I book Micky in. He can rot there whilst I find him a flight. I've still got his documents, so he's not going anywhere.

Two days later I drive him to the airport. I walk him through departures using our diplomatic passes, and I walk him onto a waiting UN plane. I go see the pilot and brief him in. I know the UN aircrews well by now, and they're all good lads.

I hand the pilot Micky's passport. 'This guy has been a real menace. I don't want him getting his passport back until he reaches Pakistan. He's been relieved of post, and I do not want him back in-country.'

The pilot asks me if he'll cause any trouble on the flight. I tell him that he won't, 'cause he's in too much trouble already. I tell Micky to behave and not to kick off, or he'll not be getting the pay that's owed him. He is very, very sheepish by now. I watch the aircraft take off and the wheels go up, and that's the end of him.

There's good reason why I've been so angry, and so determined to get him out of the country fast. If the Ambo finds out that a member of the team was pissed-up, and shooting up the compound, we may all lose our jobs. His drunken idiocy could cost us all of that. It's vital to get Micky gone without anyone realizing.

Now he's on that flight I figure it's job done. But it's still hugely frustrating. Basically, Micky was a good operator. He was great with the locals, and not a bad bloke at the end of the day. Trouble is, he has a huge drink problem, like any number of ex-Legionnaires that I've come across. It seems to go with the territory.

I am very attached to the rug that Micky spat on. It's a handmade one, decorated with various Afghan motifs that are woven into the fabric. I'd haggled and haggled for hours on end at one of the local markets, and eventually I'd got it for thirty dollars. It was infinitely better than a bare dirt floor, and far too fine a rug to gob on.

But still, I recognize that it would have been a step too far to send Micky out on a local bus via the Khyber Pass. Double Zero were right to call me out on that one. The US, British and allied forces – the ISAF coalition – are in control of Kabul and most of northern Afghanistan by now, but at some stage on that journey the bus would have passed from coalition-controlled territory to areas where the Taliban still held sway, or at least warlords aligned with the Taliban.

The signs would be subtle, but visible to those knowing what to look for. If travelling that route, I'd have been alert to any 'change in environment' – a change in my surroundings that signified the bus had crossed from friendly into enemy terrain.

At its simplest, it could be the presence of young males of fighting age, wearing the Taliban's trademark black turban. It could be compounds flying the Taliban flag, as opposed to that of the Afghan

National Army. Or it could be as life-threatening as a roadblock stopping every vehicle, and manned by Taliban gunmen.

I'd first learned the classic 'change of environment' indicators in Northern Ireland, whilst serving with the Royal Hampshires. I remember patrolling along a street in Londonderry, and noticing that loads of windows had been left open. It struck me as odd, especially as it was a bitterly cold wet winter's day.

The locals had got wind that an IRA bomb was planted in the area, one designed to tear apart our patrol. They didn't want to get their windows smashed in the coming explosion. Reading that change in environment – a classic 'combat indicator' – meant we could reroute the patrol and avoid the bomb.

If I had sent Micky out via the Khyber Pass, he'd more than likely have stumbled into a world of trouble. He could have been captured, and held hostage, which would almost definitely have brought his plight to the Ambo's attention. And that in turn could have blown the gaff that he'd been on the piss and shot up the compound.

It was fortunate that Double Zero intervened. And it was a wrong call from me to try to send Micky out that way. But the guy had tried to shoot me, and I was worried that he'd lost us our contract. And by now, I'm becoming seriously addicted to the life I'm leading here in Kabul.

Double Zero sends us out a replacement bloke, called Nick. He intimates that he's an ex-Royal Marines Commando. Well, in addition to passing SAS selection, I've also passed both Para selection and that of the Royal Marines, so I know a bit about being a Commando. I fire a couple of questions Nick's way, and it doesn't strike me that he's able to give me a straight answer. I'm doubtful that he's ever done RM selection. Either way, he's Double Zero's chosen replacement and I've got to make it work.

Nick seems a nice enough bloke, and he's a bum-on-a-seat. At least that should put the Ambo at ease that we're still a four-man CP team.

A couple of weeks after Micky's departure, we get two tree-hugger types come out to work a stint for ECHO. They're young, smart and pretty, they dress appropriately, and it's a breath of fresh air to have them around. They get billeted in the embassy residence, until we can get them out into the field.

I'm in the *salle à manger*, and the girls come to join me for breakfast.

'It's always the quiet ones, isn't it?' one of them remarks to me.

I answer her through a mouthful of fried egg. 'Sorry, love, what're you on about?'

'You know,' the other girl says. 'It's the quiet ones who turn out to have been in the SAS.'

'Like who?' I ask.

'*You know*, the quiet ones – like Nick. The little, wiry, silent ones who never say much at all.'

I nod. 'Oh yeah. Fuck yeah. Nick. Of course. D'you know he's a prize underwater knife fighter as well . . .' Apparently, Nick's been giving them the Billy Big Bollocks the night before. The bloke's a legend in his own tea break. Not to worry. I'm not about to show him up in front of the ECHO girls. If he can do his job, keep his hands off the booze, and shut the fuck up around me, I'm not going to cause him any problems. I've got enough to deal with, without making extra trouble.

My concern about our local staff is growing big time. Tribal tensions are bubbling away just below the surface. I can feel the resentment and enmity festering. I've got a file in which I'm keeping tabs on each and every one of our local staff, including who their families are and where they live. But still I'm troubled.

I figure that sooner or later someone's going to suffer a big one in Kabul – a hit on an embassy aimed at taking an ambassador and some of his staff hostage. They're the ultimate High Value Targets, and the ransom will be worth a fortune. Plus in terms of the Al Qaeda/Taliban mindset, it sends the perfect message: *No matter who you are, no white-eye infidel is safe in Afghanistan.*

With a security set-up such as ours, it's going to be next to impossible to seize the Ambo without inside help. I put my mind into that of a Taliban or Al Qaeda commander, or one of the criminal cells running the kidnap and ransom rackets. I imagine how I would go about doing the job. My first port of call would be to recruit the man on the inside.

If we have one, that is our Achilles' heel.

I figure I need a special kind of operator to help me out on this one. I need an Afghan who I can work with very closely and trust. I need a right-hand man who can be a filter where the local staff are concerned. I get him in the form of Hamed.

Officially, Hamed comes to us as a liaison officer, to open doors for the embassy. He's a rare thing in an Afghan in that he's highly educated, has spent most of his study time in France, and has lived abroad for many years. As a bonus, he's travelled all over the world.

Hamed knows and understands the ways of the West, and he's a proper gentleman. He's seen and experienced far too much to take the strictures of conservative Afghan Islam seriously. He's even been a running mate of Ahmed Shah Massoud, the late, great, legendary warlord who led the resistance against the Taliban.

Hamed shows me a photo of him with Massoud, just so I know he's not shitting me. I've had dozens of Afghans claim they were Massoud's best buddy, and mostly it turns out to be horseshit. But with Hamed it's for real.

Hamed's been up and down the Panjshir – the Five Lions –

Valley dozens of times, during the days when Massoud was fighting against the Soviet Red Army, and then the Taliban. I figure Hamed must have got some serious trigger time under his belt as well.

In short, Hamed's a top bloke, and he's got connections out the yin-yang.

Hamed, the Ambo and I strike up this great multinational partnership. The Ambo may be a Swede, but he's got a sense of humour to rival any Brit's. And whilst Hamed's some kind of Afghan–French global hybrid, he turns out to be a laugh a minute too.

I first manage to land a classic wind-up on Hamed around the time of Ramadan, the key holy festival in Islam. There are supposedly weeks of fasting during Ramadan, when nothing – not a morsel of food, nor drop of water, nor even a molecule of cigarette smoke – is supposed to pass your lips from dawn until dusk.

I know Hamed's supposed to be fasting, but I also know that the Ambo's invited the two of us for an early dinner at his villa. I sense there's fun to be had here. The Ambo's got his chef to lay on this huge spread, and I can tell that Hamed is as eager as the two of us to tuck in. But one glance out the window and it's clear the sun has yet to set.

I wait until Hamed's got his first forkful halfway to his gob, then I pipe up: 'Hold on, Hamed, aren't you supposed to be fasting? It's the second day of Ramadan, isn't it?'

Hamed freezes, the fork suspended between plate and open mouth.

The Ambo pipes up next: 'Yes, of course, Hamed. How fortunate Phil was able to warn you.'

We're both trying not to crack up laughing. Hamed glances at the two of us, and shrugs. 'You know what, guys, I'll do an extra day at the end.'

With that the fork goes in, and he's munching away, and the

Ambo and I are killing ourselves. No doubt about it, Hamed's a cool customer, and he's up for a laugh.

The following day I track Hamed to the loo. I just know he's going in there for a secret smoke. I sneak in when I figure he'll have lit up, and sure enough there are clouds of smoke billowing out from under the door of this cubicle.

I sidle up to it. 'Bit smoky in there, isn't it, Hamed?'

I hear him choking up with laughter. He knows I've got him bang to rights, and he's the first Afghan I've ever met who really gets the English sense of humour.

Over the coming days I brief Hamed on my concerns over the local staff. Hamed assures me he's on it. There is real tension between the Pashtuns and the Tajiks, he tells me. We'd have been far better advised if we'd recruited from just the one tribe, he says. And don't I bloody know it.

If a Taliban or Al Qaeda sleeper has been placed within our team, Hamed figures he can winkle him out. It's the sympathizers that are less hard to nail. There could be any number of guys who identify with our enemies, whilst not being actively involved with them. At any moment one of those guys could be drawn over to the dark side.

But we are where we are, says Hamed, and he'll see what he can do about it.

CHAPTER 27

It's around about now that the Ambo decides he needs a recce doing up near Mazar-i-Sharif, in the north of the country. That's prime Tajik territory – the late Ahmed Shah Massoud's patch – so it makes every sense to get Hamed in on this one.

The aim is to scope out a route to take a delegation of European political bigwigs there, so they can look at expanding their humanitarian work. The Ambo is right behind this venture, because it'll spread development and education, and that in turn should help bring the Afghan people on side. And that means the burden falls upon me to make sure the recce happens.

The only trouble is this: the drive from Kabul to Mazar is never an easy one, and triply so in the midst of the Afghan winter. The route north heads through the high-altitude Salang Pass, before crawling down onto the northern plains, the domain of General Dostum, one of the more infamous of the Afghan warlords, which is saying something.

Dostum is a foremost commander of the Northern Alliance, the Afghan forces that routed the Taliban post 9/11, with a little help from US air power, plus special forces on the ground. The General has something of a colourful reputation, and has been accused of some pretty nasty war crimes during the darkest days of fighting in the country.

Conditions in the mountains north of Kabul are horrendous, with ten-foot snowdrifts blocking the roads. As for the Salang Pass it is completely snowed in. We'll have to wait for a weather window, then go for it.

There's an old military adage in the units that I served with: 'Time spent on reconnaissance is seldom wasted.' And it's clearly better that Hamed and I get stuck in the frozen Salang Pass, than Hamed and me plus a bunch of European political bigwigs do. The Ambo's plan is to take the delegation up there in six weeks' time. That's the slot during which we've got to get the recce done, or fail trying. We need a weather window to open in the next month or so, whereupon we'll go for it.

I've done oodles of mountain training and operations during my time in the military, so I have an idea as to the kind of conditions we'll be facing. Whilst operating in hostile mountain environments I'd learned to live by the mantra we called 'The Seven Ps': Prior Planning and Preparation Prevents Piss-Poor Performance.

It's the Seven Ps that I'm putting into practice, as I prepare for the journey into the Salang Pass. First off, I research the 'changes in environment' we're likely to encounter en route, what dangers they will pose, and how best to avoid them.

I use local knowledge here. Hamed's been through the Salang Pass a dozen times before, though never in winter. I quiz him about what dangers we are likely to encounter, and which of the high mountain slopes are most liable to avalanche. At lesser altitudes, I want to know where we might hit deep snowdrifts, mudslides or flooding.

Whilst serving in Mountain Troop I'd scooted up many of the

higher peaks in the UK. It never ceased to amaze me the people you find on top of the hills, in the most unsuitable gear imaginable.

As with any mountainous environment, the weather in the UK can go from a roasting-hot clear day to completely nil visibility and a howling gale in a heartbeat. Yet I've been on the top of a hill carrying a Bergen full of cold-weather and survival gear, and seen a family struggling along in shorts and T-shirts. It's clear they've got zero cold-weather gear, as they don't even have a rucksack with them. The weather down in the car park was doubtless superb, but in a flash what started as a gentle walk up the hills could turn into a full-on epic death trip, if the weather suddenly turned.

I rarely if ever go into the hills – even on a day trip – without carrying at least a Gore-tex bivvie survival bag. That way, if I do get trapped in bad weather I can crawl inside, zip up and keep myself alive until the weather takes a turn for the better.

It isn't just the weather up close that you have to worry about. I'd learned in Kenya that dry wadis could flash-flood down on the plains, even when the weather was fine and the rains miles away in the mountains. In Mountain Troop I'd seen how huge drifts of snow could lie on a hillside for weeks, then dump onto terrain thousands of feet below one fine, sunny day. Likewise, mudslides and landslides aren't always triggered when it's raining; they can come days or weeks after.

The key is to get to know the weather patterns where you are operating, find out where the steep-sided mountain basins lie that are most prone to avalanche, work out where there have been incidents in the past, and avoid them.

All of this is a vital part of the Seven Ps, and it's even more relevant when preparing to make an epic overland journey into some of the remotest terrain on earth – the Salang Pass – using a dirt track that snakes between 5000-metre peaks.

People tend to think of Afghanistan as a hot country. It is, but only in the summer months and at low altitudes. On some of the tallest peaks there's glaciers the entire year round, and we are about to attempt a passage over some of the highest of them. The tallest peak in the UK is Ben Nevis, at 1,344 metres. The Salang Pass tops out at a little short of three times that altitude – rearing up to 3,878 metres. Hamed warns me that the pass is a deadly avalanche zone. The winter build-up of snow can lead to multiple avalanches, all within a few minutes of each other.

Recently, the pass has been hit by monster snowfalls. Chunks of snow and ice the size of trucks have hurtled in deadly waves down the mountainsides, burying many miles of the highway. Vehicles in the Salang tunnel have been trapped for days on end, and hundreds have died.

There is one other factor my years of soldiering make me alert to: how any natural disaster in the Salang Pass might impact upon the mood of the locals. A massive avalanche; people trapped in a snowed-in tunnel; food, water and warmth in pitifully short supply; death for many a real possibility. Under those conditions people can turn pretty nasty.

There's often little a human won't do when their very survival is at stake. And being the white-eye foreigner travelling through, I'll always be an outsider – not part of anyone else's tribe or national group. And that makes me an obvious target for being set on, robbed, kidnapped or killed.

It is immediately clear that none of our vehicles are up to the challenge of the Salang Pass. The G-Wagon's a big whale of a thing, the Pajero's a pussy, and the Discovery is far too ancient to take seriously. Instead, I manage to persuade ECHO to lend us one of their smart Toyota Land Cruisers.

The Land Cruiser comes complete with decent mud-eater tyres, snorkel for fording deep water, and most importantly a winch where you need it – mounted on the front bumper. The Land Cruiser's not an armoured beast designed for mincing around Kabul: it's built for the wild, and for going off road.

Hamed and I pack the vehicle with British Army twelve-man ration packs, which are stuffed full of some serious goodies, plus jerrycans of diesel and water. We add our own personal 'whinge kit' – jumpers, warm jackets, roll mats, ponchos and thick Afghan blankets. Lastly, we pack a satphone, our one means of long-range communication.

That done, we're good to go. Now the wait for the weather window. I'm planning to take an AK47, a dozen mags and spare crates of ammo, plus my Makarov pistol. Hamed opts to travel unarmed. He's a pseudo-dip himself these days, and packing shooters isn't his style any more.

My greatest single source of weather info is the UN pilots who are flying missions all over the north of the country. It's from them that I get the advance warning of the weather window.

I give the Toyota the once-over, and as a last thought I throw in some fresh rations – sausages and steak – in a cool box, though I'm tempted to do the Afghan thing and keep it under the carpet.

I hand over to my second in command, and at 3 a.m. I drive over to Hamed's place in the Land Cruiser. It's typical Hamed that even with an 0300 start, he's ready bang on time. That sets him apart from just about every other Afghan I've ever worked with, bar Brian the unfortunate ex-driver and sex addict.

We exit Kabul via the checkpoint on the fringes of the city and hit the route north. The going is horrendous, the road full of pot-holes that could swallow a truck. It's also totally devoid of traffic.

After some three hours' driving I'm desperate to answer the call of nature. You can't pull off the road, because the bush is very likely mined. Instead, they've built these wooden versions of a Portaloo every here and there on the roadside. Each consists of a hut on stilts, standing on what amounts to an open sewer. I pull over by one, and head inside. There's a hole in the floor to do your business, and below it a lake of rancid shit stretching as far as you can smell. There are also piles of poo around the hole where previous shitters have missed, or been caught short with the runs.

I pull my shemag – my Afghan headscarf – around my face, and jam two cigarettes into my mouth, to form a smoke screen across the front of my face. I just manage to do my stuff without vomiting, and then I make a bolt for the door.

Back in the car Hamed tells me he needs to go too. He's got a chilled can of Coke in one hand, a newspaper under his arm and a pack of ciggies in the other hand. I'm about to warn him when I think better of it. I'm dying to see his face when he comes bolting out in horror.

A good fifteen minutes later and there's no sign of Hamed. I wonder if he's died in there. Twenty minutes, and still not a sniff. It's a good twenty-five minutes before he comes strolling out of the Portaloo, looking totally unruffled.

He gets back in the car and lets out a long satisfied sigh. There's a moment's silence, then I give him this look.

'Twenty-five bloody minutes! Took roots in there, did you, Hamed mate . . .'

He gives me a look right back, and shrugs. 'What's the need to rush, my friend?'

It's fair enough. I don't have an answer for him. I guess it's time I manned up to life on the road in Afghanistan.

It's late afternoon by the time we pull in to this tiny roadside village. It lies where the plain meets the foothills, the start of the towering wall of snow-capped mountains into which we're heading. Somewhere in there lies the pass, and this is where we're stopping for the night.

Hamed is well known here, and he's warmly received with hugs and handshakes all around. Likewise with me, 'cause I'm with him. A hut's made vacant for us, and some mattresses are thrown on the floor.

Everyone here seems to be Hamed's cousin or nephew, so I figure we're safe as we're ever going to be kipping by an Afghan roadside. After all, we're their guests, and it would be a serious dishonour should anything happen to us.

I want to be through the pass in a day, for I know that bad weather is approaching. We'll need to do an Alpine start, so up at the crack of a sparrow's fart.

At first light I'm going to kick arse, and get us moving.

CHAPTER 28

I wake to a glorious dawn. As Hamed and I set off, the sun is painting the clear sky a faint blue over the horizon to the east. I feel hugely encouraged. Perhaps the weather is going to hold for us, after all.

I shouldn't have tempted fate. A few miles up the track leading into the Salang Pass, the sky darkens with clouds and the first flakes of snow begin to fall. The higher we climb the worse the weather becomes, and eventually we're driving along a dirt road switchbacking through ten-foot-high snowdrifts, and with visibility close to zero. By the time we're nearing the Salang Tunnel – the five-kilometre bottleneck that takes us into the higher reaches of the pass – it's close to whiteout conditions, with the swirling snow so thick that the Land Cruiser's headlamps reflect only a wall of white wherever they're shining.

My mind goes back to a story that Hamed told me, before we left Kabul. In the winter of 1982, during the Soviet occupation of Afghanistan, a Red Army convoy got snowed in as it attempted to move through the Salang Tunnel. A fire broke out, and the tunnel was transformed into a raging inferno, one that rapidly swept the length of its path. The fire destroyed hundreds of armoured vehicles and trucks, killing thousands of Soviet troops in the process.

It's the winter of 2002 now, and a year after the fall of the Taliban. It's two decades since the catastrophe that befell the Soviet military convoy, or the twentieth anniversary. I try not to dwell on the thought as we approach the entrance to the tunnel. But I don't have a good feeling about this place, or about what we're attempting to do here.

It's just after 5.30 a.m. by the time we pull to a halt behind a long line of vehicles. They're queuing at the gate that leads into the first of a series of tunnels, each of which is like a step that climbs ever higher into the apex of the pass itself. There's maybe fifty vehicles ahead of us, and it's the same motley collection of jingly trucks, knackered buses and ramshackle minibuses that you find everywhere on the Afghan roads.

The queue of drivers must be waiting for the tunnels to be cleared, but what are the chances of that happening? All we've seen so far is a couple of guys in flip-flops with shovels trying to clear the road. Plus there was a lone bulldozer, but overnight the fuel had frozen solid in its tank.

Most of those in the queue have spent the night here, freezing their arses off. There are guards at the gate who supposedly have communications with the gate at the far end of the pass. They are supposed to monitor conditions in the tunnels, and traffic flow, to prevent a jam occurring inside. But there's no way that I want to wait for this lot of vehicles to head into the tunnels before us.

I have a word with Hamed, and he suggests we try a little bakshish – bribery – on the gate guards. We edge our way to the front of the queue, trying to ignore the hostile glares and horning from either side. The guys manning the gate turn out to be from the local contingent of the Afghan police, and they look eminently bribable.

Hamed goes forward and has words, whilst I do my best to

ignore a couple of Afghan truck drivers who are waving their fists at me. No one seems very happy that we're queue-jumping, but the reality is that none of them is driving a vehicle that could make it over a frosted speed hump, let alone through what lies ahead. We have the only machine present with the means to get through the weather, so what's the sense in us waiting?

After some haggling, and some dollars changing hands, the guards lift the barrier and we're waved through. We leave hordes of screaming and shouting Afghan drivers behind us, those who can't afford to pay the bribes.

The first trick to driving on snow and ice is to take it dead slow, even when in a 4×4. A four-wheel-drive is only ever an advantage when one of the four drive wheels can get traction on the road. If our Land Cruiser hits ice or packed snow with all four wheels, we may as well be driving a Nissan Micra.

We press ahead, and find the route littered with vehicles that have piled into each other. Afghan truckers are having punch-ups in the thick snow outside their cabs, as each one screams at the other, blaming him for the accident.

No one seems to have brought any cold-weather gear. Instead, either they're sitting in their vehicles with the engine running and heater on full – which adds a thick diesel smog to the blizzard-like conditions – or they're dancing around in their cotton dishdashes, trying to punch the living daylights out of their fellow travellers.

I see one bloke wearing only flip-flops fighting with another bloke, trying to steal his shoes. It's carnage. Worse, I'm well aware how nothing unites a bunch of angry Afghans better than a common enemy. A white-eye driving some Gucci four-wheel-drive, complete with all the cold-weather gear you could wish for, is a top prize.

The higher we go the worse it gets. There are vehicles broken down everywhere. A large number seem to have skidded off the road as they were coming downhill, going in the opposite direction to us.

It looks as if a snowplough may have been through here sometime in the past twenty-four hours, pushing aside walls of white to the left and right of us. But with the rate it's snowing now, the road is filling up again fast. I tell Hamed to keep his eyes peeled for skidding Afghan trucks, or we're going to get splatted.

No matter how slow I take it, I find even the Land Cruiser is sliding all over the place. I keep cannoning off the snow banks to either side, and bouncing back onto the main drag. Eventually, we go into a long skid that throws the Toyota clean off the road.

I zip up my North Face down jacket, pull a thermal hat down over my eyes and slide out of the vehicle. I throw the winch into neutral, unhook the wire cable, and unroll it to the opposite side of the road. I hook it around a tree, and return to the front of the Toyota.

I flick the winch controller into drive position, hands chilled to the bone with the cold. As Hamed tries his best to steer the vehicle, the electric motor makes its high-pitched whine, and starts to reel in the steel cable. With each turn of the drum, the Land Cruiser is dragged inch-by-inch back onto the road. There's no way we could continue the journey without the winch, and I can't see anyone else making it through without one.

The tunnels alternate with a series of cuttings, and with each metre of altitude gained the conditions worsen. We're two hours into the drive when we round a bend, only to find the road thick with vehicles. A local bus has slewed across it, ending up sideways-on to the traffic. In doing so it's collided with a truck travelling downhill, plus a minibus crammed full of forty-odd people. A

Saluting the crowd aged five at Warners Isle of White holiday camp. I always had liked the Army but couldn't yet afford the uniform.

Aged nineteen on the hard streets of Londonderry with the Royal Hampshires – the regiment that felt like the first real home I'd ever had.

Out winning hearts and minds in Londonderry, by the Bishop Street Gate, just a couple of days after having been caught up in the IRA bomb blast there.

In Kenya having my first taste of the jungle and of Special Forces soldiering. I loved them both. The machine pistol was courtesy of our SF instructors.

By chance the day after I was badged into 22 SAS I met my real mother and family for the first time, and we celebrated in Tooting Social Club. Here I am – second from right – with the two brothers and the uncles I never knew I had.

En route from Kuwait to Basra, low profile and in local garb. The Arab headscarf and dish dash robe was held on by Velcro, with my usual ops kit hidden underneath.

Top: On my Kawasaki trials bike with some Afghan street kids outside the Kabul embassy we were hired to protect. Our kids at home know nothing of hardship compared to these lads.

Right: The infamous road through the Panshir Valley that leads to the late legendary Afghan warlord Ahmed Shah Massoud's gaff.

Doing a spot of public relations with the local Afghan guards on the hills overlooking Kabul. I used to while away the hours listening to the radio and drinking chai, all the while scoping out escape routes should we need to get our client out of the city pronto.

On the ranges near Kabul, training the young British soldiers on an assortment of weaponry – always a good day out. In the SAS we learned to use just about every small arms available to the world's forces.

At the Skylink Camp where we based our Basra security operation, pulling wheelies on a pilfered bike with my liberated Russian tankies' helmet.

Moving through Gaza in convoy with the UN who were officially 'not helping us' on the Karni Project. Having empty streets all around us was always a good indicator that it was all about to kick off.

In Gaza, posing with some of the Hamas operatives after we'd done a solidarity patrol with them under the Israeli's very guns. I'm second from right, and I'm smuggling in a copy of *FHM* (it's rolled up and sandwiched between my legs). Getting caught with it could well have got me killed.

The photo that made it into *FHM* . . . That's me in the centre, posing with the Gaza youth team we sponsored with free Southampton FC kit. They'd been playing in rags up until that point, but with their Saints kit they went on to win the local league.

In Gaza training the Fatah Presidential Guard. Note the wall of steel shipping containers to stop snipers from getting a clean shot at us. We weren't allowed any weapons, so we trained the Fatah lads using cardboard cut-out AK47s and yelling 'bang-bang-bang, you're dead'.

In the Gulf of Aden with a 'woody', a wooden replica weapon to deter pirates. This was the job on which I was given one roll of plain gardening wire to make the ship safe. When I phoned up the private security company to sort it out I was told: 'Nobody said it would be easy.'

In the Indian Ocean some twenty miles off the coast of Kenya. This is how anti-piracy should be done, with good blokes and proper kit. No Somali pirates were ever getting to board this ship.

Zeroing my weapon in whilst steaming through the Indian Ocean. We'd taken possession of a ship that had been ransomed off Somali pirates. In the time they'd had the vessel it had been badly damaged, and our job was to get it safely home without it being seized by pirates again!

In Cairo, after the ship had been safely delivered to its home port. In this case it wasn't the straw that broke the camel's back – it was the big bloke with the ridiculous lobster suntan and the very short haircut.

Stopping over in Jerusalem after an anti-piracy trip. My private security mate had got me in to meet Tony Blair, and I thanked him for signing off on a few jobs that I was on during his term in the chair.

large crowd of pissed-off Afghans is milling about, all arguing and scrapping with each other. It is total carnage. And everyone seems to be packing some kind of weapon. There is no doubt that it has the capacity to kick off big time.

I don't want to stop but we're forced to, as there's no way through. I go to inspect the crash, and everyone stops scrapping and yelling and stares at the white-eye instead.

The only option is to try to pull the back end of the bus around, so it's facing roughly uphill again. That should give us space enough to squeeze the Toyota through. I fetch a wire towrope from the rear of the wagon, and slide myself under the back end of the bus, searching for a tow point. The best I can manage is to hook the cable around the bus's leaf-springs – its knackered old suspension system.

As I do so, I check out the Afghan families crouching in the snowdrifts to either side of the bus, watching me. Somehow they've managed to get these fires going, but God only knows what they're burning. It smells like old tyres, from the stench of things. But the heat thrown out is feeble compared to the biting, chilling cold.

There are young people and old people and mothers freezing to death up here. Caught out in this kind of weather, a human starts to go hypothermic in thirty minutes or less. Core body temperature rapidly drops below what's needed to keep a person alive.

In the early stages of hypothermia, symptoms include shivering and mild confusion. As it worsens, an individual is unable to coordinate their movements properly, and will stumble around like a drunk. By the time it's turned severe, speech becomes slurred, and a victim loses the ability to use their hands, and to think properly. Skin turns puffy and blue, and a victim starts acting irrationally. In the final, fatal, stages they may rip off all their clothes – the so-called 'paradoxical undressing' – as the brain malfunctions, and they believe their freezing body is actually boiling hot. Victims of hypothermia may also exhibit 'terminal burrowing', where they burrow into a small enclosed space to die.

As I glance at the chaos all around me, I check for frozen individuals burrowing into the snowdrifts. I figure it won't be long now before some of them start to do so. It's total madness and buffoonery up here, that's for certain.

I finish attaching the cable, slide out from under the bus, and give Hamed this look: *What the fuck are these idiots up to? They're freezing to death up here.* Hamed shrugs. He seems pretty unfazed by it all. He's got that look in his eyes that I've seen before: *This, my friend, is Afghanistan. Better get used to it. It is what it is.*

Having hooked up the bus, I try giving the Toyota some welly, but I can't get enough traction. I grab a shovel from the rear of the wagon, and dig down through the snow, so the tyres can get some grip on the road. And finally, with wheels spinning and the smell of burning rubber thick in the air, I manage to haul the bus back into line.

As we push onwards it strikes me how alone I am up here. Whilst I've seen oodles of UN types mincing around Kabul in their smart 4×4s, there's no sign of any other white-eyes here in the Salang Pass. There's only me – with trusted Hamed riding shotgun – driving the sole vehicle that's equipped to make it through.

It's well into the afternoon, and still we're inching ever higher. We're on the roof of the world now. We crawl around a blind bend at a little more than walking pace, and an Afghan trucker steps out in front of our vehicle. He puts his hand out to stop us, and he's clearly not moving out of the way.

I pull to a halt, and glance inquiringly at Hamed.

'Another one broken down, I guess,' Hamed remarks.

I turn back to the trucker. It strikes me that he doesn't look too friendly. I've got the Makarov tucked in my belt as Hamed and I slip out of the vehicle and go to investigate.

I've barely got within screaming distance, when the trucker starts yelling at me, top volume in Farsi. I can't make out much of what he's saying, but he's clearly very angry. In fact, he's crimson with rage.

Hamed's trying to translate, but he can't get a word in edgeways. I can hear the bloke repeatedly screaming '*feringi*', the Farsi word for 'white man'. I figure it has to be some rant about foreigners having all the designer kit and the all-weather vehicles, whilst the Afghans have to make do with little better than donkey carts.

Whatever. We do not have time for this shit. There's only a few hours' daylight left, and the last thing I want is to be forced to overnight in the Salang Pass. Via Hamed I tell the trucker to get out of the way, as we need to get moving.

But he's worked himself up into such a rage that it's now he goes to whack me. I palm off his punch, and at this point I decide I have no option but to drop him. I land a clout with the Hampshire Hammer on his jaw, and an instant later he's flat out in a snowdrift. Yet he's tougher than he looks. He hauls himself out and his eyes are blazing hatred. He keeps his distance, but starts screaming at Hamed and me, vowing to track us down and kill us.

We may be armed, but we don't have the time for a firefight in these near-blizzard conditions. In any case, it's always better to avoid a firefight wherever possible, and especially when heavily outnumbered by the locals.

I tell Hamed to tell the silly fucker that with his summer robes and his flip-flops he'd be better off finding some shelter and getting a brew on. Or he's going to freeze to death up here.

But I know you should never take such threats lightly, especially from an Afghan male.

CHAPTER 29

Hamed and I push onwards for a few minutes. Finally, I'm forced to call a halt. The last thing I want is to stop here, but I'm literally falling asleep at the wheel. I've caught myself with my eyes closing and head dropping, and Hamed's had to nudge me awake more than once in the last hour.

I've been on the go in these horrendous conditions for ten hours now, either driving on snow and ice or digging and dragging vehicles free. I'm finished. I need a brew and a feed before I can continue. It's not the Taliban or the locals that's our main enemy now: it's driving in such conditions whilst totally exhausted.

We take shelter in a side tunnel and get a brew on. I use the British Army hexy fuel blocks that come with the ration packs, 'cause I reckon the canisters for our gas stove will have frozen solid by now.

Halfway through a lovely cuppa there is the distinctive crack-thump of AK fire over our heads. We're taking fire from a short way down the main tunnel, and I figure it's the truck driver and his brethren come seeking their revenge. Or maybe it's just some random trapped travellers after our vehicle.

There are bullets snapping around the Toyota, and ricocheting off the tunnel's rock walls. I can't exactly step on the gas, for there's no quick getaway possible in these conditions. I've got to get some serious fire down, and get the guys to back off, before we can make our move.

I make ready my weapon and check that Hamed's in some good cover. Bracing myself against the rough-hewn rock walls of the entrance to the side tunnel, I lean around until the gunmen come into view. I can see three figures, some two hundred metres downhill. It's near the limit of the AK's accurate range, but I'm not trying to kill anyone. Not yet, anyway. If they back off, we can all go peacefully on our way.

In Afghanistan, if you kill someone there's a blood vengeance that can last for generations. The dead man's father, brothers, cousins, sons and so on will vow revenge. The last thing Hamed and I need is a posse of enraged Afghans on our tail, as we push ahead on the drive to General Dostum's.

I open up, putting down aimed three-round bursts. I've got six mags on my person and plenty of spare boxes of ammo in the Toyota. I've got no worries about running out of bullets anytime soon.

I put down accurate fire, squirting bursts just over the heads of the gunmen. In the confined space of the tunnel, the bark of the AK firing cannons back off the walls. It's deafening. The smoke of the cordite fumes hangs blue-grey in the snow-laden air.

I creep the rounds closer to the figures, 7.62mm short kicking up gouts of white from the snowdrifts all around them. It's a great way to spot the impact of your shots, and to adjust fire accordingly.

Cthwak! Cthwak! Cthwak! I send another three-round burst punching into the snow just to the right of the distant figures. Cthwak! Cthwak! Cthwak! Another three-round burst hits the opposite side. I've shown them they're bracketed, and the next three bullets I can put into their heads.

It's a funny thing about shooting at someone that a lot of people don't seem to get: you have to aim your weapon at the target that you want to hit. In many parts of the world where I've operated the local gunmen just don't seem to appreciate this.

Instead, they treat their weapon like a firework: they point it in the general direction of the enemy, and use it to make a lot of noise and pyrotechnics. Just like these Afghan blokes are doing right now, against me.

Loosing off a whole mag from the hip might look and sound very macho, but it's going to be a very lucky bullet that hits me, concealed in great cover as I am. I guess the truckers must realize that I'm no UN tree-hugger type, and that the Toyota's not going to be an easy steal.

The firefight dies down, and the three of them scuttle off the way they came, back around the corner. I let them go. As far as I know I've not killed or wounded any of them. I wasn't trying to. But I figure they've got the message now: come any closer, lads, and I'll shoot each one of you in the head.

I make my weapon safe, Hamed and I mount up the Toyota, and we're off once more. I figure I'll keep quiet about this one with the Ambo, or field trips could be cancelled for good. In any case, there's no way in a million years we'll be bringing his delegation through this route. That's blindingly obvious.

We approach the very top of the pass at a stop–start crawl. We're inching our way forward on the winch, and clawing our way through massive snowdrifts. The last half-kilometre is mayhem, with abandoned vehicles in all directions.

There's figures scattered everywhere, and not a man amongst them doesn't seem to be packing some kind of weapon. I can sense the brooding threat here; touch it almost. All it'll take is for someone to clock us in our nice warm Toyota, churning our way through the snowdrifts, and it'll be Gunfight at the OK Corral again.

There's one advantage we've got now. It's well past 5 p.m. and the sun has long since sunk behind the jagged mountains. In the semi-darkness, and blinded by our headlamps, those we pass will have no idea what we're driving until we're gone, nor who's at the wheel. Or so I hope.

Finally, we burst through to the starlit blackness on the far side of the pass. All of a sudden the route ahead starts to slope down-hill, and it is utterly deserted. Not another vehicle is visible. I figure we're the only wagon to have made it through that day.

The only problem now is this. Either we stop where we are, and overnight here, or we break the golden rule of driving in Afghanistan, which is never to do so at night. I figure we have no choice, and Hamed concurs. We have to press on.

We're driving on lights and coming down this steep gradient at a dead slow. Nothing else is moving. I'm taking it horrendously slowly, when we have our first major slide. We end up with the nose buried deep in a snowdrift, and we have to dig ourselves out.

We do the same thing two or three times, before finally we make it out of the snowline. Ahead, the road is pretty much clear of drifts. Halle-fucking-lujah!

It's past 10 p.m. by now, and we've been on the go for over seventeen hours. I'm wrecked, dog-tired, and so is Hamed. But it's a choice of camp by the roadside and wait to get robbed, or push on through the night towards Dostum's territory.

We'll more than likely come across the odd 'Bosnian Bike' – a car or truck with only one working headlight. But both Hamed and I are of the same mind: we'd rather take the drive of death and slap into a car with no lights, than hang around here.

Hamed does his best to keep me awake as we plough onwards.

By first light we're more than halfway to Mazar town, the location of General Dostum's headquarters. It's not a bad road, considering. There's a few sections have been blown out, and the odd minefield to skirt around, but compared to the road to Jalalabad, it's a blast.

It's midday by the time we reach the outskirts of Mazar. Hamed directs me to his relatives' place, so we can get a sleep and clean ourselves up before meeting the General. But there's going to be nothing of the sort. Hamed's relatives haven't seen him for donkey's years, it seems. Everyone here is his cousin or his uncle, and Hamed's arrival is cause for a major celebration. A sheep is slaughtered. We feast on delicious barbecued meat, spicy rice, and fruit and nuts and yoghurt, and then the elder of the house breaks out the booze.

We're swiftly on to large shots of whisky, washed down with beer chasers – good old non-drinking Muslims that they are. The photo albums are dusted down and passed around. I'm shown pics of Hamed riding a sheep as a boy – or is it a camel?

'Which one's having the most fun?' I ask Hamed, pointing from his face to that of the sheep-camel.

Hamed laughs. Childhood memories. Next there's a photo of Hamed somewhere in France dressed in a smart school uniform, plus the inevitable Hamed with his first AK47.

I can't understand most of what's being said, and Hamed's done with translating, so I'm just chilling out and enjoying the buzz after the drive from hell. Compared with where we've just come from this is paradise. All it's lacking is some dancing girls, and maybe a couple of wrestling bears for light entertainment.

We're up half the night talking, drinking and laughing with our hosts. I guess we'll get around to visiting the General in the next day or so. But by the time we've recovered from the partying, we're told that the General is out of town. It doesn't really matter. The visit was just a formality.

We've got what we came for, which was *accurate information*. The recce of the route via the Salang Pass is complete. It's clear that there's no way the Ambo can take a delegation of European political bigwigs through there in winter. He'll have to fly them up, which is exactly how Hamed and I decide to travel back to Kabul.

We dump the Toyota with an ECHO project local to Mazar, and catch a UN plane heading back to Kabul. As we fly over the jagged, white-capped mountains through which snakes the Salang Pass, I can imagine the chaos and carnage going down on that snow-bound, frozen highway below.

And I can honestly say that I don't give a monkey's if I never see the Salang Pass again. The point of this trip was to prove the route and find out the ground truth. So it's mission accomplished, as far as we're concerned.

A few days later we assemble the delegation, and we're going back in. There's Jason and me acting as security, and we've got five HVTs to look after, including the Ambo. This is not how a Close Protection (CP) job should be run.

It's like trying to load ten pounds of shit into a two-pound bag. We've got the two of us and the five of them. In a CP tasking the minimum ratio should be one-on-one, operators-to-HVTs. Were the American Ambassador and his HVTs flying up to northern Afghanistan to meet with General Dostum, They'd have all the cavalry in support.

Still, this is civvy street, and you do what you have to do.

CHAPTER 30

To make matters worse two of the delegation are Frenchies. They're the types who love to munch on the garlic. You'd need the down-wash of three Chinooks to get rid of their breath in the morning.

One is a retired French Army Colonel, who's now some kind of European politician. I can't pronounce his name, so I nickname him 'Colonel Bonaparte'. Colonel Bonaparte seems to believe that he knows all there is to know about security, and the way to run operations here in Afghanistan.

The other is some incredibly pompous female Europolitician, who insists that everyone 'lower' than her must address her as 'Madame Parliamentarian'. As Jase and I are mere security opera-tors, we're the lowest of the low in her eyes, so we're amongst the first to get the please-call-me-Madame-Parliamentarian treatment.

Well, fuck that.

As far as I can tell this delegation of largely European politicians have come on a jolly to Afghan with sod-all specific to do. They've been dumped on the poor old Ambo, so he's taking them up to Mazar, where they can meet a real-life Afghan warlord – Dostum – and prod some poor people with sticks.

We head down to the airport, and Madame Parliamentarian is banging on about General Dostum this and General Dostum that.

Then she says: 'And while we are up there with him, I intend to have zee serious words with him about zee war crimes.'

For a moment there's an uncomfortable silence, which I break.

'Listen, love, and listen good. If you raise the issue of war crimes with the General, then it will probably be me who has to shoot you in the head, just so the rest of us can get out of there alive.'

Madame Parliamentarian is speechless.

'We're only there on Dostum's good will,' I continue. 'So what happens and whether we make it out of Mazar alive is in his gift. If you go upsetting him at his dinner table, when he's shown his hospitality and welcome to us, it will all go horribly, horribly wrong. And then the only way I will be able to sort it out, and save face for me and the boss – not to mention our skins – is with extreme violence against your person.'

Madame Parliamentarian turns to the Ambo in horror. The Ambo shrugs and smiles. 'I'm afraid Mr Phil is absolutely right.'

'That's how things are done up around Mazar,' I tell her. ''Cause up there it's the Kingdom of Dostum. If you want to raise the issue of war crimes, you do that in Kabul, when you have half of ISAF around you as security. But not in Mazar.'

'He's right,' the Ambo adds. 'And the same goes for everyone. There is to be no questioning of General Dostum on war crimes whilst we are in Mazar.'

Having put Madame Parliamentarian back in her box, we load up the Beechcraft light aircraft for the flight north. Two hours later we touch down at Mazar airstrip. There's no clearing customs or immigration here. Instead, a convoy of battle-worn pickups screeches out on to the runway, each of them crammed full of half-a-dozen of Dostum's gun-toting lunatics.

These blokes are far from being the scrawny Afghans we've got manning up our Kabul guard force. These are big, mean mountain warriors. They've clearly seen a lot of action, and they look the part.

We're flanked by this escort, as we make the short drive to Dostum's villa. We arrive to find the place heavily guarded, with hundreds of similar-looking gunmen on the walls. It hasn't escaped Jase and my notice that Dostum's men are tooled up to the teeth. The guys on the walls have RPGs, ammo belts and PKM light machine guns, plus there's several tripod-mounted Dushkas, a Soviet-era 12.7mm heavy machine gun.

The Dushka is designed as an anti-aircraft weapon, but it is equally devastating against vehicles or ground troops. The only thing I don't see is any of Dostum's armour. He's got a fleet of T55 main battle tanks under his command, but I figure he's got them positioned well out of Mazar itself.

It's clear that the two of us with our pistols are no match for this lot. Jase and me are obviously no threat, and there's little we can do if General Dostum decides to take the entire delegation hostage. Though frankly he's more than welcome to Madame Parliamentarian and the Froggie Colonel.

The unmistakable figure of Dostum is waiting on the steps of his villa. He's a big, barrel-chested bear of a man – your archetypal warlord. He greets each of the dips in turn, and does the same with Jase and myself. We're not dressed in suits for this mission, and I can tell that Dostum knows we're the security.

He gives each of us the once-over, as if he's weighing up our capabilities. War criminal or no war criminal, Dostum commanded men who fought alongside British and American forces post 9/11, as they liberated northern Afghanistan. They did so valiantly, and as brothers-in-arms. I can tell that he's got a certain respect for white-eye operators like us, and I for one wouldn't mind having a rumble alongside some of his lads.

Dostum announces that lunch is served, with an expansive wave of the hand. Madame Parliamentarian bustles ahead, so she can be first at the trough, and she makes it clear that the likes of Jase and me aren't wanted. The General pauses, glances behind at the two of us on the steps, and gestures for us to follow.

'Dinner is for *everyone*,' he growls. He turns to the Ambo. 'Every person on your delegation is invited to eat, including these fine men.'

Dostum gets us seated at one end of this massive table that is overflowing with scoff. At the other end he sits the Ambo and the rest of the delegation. As we eat, I make sure I keep one ear tuned in to all the hot air coming from Madame Parliamentarian's direction. If I so much as hear the words 'war' and 'criminal' in the same sentence, then it's going to be the last thing she ever says.

We finish eating and Dostum presents his five VIP visitors each with a gift. It's a traditional Afghan rug the likes of which I've got lying on my hut floor, and it's more than likely made using child labour. I make a note to remind Madame Parliamentarian of the fact just as soon as I get the chance.

There's a general chat about how pleasant the visit has been, and Dostum makes an arrangement to come and visit the delegation in Kabul, so they can have a more in-depth discussion about how European aid might benefit the north of the country – his domain.

Then it's back to the airport with Dostum's security all around us and we're on the Beechcraft heading back to Kabul. Nothing's happened to particularly spook Madame Parliamentarian, and I'm a little disappointed. But it's far from over yet.

As it happens, the Beechcraft is flying into the mother of all storms. We're climbing over the mountains above the Salang Pass, when I see these dark boiling clouds piled up before us. Suddenly the plane drops through this patch of sky where there's no air pressure, and it just keeps falling.

We're plummeting like a stone. The pilot's fighting with the controls and the turboprops are screaming. Just before we smash into the snow-capped peaks, the pilot manages to wrench the aircraft back onto an even keel. We've hit some atmosphere, and he's got some traction going so he can actually fly the thing again.

He's climbing desperately for altitude, when we hit the storm proper. The sky goes black, and we're being chucked about all over the place. One moment there's a peak to the port side, the next it's bang in front of us, as the Beechcraft is buffeted like a paper plane. I can see the pilot's white knuckles gripping the controls, as he tries to find a route through.

I glance around at the VIPs. The Ambo seems calm enough, but the rest of them are wide-eyed with terror, which does cheer me up a little. The dippy, useless French bird has transformed into Madame Shit-Herself. She's utterly petrified. I wouldn't be surprised if she's wet her knickers, which would be a result if ever there was one.

We emerge from the mountains and we're still in one piece, but the worst lies before us. Somehow, the pilot's got to land this crate in the midst of a raging storm. It's not like the UK, where you can simply divert to Stansted: here, you either put down at Kabul airport, or you plough into the mountains.

As we're coming in to land the pilot is all over the place. One moment I can see the runway out the front of the cockpit, the next it's on the starboard side. If I could persuade him to do a lap of honour for the benefit of Madame Shit-Herself I would. It would serve her right for putting the shits up me about Dostum and his war crimes.

But I reckon the pilot's got other priorities. One glance at his face and I can see he's as white as a sheet. He finally manages to slam the Beechcraft down with a bone-jarring impact, but at least we're safely on the runway. And I figure the pilot's very glad to still be in the Alive Club.

We've got one night off from the merry-go-around, and then we have to take the delegation out to Bagram Airbase, so they can 'get a look at the operations there'. It's clearly nice work if you can get it, this European politician lark. You get to fly around the world taking photos and getting feasted, and all at the expense of the tax-payer. Plus you get paid a shedload for doing so.

There is a potential threat to any convoy running the Airport Road, and I use this as my excuse to go see my mates in the US military. Recently, I've struck up a friendship with a US Marine Corps Colonel, at his base in Kabul. I love his gung-ho approach to things, plus the fact that he has all the shiny kit you could ever wish for.

I explain to him about Madame Parliamentarian's attitude problem with Dostum, the US military's brother-in-arms. Plus I outline Colonel know-it-all Bonaparte's shortcomings. I basically don't have to say a great deal. As far as Colonel Wasp is concerned they're 'cheese-eating surrender monkeys, and they're gonna git some'.

He offers up two Chinooks to do a low-level flight from Kabul up to Bagram. I tell him one should do it, and I gratefully accept.

'Soldier,' he tells me, 'let's just see the face of your Frenchie Colonel when the rotors are beating the tops off them palm trees!'

Early the following morning we shovel the delegation into the hold of the Chinook, and the pilot does this awesome flight at ten feet above ground level all the way up to Bagram. Colonel Bona-parte's face is a picture: he's shitting his load. As for Madame Parliamentarian, I figure she's realized by now she picked the wrong guys to mess with in Jase and me.

The delegation noses around Bagram for a while, whilst Jase and I load up on some burgers in the excellent US Army mess. But it's clear that after the Chinook flight the VIPs don't exactly have the stomach for this little jolly any more.

We load up for the flight back and I go have words with the pilot. 'Awesome flight,' I tell him. 'Lower than a snake's belly, mate. Let's have a bit more of that on the way back if you can manage it.'

After a second low-level dash, the pilot gives me a call. I've got the headphones on, with a radio link to the cockpit. He tells me that he's been put into a holding pattern. He asks if I'd like to see how they do their drop-offs, when they're inserting Special Forces teams into the mountains.

Oh yeah! Thatta boy!

He ramps up the turbines and we're thrown into this heart-stopping climb. I can feel the contents of my stomach – three lovely burgers – about to drop through my arsehole. There's a mountain peak rushing towards us through the portholes at breakneck speed.

At the last possible moment the pilot slows, and parks the arse end of the Chinook onto the ground. I imagine the boys piling off the ramp in all-around defence. I'm completely in my comfort zone. I'm loving it. Next the pilot pulls away from the ground, peels off and lets the Chinook fall away from the mountain.

As we plummet towards earth I take a sneaky peak at Colonel Bonaparte, plus Madame Parliamentarian. The two of them have their faces screwed up like a bulldog licking his pee off a bunch of thistles. Then Madame grabs for a vomit bag, and she's retching into it.

Great. Absolutely fabulous. It's payback time.

The following day the delegation is gone, and I go see Colonel Wasp and his team. I give them a great big box of Montecristo cigars that I brought during my last trip through duty-free. I decide to say something very American to communicate my heartfelt thanks.

'Sir, you and your guys are fucking awesome,' I tell him.

Soon as I've said it the Colonel lets out this cry of 'Hoooh-Aaaaahh!'

I stand there like a proper Englishman thinking how absolutely bizarre Americans can be. I could never imagine a British Army Colonel saying anything other than 'Thank you, old boy,' if given a box of Montecristos.

The Colonel's deputies start joining in with the hooo-aaaaahh-ing, so they're all making this weird noise like an elephant's just sat on their chest. For a moment I wonder if I should start joining in with the braying, but I just can't bring myself to.

Still, when all's said and done you've just gotta love America.

CHAPTER 31

It's early 2004 by now, so pushing three years since I started working the Kabul contract. There have been some big targets hit by the bad guys in Kabul, and across wider Afghanistan, but no one's really made a move on our embassy yet. I'm surprised we've lasted this long without taking a hit. And in a way I'm disappointed. I figure maybe it's testament to the professionalism of our set-up and our procedures. But at the same time, like any soldier, I have this desire to be tested. A part of me has been dying for the bad guys to hit us, so I can prove our defences, evacuation procedures and escape routes for real.

It's not happened yet, and I've reached the time when I figure I've had enough of the Kabul mission. The Ambo's a blast, that's for sure. But getting on for three years of babysitting dips like Madame Parliamentarian is more than enough for me.

Plus I'm burned out from the constant tension. I need a break.

I tell the Ambo that it's been good, but I'm done. I'll be handing over to Chris as team leader, so he's got a great bloke to step into my shoes. We have the mother of all piss-ups in the Ambo's villa, which turns into a completely wild party, and then I'm gone.

I head for the UK, and with just the sniff of a job in Iraq in my nostrils. Iraq post the invasion is in turmoil, and operators like me are being hired in their thousands to man up a private army the likes of which has never been seen before. The Baghdad-based security industry is booming, and a part of me fancies having a look-see. But first, it's back home for a few months of well-earned R & R.

I feel as if I've achieved something real with the Kabul mission. I've run an eighty-plus security team for over two years, with no major mishaps. I've got no education, and I've come from the roughest possible beginnings in life, but I've mixed it with high society and come out smelling of roses.

It means for the boy from the kids' home there is life after the British Army, my only real family up until now. And even in the British Army, there were times when I had struggled to feel at home.

During my months of training with the Royal Hampshires I'd found myself having a personality clash with my instructor, Corporal 'Big V' Valance. Big V was a Military Medal (MM) winner, and a bit of a legend in the Army. He also had a very short fuse and was a right lunatic.

Early on during basic training he'd cracked me around the head with the butt of a General Purpose Machine Gun (GPMG), for laughing 'too loudly' at one of his jokes. Another time he'd over-heard me going on about how light my webbing kit was. He made me wear my own plus his, and beasted me for hours around the parade ground.

Then came the breaking point. One morning Corporal Valance started upbraiding me on parade for having a dirty weapon. This was a serious offence and I knew it was total bullshit. I'd spent hours meticulously cleaning it.

Big V leant across to grab the weapon, but I thought he was trying to hit me. I blocked his arm, and in an instant we were on the floor scrapping. It was Big V's colleagues who eventually broke us up, for even back then thumping recruits was a big no-no in the Army.

I stormed off. My weapon had been perfect, I knew that. Big V had made an excuse to try to punch me out. For the first time I felt really pissed off with the whole Army thing, and was tempted to bin it.

It turned out that the Camp Storeman, a veteran soldier and a Corporal himself, had witnessed the whole incident. 'Fuck me, nipper,' he told me. 'You gave Big V a right good go there. Good on you, lad!'

The Storeman gave me a proper talking to. He persuaded me that the Army was still the place for me, and to pay no attention to Big V and his like. I found my way to the staff office, ate some humble pie and apologized to Corporal Valance. He gave me a bit of a bollocking, but after that things calmed down between us.

I consoled myself with the thought that I'd started in the Army as I meant to go on, by refusing to take any bullshit or rank-pulling. It smacked of bullying, and I'd had enough of that in the kids' homes.

At the end of my basic training, I had an interview with the regimental CO. He asked what my ambitions were in life.

'To have a good time in the Army, sir,' I told him. 'Then to move on and help others, most likely deprived kids, so I can put something back into the system.'

He was stunned. He told me that in all his years he'd never heard a soldier express such a commendable ambition. I meant what I had said. If there were two things I couldn't stand it was bullying and the abuse of kids. I'd had more than my fair share of both in the past.

During the weeks of training I'd out-tabbed (out-marched) everyone, even the instructors, one of whom had attempted SAS selection. To augment my fitness I'd started doing sessions in the gym, to build muscle. Then we were sent on our first overseas exercise, to Denmark, and I'd never been abroad before.

We went on joint exercises with the Danes, but due to a mix-up in communications I led the battalion over the start line three hours early in our Saxon armoured car. There was uproar, but as no one managed to pin it on me I never got the blame.

At the end of the exercise we were granted a night out on the town. We headed for Copenhagen's red-light area. I ended up in a whorehouse, at the back of a queue of other squaddies. I decided I wasn't about to wait for anyone.

I jumped in when the first door opened, and as the lads behind me went wild I led my lady off for a good time. I returned a while later and flicked my used rubber at one of the blokes from a rival Regiment. It kicked off instantly.

In the carnage that followed I wrenched the till from the wall and ran off with it, closely followed by my best mate in the Royal Hampshires. We dropped the till off a railway bridge, smashed it open and made a handsome profit. But the battalion got gated, and the CO had a good idea who was responsible. I got a bollocking, and had started to earn what one of my future commanding officers would refer to as a 'chequered past'.

A few weeks later I found myself heading to Kenya for our second overseas exercise. We'd taken the ferry to Denmark, so this was the first time that I'd ever been in a proper-sized aircraft. As a teenager I'd blagged myself a ride in a Cessna, in return for cleaning the South Coast Aero Club's fleet of light aircraft.

We flew to Kenya in a big old DC10 airliner. We were all dressed in our tropical camo uniforms, and just as soon as we were airborne and the no-smoking light went off and everyone sparked up.

In no time you couldn't see from one end of the plane to the other. Then the RAF stewards came out with the 'horror bags' – the RAF's idea of in-flight refreshments. Rock-hard sausage rolls were soon flying through the air, and we were having the time of our lives.

We touched down in Nairobi some eight hours later, and the doors of the aircraft were thrown open. The heat hit us like an oven. We made our way north overland to Nanyuki Showground, the makeshift Battalion HQ. A night under canvas, and we headed for the jungle. Eight hours later on terrible African roads we hit the treeline. The sun was just setting and the smell of open fires was heavy in the air in the last African village.

Our jungle instructors were two guys from the SAS. When I caught sight of them with their shaggy hair, beards, bespoke weapons and the like, I thought they looked the dog's bollocks.

The tab into the jungle was fierce, the terrain hideous and the humidity twice what it had been outside the canopy. No doubt about it, this was real man territory. But after my time roaming the New Forest I felt almost at home here.

We had to construct A-frames – a basher made of tree branches spread with a tarpaulin, and with underneath a sleeping platform raised off the jungle floor. There's little funnier than hearing the crack of a collapsing A-frame in the dead of night, followed by the howl of the occupant as he hits the jungle floor. It happened a dozen times that first night, and regularly after that.

Over the coming days I noticed how different the SAS guys were from any soldier that I'd met before. They combined a relaxed air with ultimate professionalism. There was no screaming and shouting for the sake of it. The training was hard, but their mantra was – *Train hard, fight easy*.

It made perfect sense to me.

I was eighteen years old and I applied myself 101 per cent. What

I enjoyed most was the training in the jungle for Close Quarter Battle (CQB). They also taught us how to set traps. We caught rats mainly – but these were a giant African version the size of a small pig.

We snared the odd deer, and one morning the SAS lads turned up with a monkey. It went into the pot along with the rats! For me, being in the Kenyan jungle was just an extension of my time spent living rough in the woods as a kid. I loved it there, and I would have spent my whole tour in the jungle if I could have.

The fortnight with those SAS instructors made an indelible impression on me, one that would be a driving factor in my life. One day, I decided, I was going to try for some of that.

The utter deprivation of my childhood years had made me determined to excel at the one thing I was good at: fighting and surviving. The only place to use such skills was the Army, and I was determined to be the best.

That hunger to succeed would propel me into the elite of the British military, and finally onto the circuit.

CHAPTER 32

Having signed off from the Kabul job, I'm bored after only a few months of being back in the UK. I'm craving the buzz of operations, and I'm missing the madness of the embassy contract. I get the sniff of a new job in Afghanistan, and I'm sorely tempted to take it.

It's a toss-up between that and Iraq.

I put a call through to Chris, to see what the lie of the land is out in Kabul. I want to know whether he can put me up at the embassy residence, whilst I scope out this new Afghan job. Chris tells me that it's a little difficult right now. They're not actually staying at the residence any more. In fact, it's been shot to pieces. I get the full story out of him and it goes like this.

Finally, the embassy residence had taken the hit that I'd always expected it would. The bad guys had assaulted the place and put it under ferocious siege. Our Pashtun and Tajik guards had turned on each other, and Chris and the other white-eyes were down to two rounds apiece, as they battled to keep the residence from being overrun.

They did an epic fighting withdrawal, with Colonel Wasp and the US Marine Corps coming in from the north of the city to try to link up and rescue them. Eventually, Chris got everyone out that mattered. And crucially, they used the route that I'd mapped out using my 175cc motorbike to effect their escape.

I am gutted when I hear all this. Not because the embassy's been trashed, but because I wasn't there to lead my team in the battle against the bad guys. I'd sensed it was coming; I'd just got out a few months too early is all. But fuck it, I guess you can't have everything.

As a consolation, the Iraq job that I've been waiting on comes through. I get my kit packed, pick up my flight ticket, and I'm jetting out of the UK to Jordan. At first I'm on a short-term contract, and we'll be heading into Iraq across the Jordanian border.

I check into a hotel in Amman, Jordan's capital city, and await further instructions. I've been there a couple of nights when I get a call from the company that's hired me: the job's fallen through. Luckily, there are contracts out the yin-yang in Iraq right now, and I get immediately reassigned to a job in the south of the country.

I fly from Jordan to Kuwait. I'm joining a team providing security for ITEL, the giant global Telecoms company, as they put in a mobile phone network across southern Iraq. There's a bundle of money to be made in Iraq right now, and the budget for this telecoms operations must be simply massive.

It sounds like it might be a right cushy number.

I touch down in Kuwait, and I'm through immigration and into the airport. I'm awaiting instructions on my satphone on who to meet, when I get a call telling me to take a taxi to the Kuwait–Iraq border. There I'm to rendezvous with some bloke I've never met before, who will apparently drive up to meet me from the Iraq side.

If that's the best they can do, it sounds to me like a crock of shit. The 'liberation' of Iraq is rapidly turning into the mother of all uprisings, and it's as hot as hell in there. The idea of catching a cab to the border, then hanging around with my suitcase for some bloke to come and fetch me, has less than zero appeal.

I'm going to be dumped there with no map, no intel, no body armour, no weapon and no back-up. So what's new? It's hardly the first time.

I manage to find some lunatic Kuwaiti cabbie who will drive me to Safwan, the border crossing into Iraq. It costs me a small fortune to hire him, but at least the security company running the job have agreed to reimburse my cab fare.

Mercifully, as we head through the sun-blasted desert the cabbie cranks up the aircon, so I'm not being boiled alive. Not yet, anyway. We reach the Safwan border crossing, which is slap bang in the middle of nowhere, and predictably there's no one there to meet me.

The cabbie's getting the evil eye from these teenage American grunts, who look like they've been grown in bags of manure, they're so lumbering and muscle-bound. They're manning up the border post, and they come complete with buzz cuts and sunburn. They look edgy and jumpy – not to mention trigger-happy – as hell.

Shortly after our arrival, this massive convoy of American tanks and trucks rolls up to the border. It sits there, snorting and growling in the baking heat, waiting to cross into Iraq. The American soldiers manning the vehicles are giving both my Kuwaiti cabbie and me looks that could kill.

It's not long before Kuwaiti Cabbie tells me thanks for the fare, but he's leaving. He throws out my bags, does a three-point turn, burns some rubber and he's gone in a cloud of desert dust. So there I am stuck on the border, and I don't even have a way to get back to Kuwait proper.

Nice one.

An hour later I'm getting my umpteenth lesson on how to spit chewing tobacco from Samson, my corn-fed, Bible-bashing, newest and bestest buddy. I'm just starting to master the art of hitting a spittoon at a dozen paces when a couple of 4×4s pitch up from the Iraqi side of the border.

Two guys dismount. They are clearly private operators, and I guess this is my reception party. One of them I recognize. It's Les, my old Sergeant Major from my Royal Hampshire days. In fact, by the time I served with Les the Royal Hampshires had been amalgamated into the Princess of Wales's Royal Regiment (PWRR), so strictly speaking it's from our PWRR days. But once a Royal Hampshire, always a Royal Hampshire.

With Les is a guy called Chris, another Green Army regular who's recently got out to join the circuit. I wipe the chewing tobacco juice off my chin, thank Samson for his hospitality, and then Les, Chris and me are making for the vehicles.

Once we're out of earshot of Samson and his fellow grunts, Les and Chris apologize for the hold-up. Apparently the Yanks keep changing the rules and regulations at the border, and they got snaffled in some unexpected red tape.

We mount up their gleaming 4×4, and I've got one thought foremost in my mind: *bullet-magnet.* We take the road running northeast from Safwan towards Basra, and as we do Les hands me an AK47 and some mags. At least now I've got a weapon handy if our glittering prize does come under fire.

We're driving this pristine white Toyota Land Cruiser, which is unarmoured. It practically screams out who's inside it: *Westerners, and a prime prospect for a very lucrative kidnapping.*

Halfway from Safwan to the Iraqi port of Um Qasr, we pull off the road. We're in an area called As Zubyr, and there's an old Iraqi Army camp here. It has a run-down, dilapidated feel to it, but in a sense that's not our concern. Post the 'liberation' of Iraq, the base is being run by a private security company called Generic, and we've simply got some rented accommodation here.

Soon as I've dumped my kit and got a feed, I ask Les and Chris for a heads-up on the operation that we're running. The key responsibility is a Portuguese ITEL engineer called Paulo. They have to drive Paulo into and out of work daily, which invariably means taking him back and forth from Safwan town. It's good hardtop all the way, so when the traffic's light it's a forty-five-minute drive max.

They do the run using two 4×4s. They use one as a back-up vehicle, but neither of them is armoured. They have no other wagons, and no covert vehicles of any sort. They don't appear to vary the route they drive, and they haven't spot-coded that route, or any alternatives. Plus they've not recced any escape options.

They've managed to get their hands on a selection of battle-worn AK47s, all of which are sourced locally. There are no pistols, and there's no body armour. As to the ammo for the longs, it's all locally sourced, and they have zero background or history on it.

They've recruited a team of Iraqis to help man up the operation, but they have little faith in them. It's hardly surprising. There's no system for vetting the Iraqi recruits, and the only place they have for training them is the base at As Zubyr, which is itself hardly safe or secure.

Generic have an Iraqi force standing guard on the base perimeter, but they're about as reliable as a bunch of Afghan arms dealers. At night there's gunfire sparking off in the open desert to the west of us, and it feels highly insecure.

I get Les and myself to do back-to-back stag duties on the main watchtower, so we've got one pair of eyes alert all night long. But that means we're not getting properly rested, so we can't be 100 per cent alert for the day job. Running Paulo into the office, and keeping watch in Safwan during his working hours, requires total watchfulness.

Les and Chris are driving Paulo on the exact same route at the same time each day in overt, unarmoured vehicles. In bad traffic that route becomes a nasty, honking snarl-up, with traffic backed up for miles.

I compare where I am now with the Kabul mission. It doesn't hold up well. Here we have no diplomatic plates; no diplomatic immunity; no gung-ho Colonel Wasp – Hooo-Aaahh! – to call on in an emergency; no vetting system for the local guards; and no well-rehearsed and intensively recced escape routes, for if and when it all goes to ratshit.

In short, it's a cluster-fuck.

During my days of elite soldiering we had a saying: *Fail to plan, plan to fail.* This Iraqi contract is an invitation to an almighty failure. And I'm not even getting paid any more than I was in Afghanistan.

Iraq post the 'liberation' is better for some people, but considerably worse for others. Just like Afghan was better for some people, but not for the Taliban. It's certainly better here in terms of what we in the West see as being the priorities of life: there's no more Saddam and his henchmen, and the horrific abuses that came with him. But it's not better in terms of basic security and people's ability to go about their daily lives without fear of being shot, blown up or kidnapped.

I don't worry much about whether it was right to invade or not. The question boils down to was it right for whom? And every person – myself included – takes what they can from the situation.

I don't kid myself that it's about to get any better very quickly here. But I remind myself that I'd grown tired of my Kabul job; I'd outgrown it. I'd done my bit and the operation was running itself.

I needed a new challenge.

It's very rare that you do a three-year posting in the Army even, and especially without getting bored. I'd been itching to get out of Kabul and on to pastures new. I still feel that Iraq is the place to be right now.

It's newly liberated, and anything feels possible.

CHAPTER 33

By a process of natural selection I take over as de facto team leader. I let Les and Chris know that the vehicles are next to useless. There's no advantage in driving a big, macho wagon unless: A, it's armoured, so it will stop a bullet; or B, it's unlikely to get noticed by the locals. These wagons fail on both counts.

Les and Chris have heard me when I say that we've got to change the way we operate. But it will take time. And we need the client, ITEL, to sign off on any changes we want to make that have cost implications.

A few weeks on the ground and I'm out in Kuwait sorting something for the job. A new team of white-eyes has rotated in, and I'll be going back to join them. One of them is Des, ex-Special Boat Service (SBS), the sister Special Forces regiment to the SAS. I know Des well and he's a superlative operator. He's broad and squat, with thick, dark, curly hair and a full beard. He's got a permanent tan, as he's based in the tiny Southeast Asian country of Laos. At first glance he could almost pass for an Iraqi, what with his black hair, bushy beard and swarthy features.

Des and I completed selection together (nowadays the SAS and SBS do the same selection). He's a decent geezer, well versed in the kind of work that we're doing here in Iraq. I feel more confident in the job with him on board, but still it's taking an age to change the set-up.

I return to As Zubyr, only to discover that the shit has hit the fan big time whilst I've been out. Sure enough, the daily drive into Safwan has been noted by the local bad guys, and we've been hit. The front 4×4 has been malleted by an improvised explosive device (IED), detonated on the roadside.

It's torn the unarmoured vehicle apart, and Paulo, our ITEL engineer and HVT, is dead. One of the Iraqi guards is very badly injured, and another has lost his leg. Des was in the back-up vehicle when the IED went off, and he's uninjured. But he's had to deal with the aftermath of the IED, including retrieving what remained of the bodies.

Whilst the client might always be right on a private civvy job, Des and I decide that we're pulling out of this one, unless certain changes are made pronto. First, we need to move from the base at As Zubyr to somewhere we can be assured of our own security. Second, no more using big white 4×4 bullet magnets for the operation. And third, we need to select and train up a reliable, competent guard force.

We can still use the Toyotas for operations out in the open desert, when the Telco engineers need to pay site visits, for then we're unlikely to get pinged or pinned down. But we need to ban them from going anywhere near urban areas. Plus we need some more shit-hot white-eye operators like Des.

ITEL agrees to make the changes. Before that happens, we don't want any more of their team coming into theatre. They accept that to avoid losing more of their people, they need to allow us to put the security measures in place to run the job properly. It's a multi-million-dollar contract, so it's no use having half-measures on the security front.

We relocate to Basra Airport, where Skylink, a shipping company, has a secure compound. We sublet an area of their base, and hire four cabins solely for our own use. We break them down into an ops room, a storeroom, and two cabins for the white-eye operators who are in-country manning the operation.

The two accommodation cabins have proper beds, carpets and Sky TV, so we figure this is as close to luxury as we're ever going to get. I get one of the local Iraqi guards who I figure I can trust to go and score us a beaten-up GMC pickup. It's a hulking great beast of a thing, and exactly the kind of wagon the locals drive.

We also manage to score a Chevrolet saloon car from Kuwait. It's got a 5.6-litre petrol engine, and it goes like stink. On the open road there's nothing going to catch us. More importantly, you couldn't get a more local-looking vehicle. We rough it up as much as we can, and it's good to go.

We get two new operators rotating in on the contract. There's Mac, a big, tall, wiry ex-Para who joins the operation. Mac's a capable individual, if a little sparky. It's good to have him with us. Then there's a guy called Steve Saltman, who claims to be ex-French Foreign Legion.

Bearing in mind my previous experiences with ex-Legionnaires, I'm a little wary of Steve. It's not helped by the fact that he claims to have two names, because he's been on 'deep undercover ops' back in the UK. He also says he's from some landed gentry family, and that he's got a title. He's the 'Lord Saltman of Hamby', apparently.

I sense that something really isn't right here. So does Des. We decide to keep a very close eye on Lord bloody Saltman of Hamby.

Des and I decide to try to hook up with Ahmed, a local warlord who has close ties to the Iraqi government. He's got a militia under his command that are all from the one local tribe. We're not about to fuck around with equal opportunities here. We want a guard force all from the same, close-knit tribe, and with clearly defined loyalties.

We head to Basra to meet Ahmed, driving the battered GMC and wrapped up in shemags, dishdashes and shades. We've made one crucial refinement to the beast of a wagon: from somewhere we've acquired a giant pink sofa, which we've strapped to the rear.

Our reasoning goes like this: no one will ever suspect that a pink-sofa-carrying GMC is being driven by a couple of 'white-eye' private operators. We've had time to grow beards and acquire a proper tan, and we figure we're pretty much indistinguishable from the local furniture-delivery guys.

Ahmed turns out to be your typical warlord – General Dostum with knobs on. He's got this huge office in downtown Basra, with a massive polished desk and a fine leather chair. He's surrounded by heavily armed flunkies, and he's even got a couple of local women hanging around near him, who are clearly his girlfriends.

He waves us in, and seats us before him on hard wooden stools. No mistaking the power relationship here then. As I go about explaining my proposition, I can see the fear in the eyes of the blokes to either side of him, those who have to deal with him on a daily basis.

Ahmed is clearly the Mr Big of gangsterism in Basra. If you got on the wrong side of him, I would imagine you'd end up getting fed your own foot. It's fortunate then that he likes our proposal. More than likes it, in fact. He comes bustling around his massive desk, hauls me to my feet and gives me this mafioso-style bear hug.

'My son, my son,' he's telling me, 'you train my men as you promise, they will act like your own family. They will protect you with their very lives. And you will be paying them, yes?'

I explain again that he gets his blokes trained, fed and paid a wage by us. He can turn around and tell his tribe exactly what we're doing for them, which will make him look very good in their eyes. He has a real interest in making the relationship a long and beautiful one, just as we do. Everyone wins.

'Insh'Allah – God-willing – this will be very fabulous,' Ahmed tells me. 'Like any God-fearing Muslim, I like to see my people reaping the benefits of the liberation of this Iraq, our wonderful country.'

Ahmed offers us some chilled beers so we can toast the deal. And in spite of his supposedly pious ways, he happily necks one himself, whilst all the time having a good letch at his office girls. Regardless, Des and I are happy.

We scope out an abandoned part of the airfield where we can do range work and proper training. We draw up an eight-week course that we start running a hand-picked bunch of Ahmed's boys through. We figure we need fifty to complete the course, before we're good to receive any new ITEL personnel.

And so we're six months into the Iraq mission before we finally declare that we're open for business.

CHAPTER 34

I've been formally appointed team leader by now, which means I'm officially responsible for making this Iraqi gig work. My reputation following the Kabul mission goes before me, and I don't want it torn to shreds in Basra. Des, Mac and me are kicking the operation into shape here, and I'm growing ever more confident that we'll make it work.

There's a British Army base co-located with Skylink at the airport. As I'd done in Kabul, I start looking for ways to forge links with the regular Army boys. I have a chat with their CO, and explain what we're doing here. In Basra, there's yet to be the explosion in private operators that there's been in Baghdad, so he is a little surprised.

But he accepts that we're here to stay, and that perhaps there are ways we can be of mutual help. First off, I explain about our links into Abdul and the local militia, which offer us clear opportunities for intelligence gathering – intelligence that we are happy to share with the British military.

Second, I mention that we've managed to get our hands on just about every kind of weapon the local bad guys are using, and we're happy to train his lads on the lot, if that would be helpful. In return, I wonder if we might be given access to the British Army cookhouse and the gym.

An understanding is reached, and we're free to start getting our feet under the proverbial table.

Des and I are well aware that Ahmed's guys could end up on the wrong side, *fighting against us*, so the training package we put together appears all shiny and nice, but is of limited use. A 'polished turd' is how we describe it: It looks great on the outside, but is actually full of crap.

We rehash and tone down the drills, so that we don't turn Ahmed's boys into steely-eyed bringers-of-death. We want to transform them into a force that can act as a barrier, should it all go noisy, allowing us to escape with the clients. They will be our 'combat indicators', so that we get to know when things are going wrong.

We intend to use Ahmed's guys to buy us time, so we can get the client into a vehicle and hit one of our escape routes. I have no illusions that Ahmed's lot will stand firm and fight for a white-eye for long. At the end of the day we're still infidels, as far as they're concerned.

We don't give them lessons in marksmanship, and we don't teach them to use their sights properly, or to hit a target. The average guy on our detail still couldn't hit a barn door at ten paces, even after completing the course, and I want it to stay that way. Their basic drills are to fan out and make lots of noise, whilst we get away.

We also treat them on a maximum 'need to know' basis. Whatever local force is required for a day's operations, we never let them know where they are going, or what time schedule we're working to. We change routes every day and never with any warning, or discernible pattern. That makes it hard for any one of them to get the drop on us, if they've gone over to the dark side.

By the time we get the new ITEL team in-country, the operation is going like clockwork. We're cutting around in local vehicles undetected, and we're forever changing our routes and timings. The only danger now is going into and out of our Basra Airport camp. Otherwise, once we're on the open road no one's ever going to ping us.

We've also got a good flow of intel into the operation. Ahmed's boys are providing a rich vein of local information for us to tap, which we in turn feed into the British Army set-up. ITEL soon feel confident to ship in a growing team from their side, and to start recruiting local Iraqi engineers.

It's all good. In fact, in a way it feels too good to last. Unsurprisingly, it's The Lord Saltman of Hamby who proves to be our first big undoing.

Amongst other things, 'The Lord' (as we've nicknamed him) claims to have been in the Bosnian special forces. I happen to know there are some Bosnians working as chefs in the British Army mess. I invite The Lord for a brew, and I've already keyed up one of the Bosnian lads to what I'm planning.

'Hey, BB, mate,' I announce, as The Lord and I are getting a brew. I've nicknamed the Bosnian guy 'BB', after 'Bosnian Bike'. 'BB, I want you to meet The Lord. He served with the Bosnian 1st Special Forces Brigade. I reckon he must speak some of the local lingo like.'

'Mr Lord, so nice to meet you,' BB beams. Then he goes 'Blah, blah, blah, blah, blah,' in whatever language they speak in Bosnia.

The Lord stares at BB for a good few seconds, and he's clearly lost for words. He's not understood a thing that BB's said. Just as I suspected. It's proof positive that The Lord's full of more shit than a Christmas goose.

A few days later The Lord and I are scheduled to go on a trip with some of the newly arrived ITEL guys. The drill is that no one drives around camp with a weapon made ready. Instead, we head to the front gate, take the weapons into the loading bay beside it, slot on a mag, chamber a round, flip off the safety and we're ready.

The Lord slots his mag onto his AK, but I note that he doesn't chamber a round, or flip off his safety.

I give him a look. 'Make ready then, mate.'

'Erm, I'd rather not, mate,' he replies.

'Look, unless you can bring that thing to bear and open fire in a nanosecond, you are not getting into the same vehicle as me, pal, which means you ain't going out on ops. Got it?'

His eyes are darting about nervously. 'I'll get on it if we hit any trouble, mate.'

'You don't seem to understand,' I rasp. 'We hit trouble and you're in a covert vehicle. You'll have no time to do anything other than bring your weapon to bear and open fire. So, make ready.'

He shakes his head. 'I don't want to, mate.'

I'm staring at him now. 'Either you make ready or you're not getting into that car. So let me know what's what, and I'll get someone out here who can do the job properly.'

'Best you do that, then, mate,' he mutters.

I know now that he's frightened of his own weapon. It's a case of all the gear, no idea. And how many of those bloody types have I met in this business before.

I'd sooner go out on my own driving the streets of Basra, than take The Lord with me. He's a liability. In the covert world that we're operating in, there is no time to chamber a round, flip off the safety and bring to bear. Instead, your weapon has to be firing as it comes out of its holster, or up from the vehicle's dash.

The Lord's drills are just about acceptable if you're moving around in a large convoy of up-armoured SUVs, with dozens of blokes visible and armed. With such a show of force you may get time to make ready and engage.

But not with us. We get the clients from A to Z covert and without being noticed. And if for whatever reason you do get pinged and compromised, the instant reaction has to be to open fire and put down the rounds with lethal force.

I've noted on previous jobs that on the rare occasion that The Lord came with us, he's opted to drive. And when he drives, he's going everywhere at top speed. He's like a bat out of hell on acid. I now know why: he's shit-scared, and that means he's not driving with any care.

I figure this guy's done a few years in some army somewhere, but his skill sets don't match the job he's now being called upon to do.

When I'm back at base I ping him an email, pretending to be from some private security company whose name I've just made up. I offer him the mother of all contracts, and ask to see his CV. He pings an email back, CV attached.

It makes for interesting reading. He's done everything from wrestling buffalo in Nevada to flying stealth fighter jets. In short, he's a ready-made war in a box. At least, in his dreams he is. Having unearthed the truth about The Lord, there is nothing I can do with him apart from getting him to assist with first-aid lessons for the local squad that we're training.

We get a visit from two genuine ex-French Foreign Legion lads. I take them over to The Lord's cabin, so they can try out their French on him. They're giving it the 'Bonjour', and rabbiting away in French, when The Lord starts going: 'No, no, no – *English*. Speak English.'

So he claims to have served in the Legion, but he doesn't know a word of French. Nice one. I glance at the head of his bed, and he's got this photocopy of the Hamby coat of arms pasted up beside it. I don't doubt that all of that's a crock of shit too.

One day we pitch up at the gate to the base, and there's a young soldier manning the guardhouse who hasn't seen us around before. He eyes our local dress, beaten-up GMC, plus pink sofa suspiciously. He fires some questions at us, keeping the gate well and truly barred shut.

The Lord jumps out and starts yelling at the soldier. 'Don't you know who I am? I'm Lord Saltman of Hamby! Get that gate . . .'

His sentence is cut short as Des's fist makes contact with his jaw. Des's punch knocks The Lord clean across the road, and saves us from any more embarrassment in front of the young British soldiers on duty.

Des and me have both had a skinful of the bullshitting bastard by now, and it's only by luck that Des has got to him before I did. If not The Lord would have felt the wrath of the Hampshire Hammer big time.

As team leader I'm earning a little more than The Lord, but not by much. It makes me very angry that guys like him can blag their way onto the circuit, when guys like me have made it here the proper way, the only way – *the hard way*.

Having a guy like him around means more work and less security for the rest of the team, and the client is actually being defrauded. They are paying for something they're not getting. It's hardly surprising that we're hearing stories of private operators going stir-crazy in Iraq, and blowing away everyone in their accommodation block.

Guys like this are a dangerous liability, and under pressure they're going to crack. The Lord's supposed military pedigree is all smoke and mirrors, and the saddest thing is that he actually seems to believe his own fantasies. I want shot of The Lord, but I can't get rid of him until I have something concrete to pin on him.

Before I can get that, I face a new problem, which turns out to be something of a surprise. It's Ahmed the local warlord. Like Brian the unfortunate Afghan driver, cum-sex-addict, Ahmed seems to have delusions that Des and me are somehow his newest and best buddies from the West. He keeps calling us to these 'urgent meetings' at one of his Basra safe houses, each of which turns out to be an excuse for a buddy-buddy drinking session. Having a skinful with Ahmed the Warlord is okay for intelligence gathering, but it's not necessarily great for security, or for Des and me keeping out heads on our shoulders.

From a half-cut Ahmed we glean intel on the movements of the various rival militias, and we get advance warning of serious trouble brewing in town. Even though the British Army intel guys have their own sources, what we feed them from Ahmed helps build up their intel picture.

We glean more intel from Ahmed's boys that we're training and running ops with. From them it's mainly 'gossip' that they don't realize is useful to us. We can't ask too many direct questions, for that'll make the flow of information rapidly run dry. So we probe gently and carefully.

Des and I keep what we call a 'training log', but in reality it's a notebook crammed full of the daily snippets of intel that we're picking up from Ahmed's lads. At the end of every week, we go dump the log with the intel cell at the British Army camp, so the eggheads there can do their stuff with it.

The intel picture that emerges is as follows. The threat level in and around Basra is clearly on the up, but day to day it is totally unpredictable. One moment all might be quiet, the next there could be the mother of all uprisings on the streets. All it takes is a trigger, a flashpoint, and it can spiral out of control in a matter of seconds.

And sooner or later we figure we're going to hit one of those flashpoints.

CHAPTER 35

I manage to get out with a couple of the Army pilots, flying intel overflights with them in a Lynx. Travel by air is supposedly the only truly safe way to get around in Iraq these days. It doesn't feel particularly safe or secure to me.

We're doing a day flight, with the doors to the helo wide open so we can clock what's going on below. All of a sudden there's this deafening roar, and a flaming great projectile comes shooting past the starboard side of the helo, missing us by inches.

The pilot throws us into evasive manoeuvres, and the decoy flares are firing off in a comet trail behind us. The door-gunners are hunched over their guns, searching for a target, but there's no sign of the launch site below.

I make ready my weapon, but there doesn't seem a great deal of point in doing so. We're highly visible buzzing around in the air like a great big bumblebee: matey down there with the launcher is well hidden amongst a thousand-and-one palm trees. Anyway, I'd rather get the hell out of his airspace before he can rearm and have another pop at us.

One of the passengers has been filming with a video camera, for intel purposes. Once we're on the ground we review the tape: he freeze-frames it on the projectile going past. Whatever it is, it doesn't look like a common or garden RPG. It's more like a SAM7 or a Stinger – simple but highly lethal man-portable surface-to-air missiles.

Whilst travel by air is looking ever more dodgy, so is travel by road. Basra's seething with armed and dangerous militia gangs boasting increasingly sophisticated weaponry. It's starting to feel uncomfortably like a pressure cooker out there. Ahmed has warned us that the militias are planning a big hit on coalition forces, or their private security contractor allies. At some stage we're clearly going to get some.

More and more of the big private military companies (PMCs) are moving into southern Iraq. Few run operations like we do, covert and low-profile. Most burn around in big convoys of SUVs, with weapons sticking out of the windows, making like they own the country. It's only a matter of time before someone takes a major hit.

Des and I know that there's a second plank to what we should be doing here that we're not doing. Staying covert is the first priority, and rightly so. But as with the Kabul mission, hearts and minds should be the second. We're doing none of that, and we need to get some kind of psychological operations – psyops: hearts and minds – up and running amongst the locals with whom we operate.

I've always been a keen football player, so when Omer, one of our more capable local force commanders, asks me what team I support, I see an opening. It turns out that Omer and I share a love of the beautiful game. I ask him about his kids, and whether there's a local youth team that they play for. Omer tells me there is. Safwan United are the local under-14s squad, and most of our guard force have lads playing in the team, or trying to get a place on it.

Omer asks me if I'll go down one Friday to watch Safwan United play. I tell him I'd like nothing better. I'd been a talented player myself in my youth, but when I should have concentrated on developing my game, I was running away from the kids' homes and causing mayhem instead, so my talent had never been nurtured.

Des and I head out to watch the Friday match. The pitch is actually a patch of bare and beaten mud, with a couple of goalposts leaning at crazy angles at either end. None of the kids has any of the right gear, and the football's been repaired so many times it's more patch than it is ball.

But the kids play like kids do all over the world, with real gusto and a wild will to win. As we watch the ebb and flow of the match, Des, Omer and me are talking nineteen to the dozen with the other football dads – many of whom serve on our guard force – about the English Premier League. Because we're English, they presume that David Beckham has to be our best mate, and Rooney lives just down the road.

The following Friday Des and I get down there early, and we run a proper warm-up session with the Safwan United lads. We sort them into two sides, and start doing some organized training exercises. Before now, all they have ever done is gather at the footie pitch for the weekly kick-around. But they've seen their heroes in the Premier League on TV doing the kind of stuff that Des and I are now teaching them. They sense this is the real deal, and they're lit up by it. And so, we notice, are all the football dads.

Des is not massively into football, and he only lasts a couple of weekends. In any case, he's the main sponsor of his local football team. When not cutting around Iraq, Des lives in Laos, a tiny Southeast Asian country. He's shown me the photos of the Lao team's sponsored T-shirts. Instead of Sony, they've got 'Mr. Des' emblazoned on the front of them.

Des figures he's doing his bit sponsoring Mr Des's Lao team, so he leaves the bulk of the Safwan United (SU) coaching to me. I'm down there regularly now, and I keep the SU lads at it. Omer's joined me as my makeshift assistant coach, and together we're licking the lads into some form of shape.

I strike up a kind of father–son friendship with the young lad who's the captain of the team. He's called Naquibullah, or some such completely unpronounceable name. As he's the spitting image of Ronaldo, that's the nickname I give him, and he loves it.

I do a couple of runs to Kuwait, to pick up cash to pay our local guard force, and I bring back with me some brand-new footballs. When I present them to Ronaldo and his team, Big Phil feels like Santa Claus all of a sudden. I've also managed to score a couple of Manchester United T-shirts, which are like gold dust to these young lads.

I have never been anywhere in the world where you can't find a Man U shirt. Professing to be a Man U fan – which I am not – is a universal icebreaker, no matter where you are on earth. Every one of the Safwan United lads wants one of the shirts that I've brought with me.

I tell them the score. They've got three more games coming up in the local under-14s league. If they go on to win the league, the team gets the Man U shirts. There's one for Ronaldo, the captain, and three more for the man of the match in each remaining game. But only if they secure pole position.

Safwan United do go on to win the league. Des, Omer and me are there to see them do so, and we present Ronaldo and the others with their Man U shirts. It's a pretty special day, and it's Des and myself and our operation that take the credit for getting the team to the top of the league.

It's a top fluffy feeling all around, not to mention top-notch hearts and minds work with the locals. But neither Des nor I kid ourselves that it'll be enough to keep the real fanatics off our backs. There are some real nutters out there, and tensions in Basra are reaching breaking point.

Some militias, such as the so-called Badr Brigade, are operating pretty much openly on the streets of Basra by now. They're beating and murdering young women for showing a flash of flesh on the streets, and wiping out their rivals. It's like the Taliban have been kicked out of Afghanistan and somehow jetted into Basra instead.

Neighbouring Iran's also got its evil finger in the pie, sending suicide bombers and sophisticated IED devices over the border into Basra, in an effort to hit the British military, or the private operators. And then there's the lunatic Muqtada al-Sadr's Mahdi Army waiting in the wings to foment extreme violence against 'the infidels'.

One night we're driving back from a late session with Ahmed the Warlord, one that's been full of dire warning about how Basra's poised to blow. We opt to take a dirt track that loops north through the open desert, and back to our base at Basra Airfield. It's one of the many routes that we've recced, as an alternative to taking the main drag.

We're in the GMC, sun-faded sofa still strapped to the rear, and barrelling through the flat desert sands. We're following the dirt road, the way ahead looks clear, and the sky above us is so star-bright it dazzles. Another time, another mission, and this country could be captivating.

As it is, we slow the vehicle and slip into a shallow wadi. The track crosses the dry, sandy bed of the wadi, and climbs up a blind rise on the far side. As we crest it, we're suddenly confronted by the mother of all insurgent gatherings.

We are in the midst of the open desert, and there are crowds of

Iraqis milling about and tooled up to the eyeballs. If we stop, or hesitate, or try to turn back, we're toast. We'll immediately betray the fact that we're not supposed to be here, and our cover will be blown. We'll get an RPG in through the window, and a posse on our tail.

There's a dozen or more Toyota pickups parked up here. They're faster than the GMC, and more manoeuvrable, plus there's a number with heavy machine guns mounted on the rear. They'll come burning after us through the open terrain, playing shoot-'em-up for fun.

There's not a word spoken between Des and me, nor a flicker of indecision. Without slackening our pace we keep driving ahead. We've trained for this countless times before, and we both know the drills.

We'll force ourselves to head on through as if we have every right to be here, and if it all goes noisy we'll be straight into our fire drills, in an attempt to fight our way out. But if it does come to a firefight, I rate our chances of getting out of this one just about zero.

Neither speeding up nor slowing much, we keep pushing ahead. The crowd shifts, restlessly, and for a horrible moment I wonder if it's going to allow us through. Des and I force ourselves to talk, as if we're chatting away to each other without a concern in the world, instead of totally shitting ourselves.

I flick a brief glance at Des. 'Reckon we can sell them the fucking sofa, mate?'

He shakes his head, keeping his eyes on the road. 'Nah mate. It's the wrong colour. Doesn't match the curtains.'

It's less than a minute's drive, and we're finally through the far side of the crowd, but still it feels like a lifetime. As we pull away from the heavily armed throng, I'm expecting to see tracer rounds come fingering after us, and tearing into the rear of the GMC.

Instead, the darkened desert remains blissfully silent and still behind us. We've been incredibly, insanely lucky.

It strikes the both of us that we mightn't be so fortunate next time.

CHAPTER 36

A couple of weeks later our fears about how narrowly we've escaped a desert lynching are confirmed, and in the worst possible way. Two British soldiers are captured by a mob in similar circumstances, driving an unmarked local car through Basra. They've been ripped from the vehicle, savagely beaten and kidnapped.

Fucking hell, is my first thought upon hearing of what's happened. *That could have been us.*

It's 19 September 2005, and it's our British Army pals in Basra, plus our contacts in the local militias, who put us in the picture about how those lads have been seized.

For months now the British military has been running covert operations in and around Basra. As private security operators we don't need to know who or where they are or even what they're up to. But in essence, their missions have been similar to our own in style and appearance. They keep a very low profile and cut around getting the job done.

Their mission is the main difference in terms of how we do things here in and around Basra. Whilst Des, Mac and me are here to earn an honest dollar, and to protect ITEL's engineers and operations, the British army lads have been building a 'pattern of life picture' around one specific individual.

Early on the morning of the 19 September the two British soldiers were driving through one of the main thoroughfares, to the east of the city. They approached an Iraqi police checkpoint, and for some reason their unmarked car was waved to a stop.

A firefight erupted, during which the two blokes had managed to escape. But with Iraqi police vehicles in pursuit they were outrun and cut off. Surrounded, the two soldiers had opted to lay down their weapons and try to talk their way out of it.

Instead, they were bundled into an Iraqi police wagon and driven off at high speed. The British military scrambled a Sea King surveillance helicopter, and got it overhead providing a live video feed. Stripped of their equipment and badly beaten, the two lads were in danger of being 'disappeared'.

The Iraqi police video taped the British soldiers plus the captured weaponry, and released those images to the media, accusing them of being 'terrorist spies'. The British Army sent in its Quick Reaction Force (QRF), and threw a cordon of men and armour around the Jamiat police station, where the two lads were being held.

At the same time angry crowds gathered, their hatred fuelled by rumour and misinformation about the 'two British terrorist-spies'. The screaming crowd started hurling petrol bombs at the Warrior armoured vehicles, and soldiers were engulfed in flames. Gunfire erupted in both directions, as the British tried to hold the cordon, and the Iraqi mob did its best to break it.

Kids as young as Ronaldo from Safwan United were fighting running battles with British squaddies. In short, what we had feared for months had finally come to pass: the fuse had been lit, and Basra had exploded into flames.

Mercifully, we got the warnings early about the troubles and from multiple different sources. The British Army ops room; Omer my force commander; Ahmed the warlord: from all directions we learned that the shit has hit the fan big time in Basra.

Immediately, we pulled all our ITEL people back in to the security of the base, and we stood-to all the guards that we could muster. We were in lockdown mode, and we would remain like that until the trouble died down.

That evening the Sea King surveillance helo secured images of the two captured British soldiers being moved. They were bundled into a vehicle with blankets over their heads, and dressed in local dishdash robes. They were driven a short distance, and handed over to a known Iraqi Hezbollah group, which is one step closer to Al Qaeda.

That was the catalyst for the British assault force to go in. Whilst the main body of British armour smashed its way gloriously into the Jamiat cop shop, crushing vehicles and flattening walls as it went, a squadron of airmobile British troops hit the Iraqi Hezbollah building.

Blowing in the doors and windows, they discovered that whoever had been holding the two captives had fled. The lads were discovered in a locked room, bloodied and beaten but still very much alive. They were pulled out, and the entire British force was withdrawn. And Basra city was left to stew in it's own, very angry, hate-fuelled juices.

I didn't know those two soldiers personally, but their reputation was of being veterans of covert recce operations. Operating in and around Basra is starting to resemble the very worst days of Northern Ireland, when hatred stalked the Belfast streets, and any British squaddie was a prime target for a killing.

Having served in Northern Ireland, I can remember those days well. It was after the Kenyan jungle training that I was warned off to deploy to Londonderry for two years. Thank fuck for that, was my reaction. At last a chance to do some real soldiering.

The Northern Ireland tour had three stages: Guards and Duties, The Waterside, and a City Tour. That last was Belfast. We would operate from a small patrol base in a Catholic part of the city, and it was there that we reckoned the real action would be had.

But as things turned out, the first two stages of the tour proved pretty eventful too. One evening we were carrying out an aggressive foot patrol on the border, and stopping suspect vehicles. Unbeknown to us, the IRA had forced a man to drive a van packed with explosives, by taking his family hostage. They had sent him towards a fortified British border outpost – Fort George – where they would detonate the van by remote control. It was an evil operation, and sadly we didn't get to stop it.

On that occasion the IRA pulled it off, killing several British soldiers. The first we knew about it was when the horizon flared red in this massive explosion, followed by a withering barrage of machine-gun fire, as we went in at night to try to hunt down the killers.

After that we deployed to Belfast. We were sent to Masonic, a British Army post overlooking the Bogside. On guard duty in the sangar above the Bishop's Street Gate it was clear that you couldn't afford to switch off for a second. People swarmed the streets and you had to have eyes everywhere.

The Battalion's Close Observation Platoon (COP) was looking to fill some vacant slots, so I decided to give it a go. I passed the course, and was now in with the battalion's best. The work was specialist and dangerous, and none of us were allowed to discuss operations outside of the Platoon. Nine of our number from the COP would go on to join Specialist Military Units.

I became friendly with a local Belfast lass named Dorothy, and got clearance to visit her at her flat. But one day the IRA placed one of their men outside in a car. Luckily, I spotted him first. I called the base, and they sent out a patrol to bring me in. As I left the flat I gave the guy a big smile, and he sped off in a cloud of burning rubber. I wondered what he might have had in his vehicle for me: a short, a long or a grenade? Either way, killing a British soldier was as good as it got for those boys, no matter how you went about it.

I also wondered who it was who'd reported on me to the IRA. Even my girl, Dorothy, wasn't above suspicion. You never knew who might be about to betray you on the grim, rain-lashed streets of Belfast. Which made it pretty similar to operating on the dusty, sun-blasted, hate-filled streets of Basra.

Only Basra is far worse. We don't share the same history, culture, racial origins or beliefs as the Iraqis. We're the white-eyes and the infidels. And worse than that, we're increasingly being seen as the invaders of their country.

A few days after the capture of the two soldiers, I'm passing through the centre of Basra with Mac. We're keeping our movements to a minimum now, but some trips – like this one – can't be avoided, if we're to keep delivering on the contract with the clients.

The suffocating, fifty-degree heat of the day has dropped into the near-cool of the Iraqi night. But the streets are still poisonous, and boiling up with anger. You can sense it on every road junction that you pass.

We've covert, dressed like locals, and with our weapons made very, very ready. There is no other practicable way to run the ITEL contract and to make it work, here in southern Iraq. We turn a darkened street corner, and up ahead the road is bathed in the orange glow of street lamps. At night we avoid the light like the plague. We seek out the shadows and the darkness, which provide an extra cloak of anonymity.

Normally, we'd speed up and pass quickly through a well-lit area like this one. But not tonight. Up ahead there's a solid build-up of traffic. We're in the Chevrolet for a change, and Mac slows it to a stop behind the rearmost vehicle, the throbbing beat of the engine dying down to a throaty idle.

All of a sudden I've got that feeling: a horrible, tingling sensation running up and down my spine. *Danger.* I see the first finger stabbing the air. It's a kid of about Ronaldo's age, to the left rear of the vehicle. He's pointing at Mac and me and yelling, his eyes wide with bloodlust and hatred. In an instant, the first rocks are flying towards our rear window.

Fuck knows what the flashpoint's been, or how exactly we've been rumbled, but it's all going rapidly to ratshit. I see hands lifting the distinctive shape of an AK47.

Either we get the hell out of here now, or we're dead.

CHAPTER 37

I'm yelling at Mac to get the Chevy moving, but he doesn't need me to tell him. He's alert to the danger all around us, just as soon as I am. He's searching for an escape route, but we're surrounded by a solid wall of traffic. Mac's edging forward and trying to force a way through the jam of vehicles. He's bumping cars ahead of us and trying to shunt them aside, but we're not moving far enough or fast enough.

Within seconds a screaming mob closes in from behind, and the first brick smashes down on the rear window. I clamber into the back seat, so I can take up a fire position covering the crowd. Every second the seething mob is growing, both in terms of numbers and the level of pure animal aggression it's about to unleash upon us.

I raise myself into a fire position and bring my muzzle up to bear. I've got a big, beautiful Hechler & Koch G3 in my hands – the 'Barking Dog' we used to call it. It's a large, fearsome, intimidating piece, the perfect crowd-control weapon. Staring down that dark, gaping muzzle is like an invitation to hell.

It's already made ready to fire before I bring it to bear. But I'm hyper-alert to the fact that in the vanguard of the mob there's mostly teenage kids. *Iraqi Ronaldos.* The real bad guys are hanging further back. If I shoot a kid and we don't get our arses out of here, they'll torture us and crucify our souls.

There's an earsplitting crash as another brick hammers down on the window, half smashing it in. An iron bar follows, ripping through the glass. The noise of the screaming assault right in front of my face is deafening.

I use the muzzle to smash away the broken glass, so I've got a clear field of fire. I'm instantly in the aim. I'm finger on the trigger, poised to blow away at point-blank range the next group of teenage mobsters who come for the vehicle.

There is no fear in my eyes. *Show fear and you're finished.* Instead, there's the look of the school kid – 'Kevin' – who smashed the floor buffer down onto Cornelius's skull. I'm a steely-eyed bringer of death. *Come and get some.*

There must be something in my demeanour – a locked and loaded white-eye operator ready to wreak havoc on his attackers – that for an instant makes the crowd hesitate. And in that moment Mac sees his chance. He spots a momentary break in the wall of cars before us, floors the throttle, and with a screech of tyres we lurch ahead. I feel Mac gunning the engine, and we career into two cars in front of us, cannoning off both of them. There's a scream of metal tearing metal, and then we're powering ahead.

Through the shattered rear window I see figures racing after us, and the spark of muzzle flashes from the darkness either side of the Chevy. They've placed gunmen up ahead of where the mob set upon us, to prevent us making our getaway.

I yell out a warning that we're under fire. Mac weaves and races the Chevy, as I unleash rounds from the G3, pumping a storm of lead in the general direction of the muzzle flashes.

As we pull ahead, I drop the G3 and grab my MP5 sub-machine gun. I've got limited ammo for the G3, and a couple of shots from the Barking Dog are all I can afford. Plus I may need the G3 later if we're pursued, 'cause it's got better accuracy at long range.

For now, I make do with the MP5, targeting the muzzle flashes that are fast receding into the distance, shooting through the shattered hole in the glass. A few well-aimed single shots and the gunmen go quiet, and then we're speeding out of there.

We go tearing around a corner practically broadside-on to the road, which puts us out of our attackers' line of fire. Up front Mac keeps the pedal to the metal. Soon we're speeding out of town towards the airport road. We're unsure if we've got any vehicles in pursuit, but either way they won't outrun the Chevy at full blast.

I stick to my fire position until I'm certain there's no one following us. Then I sink back into my seat, pulse thumping in my ears like a jackhammer. I can't believe we've made it out of there. It's a miracle we're still at liberty and alive.

We reach the base. Never have I been so pleased to see a bunch of British squaddies, as the lads on stag usher us in through the gates. *Welcome home.*

Both of us know that if we hadn't made it out of there when we did, we'd have been toast. We'd have been beaten to death on the spot, or taken into the insurgents' custody, which would have been far worse than a quick bullet on the roadside.

We don't make a big deal out of it with the Green Army lads. We don't need telling twice that we should consider going out less on the streets of Basra.

It's luck that's got us out of there, pure and simple. If the gap hadn't opened in the traffic when it did, we'd have been finished. Lady Luck was with us today, just as she hadn't been with the two British Army lads captured by the Iraqi police thugs.

Another thing is crystal-clear to us. The British have lost control of Basra city, and they've lost the spirit for the fight. Plus we've more than lost the battle for hearts and minds here. I figure it's time to get the hell out of southern Iraq.

But first, there's news of a kidnapping.

The Kidnap and Ransom (K & R) industry in Iraq is brutal and booming. God only knows how many K & R victims have been zipped into orange boiler suits and had their heads hacked off. The international kidnappings make the big global headlines, but the thousands of Iraqis taken go all but unreported.

The hardline Islamist terrorist groups are executing their victims live on the internet, in an effort to force the white-eyes out of Iraq. The more criminal elements are seizing hostages to solicit multi-million-dollar ransoms in return for their release. There's millions of dollars in ransoms being handed over, and the more money paid the more it fuels the industry. It's a vicious circle, and the insurgents and criminal gangs can't get enough of it.

There's not been a massive amount of kidnappings down in our sector yet, but that's changing. The first big incident was when a bunch of locals dressed as Iraqi coppers – or more likely they were some rogue Iraqi cops wearing their own uniforms – tried to take a bunch of white-eye private operators hostage.

The Iraqi cops had 'arrested' these guys from a PMC called Securiforce, down near the Safwan border crossing. The Securiforce blokes had been transferring from one job to another, and they quickly realized that something wasn't right with the coppers who'd taken them. They could sense that they were being driven off for the big interview without coffee. They managed to knife one of the drivers and make their getaway, but not before a couple of the Securiforce lads had got badly shot up.

Word of that attempted kidnapping ran like wildfire around the private operators working the circuit here. We're alert to the fact that kidnap and ransom is a very real threat, and that private operators like us are seen as prime targets.

I'm relaxing on my basher in the camp when I get the call. By now I've managed to get an Iraqi mobile that gets an intermittent signal on camp. I check the caller ID. It's my good mate Jack, a fellow private operator on contract to the UN. He's their Baghdad security coordinator, and I wonder why he's calling.

'Mate, I need a favour,' Jack tells me, over a line buzzing with static. 'I'm on this helo flying down from Baggers, and I need someone with a vehicle who can get me out of the Brit Army camp. I need to RV with a K & R victim who's just been released. No one else seems interested in bringing him in, so I thought of you.'

'No worries, mate,' I tell him. 'What d'you need?'

'I need wheels to get out of camp, to see if I can find him. I need a driver with a vehicle plus weapons, someone who's willing to go bring him in with me . . .'

'I'm on it, Jack mate. I'll meet you at the airstrip. What's your ETA?'

I find out when Jack's expecting to touch down, stuff the H & K Barking Dog into the Chevy, plus my pistol, and drive out to meet him.

Jack is an ex-Royal Marine. I first ran into him when working the Kabul contract. He's short, wiry, with a goatee beard, and he's got the build of a hyena. He's been around the block a few times, and he's one of the nicest blokes I've ever met. Under the sparky exterior lies a heart of gold. He's also totally fearless.

Jack and I both live in Southampton. One time we were in this local bar, and Jack couldn't find his sunglasses. He went up to the bar and told the barmaid to turn the music and TV off. Jack can be very persuasive, and eventually she did.

In the weird silence that followed, Jack climbed onto the pool table, removed one sock and placed a couple of pool balls inside it. Then he made an announcement to the entire pub.

'One of you fuckers has stolen my shades,' he said. 'Unless you return them to me now, this sock goes through that TV screen, and there's no more watching the match.'

There were forty-odd people in the pub, and they were stunned. Jack's only four-foot-four and a fag butt high, and he'd just called the whole pub out. Then this young bloke spotted a pair of sunglasses lying beneath our table.

He held them up: 'These yours, mate?'

Jack stared at the glasses. 'Yeah, they are.' He took them, then announced to the pub: 'Carry on, everybody.'

I know from experience that Jack would never see one of his mates down and out. He'd always help you out. So I don't hesitate when he asks for my help bringing in the kidnap victim.

I meet him off the helo, get him in the Chevy and we're driving towards the camp exit. En route, he briefs me in on the kidnapping. There's this fabulously wealthy Turkish businessman called Kahraman Sadikoglu, who was taken hostage down at the nearby Iraqi port of Um Qasr.

Sadikoglu is President of the Istanbul-based Tuzla Shipyard. He'd left Basra to travel to Um Qasr, to assess how to clear the port of sunken ships. Whilst there he'd been warned by the locals about a kidnap gang targeting him, but he'd refused to leave. In due course he was snatched off the streets, and disappeared. His kidnappers have been seeking a $25 million ransom to release him. He'd been working on a joint UN–Iraqi government contract to clear the port, so both the Iraqi government and the UN are desperate to get him out of the kidnappers' clutches.

Ninety days into the kidnap ordeal, and the UN got the call that Sadikoglu was getting released. A ransom had been paid, and he was going to be set free somewhere in Basra. Trouble is, no one from the local British Army contingent seems to have the will or the wherewithal to go bring him in. Hence Jack got the call, and he in turn called me.

I've got the vehicles permanently kitted out with medical packs, food rations, water, blankets and ammo. It's a basic survival kit, and it makes sense to carry it at all times when running a show like this one. You always have to be ready to deal with the unexpected – like right now.

Jack's got bugger-all information on the release, because no one seems to have been able to give him any. All he does know is that the UN got the call from Sadikoglu's wife, and that the kidnap gang had told her he was being 'handed over in an hour's time'. With the time it's taken to get a helo cranked up and Jack flown down here, Sadikoglu's been turned loose over thirty minutes ago. But as to where they've dumped the poor fucker, or where we're supposed to rendezvous with him, we have zero idea.

Jack and I reach the camp gate, we make ready our weapons and exit the base. We take the main road heading into Basra. All we can think of doing is driving towards downtown, and hoping we can spot him. It's not much of a plan, but it's all we've got.

As I get the Chevy shifting, it crosses my mind that the entire thing may be a set-up. The kidnap gang may simply be trying to lure in some more kidnap victims – *us*. But if it is genuine, there may well be a big fat reward at the end of it.

I'd have done the job anyway, 'cause Jack asked me to and it's the right thing to do. But the promise of a payoff is an added incentive.

There's also the question of who Sadikoglu is being handed over to. As far as Jack knows, no one else has been tasked to go in and get him. And if the good guys – and in this case that's Jack and me – don't get to him first, an ultra-High Value Target like Sadikoglu is rich pickings.

With Sadikoglu wandering the streets of Basra, one of the ultra-hard-line kidnapping groups allied to Al Qaeda might very well take him. And if that happens, there'll be no reward for us, 'cause Sadikoglu's going to lose his fucking head.

CHAPTER 38

We hit a major road junction, and we pull up on a bridge overlooking the main highway. We figure we'll stake out the road for a bit, and see what we can see.

It's Jack who spots him first. Way down this wide, fast-flowing dual carriageway there's a lone figure. He appears to be walking and stumbling unsteadily out of Basra, that's in our direction. We study him for a few seconds. We have no idea what Sadikoglu looks like, but sure as eggs is eggs it's got to be him. He's the only pedestrian on the entire highway, and no one ever walks this road alone and unarmed.

He also looks to be in a totally shit state. He's wearing a Western-style shirt and trousers, but they are stained and dirtied and half in tatters. He's itching and scratching himself as he walks, and every other second he keeps looking over his shoulder. He's clearly very worried. No doubt about it, this is our man.

Walking down that road in broad daylight as he is, he stands out like a dog's bollocks. He's clearly a foreigner, and he's an invitation to a second kidnapping. Either that, or he's the bait to lure Jack and me into a well-set trap.

We drive a couple of circuits around the lone figure, seeing if we can spot a watcher vehicle. But there's nothing obvious. We figure we've got to bring him in now, regardless of the risks, or we're going to lose him.

We drive a third loop, and at the end of it we pull up next to the lone figure. He glances behind, sees the beaten up old Chevy, and he starts to run. Jack's half out of the window screaming at him in English to get the fuck in.

The figure hesitates, and Jack and I rip down our shemags so that he can see our faces. He clocks the fact that we're white-eyes, and that we're yelling at him in English. We see this look of terror on his face transform itself into amazement, and then into disbelieving hope.

The figure turns, races for the vehicle, Jack opens the rear door and he dives in. An instant later I'm gunning the Chevy, and we're burning rubber out of there.

Jack turns around from where he's riding shotgun and flashes the figure his UN badge. 'Kahraman Sadikoglu? You are Kahraman Sadikoglu? We're from the UN . . .'

The next moment Sadikoglu's lunging forward and hugging Jack, and crying out for joy. For an instant I clock the figure in the rearview mirror. He's got this grin on his face that's going to split it in half, and his cheeks are running with tears. But for a bloke who's been in the hands of an Iraqi kidnapping gang for ninety days it strikes me he's holding up remarkably well. He looks to be in pretty good shape, and I figure Kahraman Sadikoglu must be made of strong stuff.

I don't have much time to savour the moment. Instead, I'm concentrating on driving the Chevy fast and aggressively, and getting us back to the base, whilst trying to check that we're not being followed.

We reach the camp without incident. By now the Chevy's well known here, and we're waved through the front gate. But the RMP guys manning the guardhouse seem typically confused, and unable to grasp what we have just done. We've got this Turkish civilian in tow who looks to them like a hobo, and they're trying to argue that they're not permitted to let him onto the base.

During the helo flight down here Jack had called the base to explain what we were up to, but the message clearly hasn't got through. It's a typical Army SNAFU: Situation Normal All Fucked Up.

I broker a deal with the RMP idiots to let us squat with Sadikoglu in the guardroom, at least until they can get their heads around what's what. But they make Sadikoglu stay in the rear cubicle, where the Iraqi staff are searched by the RMPs, before being allowed onto the base.

So Sadikoglu's been plucked out of one cell and fed straight into another. It's nice work by those RMP wankers. He seems traumatized, and incapable of thinking or acting rationally. He vacillates between being unable to grasp that he's actually free, and hugging and embracing his 'saviours' – that's Jack and me. I guess it's hardly surprising: we're the first friendly faces that he'll have seen in ninety days of hell.

I make a brew using the guardroom kettle, and we get some sugary tea and biscuits into him. Gradually, the story of what's happened over the last few hours starts to emerge.

A couple of hours ago, the kidnap gang – all wearing masks – hauled him out of the cell where he was being held. They bundled him into a vehicle with a sack over his head, and drove him into the centre of a noisy city.

They stopped, pulled off the sack, thrust $800 into his hand, and kicked him out of the vehicle. Sadikoglu found himself somewhere on the streets of what he presumed was downtown Basra. He was deep in shock, and understandably terrified of being taken hostage again.

He waved down a passing cab, thrust the $800 into the hands of the cabbie, and told him to drive to the 'nearest British Army base'. The cabbie had duly set off for Basra Airfield, but he'd got cold feet along the way. He was worried that the British soldiers might mistake him for one of the hostage takers.

The cabbie had refused to drive to the base proper, and finally he'd kicked Sadikoglu out on the airport road. That's where we'd found him, wandering along confused, distraught and penniless, and going in what he hoped was the right direction for the British base.

He'd been convinced that he was about to be picked up by some more of the local bad guys, or that the cabbie had phoned his brothers to tip them off. And so it was that when we'd pitched up in the Chevy, he'd put two and two together and decided to make a run for it. *The poor fucker.*

Whilst we're talking to him, Sadikoglu keeps going on about his multimillion dollar shipping business. He tells us he owns the biggest yacht in the Aegean, and he keeps telling Jack and me that we're welcome to come stay on it any time we like. He strikes me as being a decent kind of bloke, and I'm tempted to take him up on his offer.

Neither Jack nor I are trained in debriefing hostages who've been through such a horrific ordeal, so we don't push him to unload a great deal more. We just reassure him that regardless of those RMP muppets he's safe now, and that all is going to be fine from here on.

Sadikoglu makes it clear that the one thing he's dying to do is to call his wife. I'm genuinely touched by his burning desire to phone home, and I offer him the use of my Thuraya satphone. Unlike a local Iraqi mobile, the Thuraya can pick up a signal pretty much anywhere in Iraq, and it's good for overseas calls.

I flick up the donkey-dick-like antennae, and show him how to work it, then he's punching in a number that he clearly knows by heart. He's smiling and wiping his eyes, and glancing up at me in gratitude, as he starts chatting away in Turkish to what I guess must be his missus.

As he's doing so, a duty sergeant pitches up to investigate what we're doing here. Fuck knows what he's been briefed by the RMP idiots, but he clearly thinks that the three of us are a bundle of unwanted trouble.

'Who are you lot?' he asks. 'And why is a Turkish civvy, plus the UN, on this camp?'

As patiently as I can I explain that Jack and me are private contractors, and that we've just rescued a Turkish businessman who's been held hostage for ninety days somewhere around Basra.

'At the very least, you need to get this guy in and debrief him on what he knows,' I tell the duty sergeant. 'You need to find out who held him, where and what group it is. There may be others being held hostage by the same people and in the same location.'

The duty sergeant's thicker than a whale omelette. He just doesn't seem to get it. He's fixated on why a UN contractor and a foreigner are here on a British Army base.

Finally, I decide I've had enough. 'Look, mate, can I speak to the organ grinder, 'cause I'm tired of speaking to the fucking monkey.'

He tries getting shitty with me, but everyone knows me on this base by now. I've been training the British Army TA lads on a raft of local weapons. We've built up a good armoury for our operation, including AKs, Barking Dog G3s, belt-fed RPD light machine guns, rocket-propelled grenades (RPGs), old bolt-action .303 Lee Enfield rifles, and even a Soviet-era Dragunov sniper rifle.

The British Army just doesn't have that kind of kit kicking around to train their lads on. It's amazing how attentive the TA lot have been. I guess it makes you hungry to learn when you know that if you don't master a new weapon, you may end up getting slotted by it.

After a good deal of huffing and puffing, the duty sergeant bustles off to fetch 'an officer'. I explain to that officer what I've just explained to him.

'This guy is a Turkish businessman who's been held hostage for ninety days. The UN negotiated his release, and me and Jack here have gone and picked him up from where the kidnappers dumped him. So can we please have someone competent to process him.'

The officer promises to go fetch the Colonel. When finally the Colonel pitches up, everything changes. Suddenly someone realizes what he's got on his hands in Sadikoglu. The Colonel starts offering to put him up at the base, whilst they work out exactly what they're going to do about him.

Jack and I rapidly get thinned out, without even so much as a 'Thanks, lads' from the Colonel. The British Army and the UN go on to parade the Sadikoglu rescue before the world's media, as if they'd been responsible for bringing him in. In reality, they had barely lifted a finger.

At the end of it all the kidnap gang has made a small fortune. And rescuing Kahraman Sadikoglu has cost me the price of one very long and very expensive call on my Thuraya satphone.

Nice one.

I'm reminded of a saying that I've used a lot in my life: *No good turn goes unpunished.* But I've no regrets. I'd gone in to rescue Sadikoglu because Jack needed back-up, and because I couldn't stand to see people refusing to act. Sadikoglu was an innocent man and he'd suffered more than enough. In my book leaving that poor bastard to his fate just wasn't acceptable after all he'd been through.

*   *   *

I'd opted to do the right thing, and I could look myself in the eye the following morning. And that's important to me. I never have been one to stand by and watch the weak or defenceless or the underdog suffer. It didn't matter who they were or where I might be – if the strong were messing with the weak, I'd wade in every time.

Although I didn't always come out of it smelling of roses.

I was in Belfast with the Royal Hampshires, when I'd got one of my worst ever bollockings for doing my Good Samaritan act. I was drinking in a local British Legion bar when I saw a bloke abusing a pregnant woman.

It had started as verbal abuse, but in no time he was shoving her about. I wasn't having any of that. I stepped in and tried to stop it verbally, but the guy started abusing me. So I knocked the crap out of him, which was what I figured he deserved.

The Royal Ulster Constabulary (RUC) – the then Northern Ireland police force – was called, and the RUC officers tried to arrest me, along with the bullyboy. When they failed to get near me, they called the Royal Military Police (RMP).

I was only a couple of years into the Army by then, but already I'd built up a pathological hatred of the RMP. None of them could lay a hand on me, and it took a visit from my Guard Commander, a guy who knew me well, to persuade me to surrender.

I was locked up back at base, and the following morning I was hauled before the CO in my No. 2 dress. I got twenty-one days in the nick. The CO was a tough, no-nonsense individual, and he was determined that anyone sent to the cells was to get it ten times worse than the lads out risking their lives on patrol. Which was fair enough, really.

The corporals who ran the nick were evil. That first morning the corporal on duty ordered me to pull the fire cart to and fro. So be it. I did it with such gusto that he couldn't keep up.

I was running in front of him and taking the piss, much to the amusement of the other prisoners. Even the cleaners seemed to appreciate the joke: they started leaving cigarettes for me hidden in a plant pot just outside my cell door.

Once I'd completed my twenty-one days I was sent to see the Regimental Sergeant Major (RSM). The RSM announced that the pregnant woman had been in to the base, to explain what had happened. She wanted to thank me for saving her from the lunatic who'd been abusing her in that bar.

The RSM told me that any other bloke would have been released, but not me. He had a good idea just how much wrongdoing I hadn't been done for, so I'd been left to serve my full twenty-one days. I was punished further by being removed from the Close Observation Platoon, and sent to a bog-standard rifle company.

So there it was: a case of *No good turn goes unpunished* again.

There was a fatty of a bloke on the rifle company who was slated for Royal Marines (RM) selection, at Lympstone. The Commando had asked our CO to make sure the bloke was ready for selection, and the CO was forced to report that he was not.

By chance I was in the CO's office at the time. I seized the opportunity and told the CO that I was in great shape and ready and willing to go for selection. It gave the CO a great let-out, so that was me off to pack my kit for Lympstone.

At first, Commando selection was a lot like being back in basic training – loads of screaming, shouting and bullshit. The instructors nicknamed me 'Pongo Phil'. It was some in-house joke about 'Everywhere that Phil goes the pong goes too.' I never did get it.

The course itself was fantastic and I loved every minute. My fitness level was second to none. The one downer was this smart-arse Sergeant doing selection, who decided to book a coach to get everyone to the start of the endurance stage.

We were supposed to walk there, and getting the coach had seemed like a blinding move at the time – that's until we realized he'd booked it via the Royal Marines' own motor pool. The instructors were there to meet us off the bus, and they beasted the hell out of us for the entire day.

We were forced to race in teams carrying massive logs, and then do it all over again. Still, I got through it, completing my thirty-miler in top time, and I earned my Commando green beret with enormous pride.

Having passed RM selection, I asked my CO for a transfer to the Royal Marines. Having made such a fuck-up of my childhood and my education, I was hungry to make something of myself now. I was eager for the next challenge, and I desperately wanted in with an elite unit like the Commandos.

But my CO refused the transfer. Instead, I was returned to my battalion, now based in Colchester, and promoted to Lance Corporal. But upping my rank didn't do it for me. I felt as if I was stuck in the regular forces, where my fitness, survival skills and fighting prowess couldn't best be utilized.

I was feeling increasingly frustrated, like a round peg in a square hole. I yearned to serve in an elite unit, earning the kind of experience that would enable me to operate at the cutting edge of military operations.

And including – eventually – the circuit.

CHAPTER 39

Before Iraq, the world of the circuit was a closed, secretive affair, one reserved for operators hailing from elite units who could handle the sort of missions we were tasked with. But in Iraq the industry exploded, and every guy who'd ever had an itch to carry a gun was there.

There were ex-policemen, bodyguards and nightclub bouncers posing as elite warriors. As long as they could stick to the main bases ringed with guard posts, or the big convoys of up-armoured SUVs, they figured they were safe enough and would never be called upon to use their weapons.

For those who could bluff it, it was easy money. A thousand dollars a day, and no questions asked. It also had all the whiff of adventure and secretive intrigue – that's until the bullets started to fly.

In southern Iraq at least, it wasn't just the private operators who were being found wanting. The British Army seemed to lack the firepower, or the will, or the political clout to clamp down on the insurgency. Instead, Basra had become pretty much a militia free-for-all.

I'd had a bellyful of the Iraq mission by now. And it's Jack – the guy with whom I'd rescued Sadikoglu – who offers me the perfect way out. Jack tells me that he's putting a team together to go into Gaza, to train up the Presidential Guard, which in effect means training Fatah. As Islamic militias go, Fatah are one of the least extreme, and their political party has recently won the elections in Gaza.

The job is labelled 'the Karni Project', and it's backed and funded by the US and various European governments. But due to sensitivities with Israel – who won't go a bundle on British ex-special forces training up Fatah – the whole thing is being run pretty much as a covert operation.

No one can be seen to be doing the kind of work that we are about to undertake, so the Americans have outsourced it to the UN. But the UN are worried about compromising their 'impartiality', so they in turn are quietly contracting a team of private operators. The objective of the mission is to get 250 Fatah lads up to a level of training where they can open, and keep control over, the Karni border crossing into Israel. Hence the name – the Karni Project.

Karni is crucial. Hundreds of thousands of Palestinians depend on that border crossing being open. It's the main conduit through which food, medicines and other vital supplies go into Gaza. Plus the few key exports that the Gazans produce – fruit, tomatoes, flowers – need to be trucked out that way to markets.

Trouble is, Karni has also been used several times to smuggle truck bombs, and suicide bombers, over into Israel. The Israelis are reluctant to get the border crossing up and running at full capacity, and operations there are running on a hair trigger.

The Karni Project's been conceived by a US Lieutenant General Dayton, who is the regional security coordinator for the Americans. America is at loggerheads with Fatah's arch-rivals, Hamas, the more extreme Islamic militia in Gaza. Hamas is listed by the

US as a terrorist organization, so I figure they're the really bad guys.

Hamas and Fatah are regularly clashing in Gaza, in a bitter struggle for power. Sporadic gun battles threaten to explode into all-out civil war. Sending in a bunch of elite operators like us to train Fatah is going to provoke Hamas big time. They'll know about it just as soon as we've got boots on the ground, and they'll be onto us.

I've never worked in that part of the world before, so there's the draw of pastures new. Plus I've got this burning desire to get out of southern Iraq. So in spite of all the challenges, the uncertainties and the intrigue with the Karni Project, I tell Jack I'll take the job.

Jack is out there already, as team leader. It's the autumn of 2006 when I fly out to meet him, and link up with the other lads on the project. There are two, in addition to Jack and me.

First there's big, stocky Eddie, with his giant, Zorro-style moustache and goatee. He hails from the Paras, plus he's also ex-SAS, and I sense that he's a tough operator. I've never worked with Eddie before, but he strikes me as being a top bloke.

Then there's Paul, an Aussie ex-copper who I've never worked with before. The first time we meet, Paul keeps shaking my hand until it's about to drop off. It strikes me that Paul has all the charisma of a butterbean. I wonder if he's got the operational experience to take this job on, for it has all the promise of going noisy and nasty big time.

Stage one of the mission is to train a handpicked unit of eight lieutenants and majors from Fatah's Presidential Guard. They'll form an officer cadre that will be trained as trainers, to continue the project once us lot are gone. That's the theory, anyway.

There's a Karni Project desk been established in the US embassy building, in Israel. Orders come direct from Condoleezza Rice, the US Secretary of State, and this is definitely her baby.

There's a news blackout on what we're doing, and each of us has been recruited individually, rather than via the normal channel, which would be to contract us under a private military company (PMC). The Karni Project has all the signs of being a 'deniable operation'.

The officer cadre is brought out of Gaza for this stage one training. We're billeted in some deserted five-star hotel in the West Bank, and that's where we start the job. We try to teach the officers the basics of controlling a platoon-strength unit of troops, without having the men around to do the practicals. We aim to give them the skills to set up and command a small base on the Karni crossing, to monitor and control security on their side of the border.

Jack, Eddie and me have all served in Northern Ireland, so we run the training as if we're preparing to man up a small patrol base on the border with the South. We work on the scenario of a guard force on rotating duties, with goods and personnel moving across the border, and going into a holding cell for security checks.

If we can get good, capable officers trained to command a genuine security-screening operation like this one, the Israelis might gain enough confidence in the Gazan side to open up the Karni Crossing properly. That's the hope.

The Gazan officers are okay. They're not at Sandhurst level, certainly, but some have trained overseas with the Qatari military, and they're smart and capable. In British Army terms we're teaching officers to do the stuff that senior NCOs would do. But it's impossible to keep something like the Karni Project quiet, especially when you're operating on the Israeli–Gaza border. The Israeli–Palestinian conflict is big news, and the region crawls with journalists. Rumour fuels rumour, and finally a story hits the media that a team of British ex-special forces is training up Fatah.

No one wants the story out, but it's broken anyway. Everyone's trying to keep their head well down. Neither the Americans, the British, the Israelis nor the Palestinians want to stand up and be counted on the fact that the Karni Project is up and running.

Meanwhile, we're about to head into Gaza proper, to start training the border force on the ground. It looks like we're going to have zero back-up if and when it all goes tits-up, running a training op in Gaza that everyone's trying to deny.

Nice one.

To make matters worse, we're going in unarmed. It's bad enough that we've now been publicly exposed as *training* the Fatah lot. If there is the slightest hint that we are going in to *arm* them, the Israelis will shut this thing down pronto.

So the four of us head down to the Karni Crossing, armed with our 'official' British embassy accreditation and fuck-all else. Karni is this massive, space-age-looking transit point, consisting of a mass of warehouses, fences and solid, blast-proof walls.

The Israelis want the Karni Project gone, but they have to be seen to be cooperating with the Americans. So from day one their aim is to make it as difficult as they possibly can for those running the project on the ground – that's us.

The young Israeli guards have complete control of the border here, and they are well armed. Their attitude seems to be that anyone helping the Palestinians is, by definition, scum. Their senior commanders seem to share that attitude, apart from one or two who are strangely over-friendly with us.

That first day, as we're trying to explain for the umpteenth time why we're here and why they need to allow us through, there's a couple of Israeli commanders trying to do the nice guy act. We figure they're Israeli intelligence, and that it's all in an effort to gain intel for their superiors.

From the get-go we decide to be as frank and open as possible. They all know why we're here, so what's the point in trying to hide anything? We've been followed and placed under surveillance ever since we arrived in Israel, and we've been tailed down to the border today.

They split the four of us up, and start these mini-interrogations.

First question: 'What are you doing here?'

'You know exactly what we're doing here,' I answer. 'We are training the Palestinians.'

'Which Palestinians?'

'The Presidential Guard. Their army.'

I don't feel particular sympathy for either side in the conflict. The Israelis treat the Palestinians worse than animals, but the Palestinians have committed hideous atrocities against the Israelis in turn. So both sides are at fault. I just want to be allowed through the border and get on with the job.

One by one we're prodded inside this massive, warehouse-like hangar, and the electric doors whir shut behind us. They prod us into a pit where they inspect the convoys of food aid lorries that are allowed across, to check they aren't carrying hidden arms or explosives.

They fuck us around as much as they can, putting us into special X-ray tunnels, then stripping us down and poking us all over with metal detectors. They treat us worse than animals – just like they treat the locals – in an effort to make us snap.

Finally, we're spat out the Israeli side of the Karni terminal, and into the Gazan side. We're met by Khaled, one of the ablest officers from the Presidential Guard cadre. With him is Hassan, a Palestinian lawyer who's acting on the quiet as the UN's liaison with the Karni Project, plus our informal interpreter.

Hassan is an educated, urbane individual, who's travelled and worked all over the world. Khaled is a capable, professional, respected officer in the Presidential Guard (PG), and he's 100 per cent loyal to the Gazan/Fatah cause. The guys have become good friends over the last few days that we've been training with them.

Khaled leads us through to this vast, echoing, open-sided hangar. There's eighty young PG recruits gathered in there, sitting cross-legged on the concrete floor. They're dressed in a motley collection of T-shirts, khaki trousers, and training shoes or black Army boots.

They're keen and attentive and eager to learn, but the first issue has to be security. It's a given that Hamas know what we're doing here. So, we figure, will the rest of the Islamic lunatics that thrive in the cauldron that is Gaza.

Islamic Jihad are here. So are Hezbollah. So, we figure, must be Al Qaeda, or one of their local franchises. Probably 'Al Qaeda in Gaza', or some such name.

The warehouse is open-sided and overlooked by high ground, and by some of the high-rise buildings inside Gaza. It's a bullet magnet, as is what we're doing here. As a first priority, we get some heavy lifting equipment in, and construct a solid wall of steel shipping containers around the exterior of the warehouse. They probably won't stop a high-velocity bullet, and certainly not an armour-piercing round, but what they will do is shield the trainees – and us – from view. It's hard to target and kill a man when you can't see to aim at him.

Our second priority is to acquire some 'weapons' to train with. It sounds pathetic, but we get the trainees to make some cardboard cut-out AK47s. We can then start doing weapons drills with them, and train them as a Quick Reaction Force (QRF), to respond to any trouble that flares up.

At first the trainees are embarrassed when they have to wield those mock-up guns, going 'Bang! Bang! Bang!' But I explain to them that we've all done similar in basic training with the British Army. We get them rehearsing an attack, moving forward and taking cover on the deck.

They're aiming their weapons, and yelling: 'Bang! Bang! Bang! You're dead!'

As it happens, we've got the wall of steel shipping containers up not a moment too soon. Barely has the last one been slotted into place, when we get a sniper round tearing into the warehouse. It clangs into a shipping container, punches a hole clear through and embeds itself in the wall on the far side.

Welcome to Gaza.

CHAPTER 40

The Karni Project is the biggest thing that's happened in Gaza for decades. What we're doing will help 1.4 million Gazans get basic survival supplies in, and get their exports out. It's vital to their wellbeing, and it's big news here.

Hamas knows all about the Karni Project, and they doubly hate it because it vindicates Fatah. They're desperate for it to fail. Then they can say to the people of Gaza: *Look, we told you so, Fatah couldn't organize a piss-up in a brewery.* The propaganda victory would be huge.

Even more than the Israelis, Hamas have huge interest in the project going pear-shaped. As for Islamic Jihad and the rest of the lunatics here, they just want to drag everything back to the Dark Ages. They're against doing anything of any worth in Gaza.

We try to instil some basic security procedures into our eighty Fatah recruits. We warn them not to wear what scraps of uniform they do have on the way to work. We tell them to vary the route they take, so as to make it harder to follow them. And we urge them to tell no one – not even their families – what they're doing here.

We are acutely aware that what we're doing – walking across this border every day; having the Israelis usher us into this vast, echoing chamber and close the doors behind us; having the Gazans open the doors to let us through to their side – is totally unprecedented.

No one walks across the border into Gaza. *Ever.* So we're breaking the mould just by being here, let alone by doing what we are doing. It's obvious we're going to draw serious attention from the bad guys.

We start getting more and more sniper rounds pinging into the warehouse. We warn the trainees not to linger close by the shipping containers. It's clear that whoever's targeting us – Hamas most likely – is starting to ratchet up the pressure.

The Americans and Israelis have agreed strict rules for the running of the Karni Project. There is to be no Israeli scrutiny of the training programme, once we're on the Gazan side. But the Israelis won't allow us to enter Gaza proper, so we're allowed no further than the border-crossing complex.

A mouse can't fart in Gaza without the Israelis knowing. They've got these barrage balloons tethered every kilometre or so along the border, with observation pods slung beneath them stacked full of cameras and listening gear. Their eyes in the sky.

Plus they have unmanned aerial vehicles (UAVs) – pilotless drones – flying recce sorties over Gaza. And there's Israeli fast jets and Apache attack helicopters thundering through the skies. A day doesn't seem to go by without hearing the crump, crump, crump of cannon fire or bombs, as an air attack goes in.

After a few days' training with cardboard cut-out AK47s, it's pretty obvious we need to move on to some real weapons. Not far behind the Karni Terminal Fatah has a range, which would make a fine training ground. The trouble is, we're not allowed inside Gaza.

We tell Hassan and Khaled that we need to get through, and get out on the ranges with their lads. Together, we cook up a cover story for the Israelis. We tell them that we've got to go and speak with some of the top leaders in the Presidential Guard, to discuss the next stages of training.

The only way in to Gaza proper, we're told, is to use the border crossing at Erez. We have to clear the journey with the Israeli ministry of the interior, clear it with the US embassy, score ourselves some diplomatic passes, plus cars with diplomatic plates on.

Eventually we're done, and we mount up the 4×4 vehicles and drive down to Erez. There's a good hour checking our permissions and paperwork, but the border guards can't argue with our diplomatic credentials. Finally, we're waved through.

Without that kind of clout behind you, you have to walk across at Erez – that's if they allow you through at all. And if you're on foot, you have to go via the tunnels. They are these long, subterranean passageways that snake beneath the ground, taking you from the Israeli side of the border into no-man's-land. You emerge halfway to Gaza, and you have to complete the final few hundred yards of the crossing in the flat, open, sun-beaten, empty desert.

As it is, we arrive in Gaza proper with a grunting of our powerful 4×4 diesel engines, and a cloud of dust. We're met by an official Presidential Guard reception party, and blue-lighted through the streets.

While we're barrelling along the roads, what strikes me most is how totally blasted apart the place is. Every building we pass is riddled with bullet holes and craters, evidence of recent fighting with the Israelis, or infighting between various Palestinian factions.

Gaza looks ten times worse than Kabul did after decades under the Mujahideen and the Taliban. It is completely smashed up. It is nowhere near as large an area as Kabul, but you'd be pushed to find a street that isn't riddled with bullet holes. Each main arterial road has these huge chicanes made of sand piles. Hassan tells me that they're packed with explosives, so if the Israelis come in with their armour, Fatah can blow the chicanes (and the Israeli tanks) sky-high.

It's like a cross between the ruined moonscape of the worst parts of Kabul, and the bitter and savage sectarianism of Northern Ireland. Driving here reminds me of patrolling Belfast, and transiting from an area where the kerbstones were painted red, white and blue – Loyalist territory – to a street decked with green, orange and white. We knew instantly when we'd crossed into IRA territory, whereupon we'd suddenly gone from being the good guys to enemy number one. Gaza has the same divided feel to it, only now I don't have a clue how to read the various sectarian graffiti and flags.

I can spot the differences between Hebrew and Arabic writing, so as to identify which population controls which area along the Israeli border. But here in Gaza it's all Arabic – with the odd phrase of broken English thrown in – and I don't know where Fatah ends, Hamas begins, or Islamic Jihad takes over.

I need to learn this shit, and fast. I need to recognize who is who – and the various degrees to which they're friendly or hostile: Fatah, more or less on-side; Hamas, unfriendly – very; Islamic Jihad, totally fucking murderous. The crucial thing is to recognize the transition from one stretch of territory to another.

Hassan tells me proudly that below the streets we're passing through, Gaza is honeycombed with tunnels like nowhere else on earth. Gazan fighters use them for moving around without being seen by the Israelis, and for launching surprise attacks into Israel.

I've heard about these tunnels. Some are rumoured to go for many miles, crossing the border into Egypt and elsewhere. The most infamous tunnel-building incident happened just a few months back, when the Gazans burrowed five kilometres into Israel.

In a dawn assault they came up right under an Israeli guard post. They blew apart a tank, killing two soldiers in the process, and seizing one alive. That soldier, Corporal Gilad Shalit, was spirited back into Gaza. Militants linked to Hamas claimed responsibility for the attack and kidnapping.

The captured Israeli soldier is still being held hostage. There's a whopping great five-million-dollar reward on offer for bringing him out of Gaza alive. Five million dollars is an awful lot of bread. No harm in keeping my eyes and ears open, I tell myself.

As casually as I can I ask Hassan if I can pay a visit to the tunnels, but he tells me it's best not to go there. They're top-secret, as far as everyone's concerned. Asking about the tunnels, *and if I can see them*, might suggest I'm linked with the hated Israelis.

We reach the ranges without incident, and have the lads throw down their cardboard cut-out AKs and pick up the real deal. We get them rehearsing their drills, and putting rounds down the ranges, and they're doing very nicely. But not long after the firing starts an Israeli drone pitches up, flying orbits high above us.

I guess that's us lot caught on film doing exactly what we've been forbidden from doing. It wouldn't take a genius to figure out why on the day we go across to 'meet the Presidential Guard leadership', Fatah's ranges are suddenly buzzing with live firing. And now they've got the pics to prove it.

That evening we blue-light it back to the Erez crossing. There we're given the worst going-over yet by the Israeli border guards. They prod, poke, insult and provoke us for hours on end. It's only the diplomatic credentials – and the diplomatic immunity that comes with it – that get us through.

By now we've hired an apartment for the four of us to stay in, in the Israeli town of Ashkelon, and we're late back. I get a big bacon fry-up going. I've got half a pig sizzling on the stove, when suddenly I have a brainwave. I get Eddie to go to the lift that serves the apartment, and jam the doors open. Then I take the pan of frying bacon, and waft the hot fumes into the lift shaft.

In no time the entire apartment block is full of the mouth-watering smell of frying pork. Or at least *we* think it's mouthwatering. The rest of the apartment block doesn't seem to agree. As with their Muslim brothers, Israeli Jews believe the pig to be an unclean animal, one that their religion bans them from eating.

The entire block is in uproar. As for Eddie and me, we're back in the apartment killing ourselves laughing. Juvenile it may be, yet revenge feels good after all the shit we've taken from those border guards.

But as it happens, they haven't even started with us yet.

There's shit in truckloads coming.

CHAPTER 41

We're a couple of weeks into the training proper when Hamas start to flex their muscles. They ratchet up their attacks against Fatah, whilst at the same time picking a fight with the Israelis. They start slinging these big Qassam rockets into Ashkelon, the nearest Israeli town.

The Qassam is named after the Izz ad-Din al-Qassam Brigades, the armed wing of Hamas. It is a cheap, easy-to-make weapon that can be manufactured in Gaza. Its propellant is a mixture of sugar and potassium sulphate, a common fertilizer. The warhead is packed full of urea nitrate, another fertilizer, plus dynamite.

In spite of its home-made origin, the Qassam packs a punch. The Qassam-3 is two metres long, carries a ten-kilo warhead, and has a range of over ten kilometres – which means it can reach well into Israeli territory.

As the Qassams slam into the outskirts of Ashkelon – the town in which us lot are staying – so the Israelis launch their response. State-of-the-art Israeli Merkava-3 main battle tanks rumble into Gaza, hunting for the missile launch sites.

The 65-tonne Merkava is an evil-looking machine, with stream-lined, angular, stealth-like armour. It packs a 120mm main gun, three 7.62mm machine guns, and a 60mm mortar. It is one of the best-protected tanks in the world, with modular armour systems that can be changed in the field. As squadrons of Merkavas thunder and churn their way around Gaza, there's little that Hamas, or any of the other militias, can do about it. And there's little training that we can do with Fatah.

We operate on the basis of whatever intel we can glean on the day, and increasingly we're getting called by Khaled or Hassan and told not to come over. Rarely do we get a call from the Israelis warning us there's an offensive going down. We figure they'd like nothing more than for us four to get smashed in the crossfire resulting from one of their land operations. We'll have been done for, and the Israelis can say to those masterminding the Karni Project: *We told you so.*

There are three-, four- and five-day periods when we can't go in. We sit and kick our heels in Ashkelon, as Fatah and Hamas knock seven bales of shit out of each other, and the Israelis go hunting Qassams. It's chaos and carnage out there.

There are increasingly longer gaps in the training programme, and we're soon down to one visit a week. A lot of the days it's an on-the-truck, off-the-truck kind of thing. We head down to Karni in the 4×4s, only to get there and find a column of Israeli troops and armour lined up to cross the border. Then we know we're going nowhere.

On the rare days that we do get across, we notice that the number of trainees keeps dropping. Hamas are ratcheting up the pressure, and every day fewer and fewer Fatah lads are turning up. Finally, we're working with just a handful of blokes with cardboard cut-out AKs and ragtag uniforms, as the gunfire and explosions echo all around us.

We start trying to plan for the attack that we know is coming, but there are zero options open to us. We can hardly disappear into Gaza proper. The Israelis won't let us, Hamas will hunt us down, and there's nowhere to escape to from inside Gaza.

Gaza is as closed and escape-proof as your average high-security prison. The Israelis control every overland border crossing. Plus they have fast patrol boats enforcing a 12-mile cordon at sea. There's no way out, not even into the ocean.

The Fatah trainees won't be able to defend us against a Hamas assault, not with their mocked-up Kalashnikovs. And even if we do manage to make it to the Israeli border post, they're hardly likely to let us back through, not with fighting raging on their very doorstep.

So in essence there is no escape plan, 'cause we can't think of one.

This is a very heavy tasking now. Any serving military team that might have fronted it would have gone in with proper logistics forward-mounted, and be here with bundles of weaponry, plus back-up. We, needless to say, have none of that.

We've been out of Gaza for two weeks, and we're going stir-crazy in Ashkelon, when finally we get the word. Hassan calls us, his voice edged with panic. Hamas has launched a massive push against Fatah, and it's all-out civil war. The Fatah lads we've been training are fighting for their lives now.

As Hamas push home their attack, we can hear the staccato crackle of small-arms fire and the crump of RPGs echoing from inside Gaza. One by one the Fatah camps fall, until Hamas have the Presidential Guard compound surrounded and under siege.

In a matter of hours Fatah's last bastion of resistance crumbles. We take a call from the British embassy, and we're told that the Presidential Guard has been defeated. Hamas have seized control of all of Gaza.

The Israelis have stood quietly by and let the two sides fight it out. The bad guys have won, just as the Israelis predicted they would. All border crossings into Gaza have been closed, and it's all over for the Karni Project.

The Project was about training a guard force to keep the border open. With its closing our reason for being here is gone. No one wanted the Karni Project to work: the Israelis couldn't abide it; Hamas hated it; Fatah were too weak to make it last. Only the Americans had energetically backed it, and that was not enough on the day.

From those who hired us, we get a 'Thanks guys, but you're out of here.'

Before leaving for the airport, we manage to make contact with Khaled and Hassan. They've managed to hide from the rampaging Hamas gunmen, and they're both okay. But as to the rest of the Karni Project trainees, they have no idea what has happened to them.

A few days later I get a video emailed to me from inside Gaza. I'm back in the UK, and I watch it on my laptop. A line of young Fatah blokes is lying face-down on the dirt against a wall, getting machine-gunned to death by Hamas.

Three Hamas operatives run up and down the line, cheering and grinning maniacally as they spray off on automatic into the twitching, writhing figures. The Hamas gunmen are yelling 'Allahu Akhbar!' – God is great – as they keep their fingers on the trigger. The pink mist of flesh, blood and brains getting pulverized by rounds fired at near point-blank range is clearly visible. It hangs in the air. And over those video images triumphant Islamic-style music is playing in the background.

All the achievements of the Karni Project are worthless now. It's all fucked. And it crosses my mind that had the four of us been in there, training the Fatah lads on the day that Hamas struck, we'd likely have featured in the pink-mist video ourselves. For me, it's yet another narrow escape from death in a life defined by such things.

The first time I truly cheated death I was with the Royal Hampshires, doing another nightmare posting in Belfast. When not on guard duty in the sangar, our platoon served as the Quick Reaction Force (QRF), providing mobile back-up to any patrol that got hit.

A few weeks into the posting the IRA blew up a pub near our base. It was 0400 hours, and being the QRF we were sent in to check out the scene of the attack, knowing all the time that the IRA had likely set a second, much larger device – a 'secondary' – to nail us.

We screamed down there in our thin-skinned Land Rovers, and sure enough, as we dismounted and went to surround the pub, there was this massive, ear-splitting explosion. I managed to dive beneath one of the vehicles as a tidal wave of shattered glass, concrete and bricks tore through the air, and smashed down all around us.

It was a miraculous escape for me and the rest of the lads. The terrorists had fucked up. For some reason they'd set the bomb in the upper floor of the pub, so the blast hadn't hit us full-on at street level. Had they placed the bomb on the ground floor, I and my fellow patrol members wouldn't be here today.

Up on my feet again, I helped a couple of the injured soldiers into the vehicles, so they could be rushed back to base. Then I and the other lads still standing legged it to secure the perimeter, in the hope of catching one of the bombers.

As we did I ran smack bang into this bloke fleeing the scene. He was covered in a thick film of white dust from all the blasted masonry. I figured he had to be one of the bastard bombers. In an instant I'd smacked him to the ground. I hauled him up by his scruff. 'Who the fuck are you?' I yelled in his face. 'And what the fuck are you doing out at four in the fucking morning?'

The guy was shaking like a leaf. It turned out that he was a baker on his way to work, and he'd been caught in the blast.

We didn't manage to net any of the bombers, so as a consolation prize me and the other lads robbed the pub of several armfuls of booze. We hid it under the Platoon Commander's bed in preparation for our pre-leave piss-up.

In due course the landlord reported the loss to the RUC. The RUC sent in a man with a sniffer dog, which went straight to the Platoon Commander's bed. The dog stuck his nose beneath the cot right where the booze was hidden, went down on its belly and froze.

Amazing how it managed to sniff out a few bottles of hooch like that. We managed to distract the dog by getting down on all fours ourselves and barking at it wildly. Faced with us lot of lunatics fresh from being blown up, the RUC bloke decided discretion was definitely the better part of valour, and left.

The drink was mainly an Irish brew called something like 'Mundies', and it went down a treat with the lads. As we proceeded to get thoroughly pissed I wondered how it was possible to be in the midst of a massive blast like that which had torn apart the pub, and emerge more or less unscathed.

Getting blown up: it's amazing what the human body can walk away from.

But when I'm asked to return to Gaza, I'm seriously questioning whether there'll be any walking away from this one.

CHAPTER 42

A month after my escape from Gaza I'm asked to go back in again. If our previous mission was deniable, this one is ultra-deniable. The tasking is to go in under the auspices of the new rulers of Gaza: Hamas, the producers of the pink-mist video.

Hamas are listed as a proscribed terrorist group by the US, British and allied governments. They're a bunch of Islamist fanatics by anyone's reckoning. The job I'm being asked to do is to join a team securing a Gazan power station that's been bombed by the Israelis.

The Israelis have hit a steam-turbine-driven power station in an area called Dir Al Balla, in the midst of Gaza. But they're growing increasingly fed up with having to bow to world pressure to provide electricity to the Gazans, so they're allowing someone in to repair it.

I've got zero idea who's funding the operation to fix the power station, but the only company in the world that can get it working again is the Swedish company that built it. And the only private security operators with the clearances to go into Gaza at short notice are the four of us who ran the Karni Project. Our documentation – visas, accreditation and permissions – is still current, which makes us the ideal team to do the tasking.

The risks on this one are insane. Just a few weeks back we were out there training Fatah, and our going back in again is akin to the SAS being sent in to train the IRA, it is that much of a no-no. But the pay is also insane, and because of that I agree to take it.

We reassemble the Karni Project team. There's one new bloke being sent out to join us. Brian is a British ex-copper who served some time in Panama, training their police force. He's being parachuted into our team by the private security company running the contract, and he earns the nickname 'Panama Plod'.

The only way into a Gaza torn by upheaval and bloodshed is on foot via the Erez crossing. But we have zero chance of securing diplomatic status on this job. And that means going in via the tunnels, and walking the 600 metres of no-man's-land.

The Israeli border guards at Erez are young conscripts, serving their compulsory year in the Israeli Defence Forces (IDF). They don't want to be in the IDF, let alone manning a border post in a place close to hell, one that gets hit every day. The level of attacks is high, and growing ever more vicious since Hamas seized control.

Unsurprisingly, they're less than pleased when they see the four of us from the now defunct Karni Project reappear at their border crossing. This time we've got no diplomatic status to safeguard us, and no power of the US government's backing. The pimply young border guards are visibly gleeful, once they realize they'll get to shove us into the tunnels and make us do the walk.

On the far side a Hamas reception party is supposed to be waiting for us, to run us to the power station. How nice. Our one hope is that Hamas are responsible for getting the power station repaired, so they have something to prove to the world here.

There's one other tiny snifter of safety. Along with the Hamas lot, we're linking up with the United Nations security representative. He's offered us a couple of UN Toyota Land Cruisers, on the

QT. He's done so because he wants the power station up and running again, so the UN can get their electricity back.

The Land Cruisers are thin-skinned, and they're painted a bright white with 'UN' emblazoned in big black letters on their sides. The hope is that if we have to evacuate the power station, the UN markings will prevent us from getting taken out by the Israelis, or any other crazies that might be after us.

To be honest, we're going to be grateful for any friendlies we can find once we're in there. If we have to run we can't get out, so we're going to need somewhere to go to ground inside Gaza. The UN headquarters looks like the only place to run to.

But first, we've got to get across the border at Erez.

Of the five of us I'm last into the tunnel, with a sneering teenage Israeli gunman jabbing an M16 into my back. Then begin the mind games in the darkness of the tunnel, which culminate in my encounter with the prone figure lying on the stretcher, the one who pleads at me in Arabic: *sick; help; doctor.* The one who could be a genuine member of the injured or the dying, or could just as easily be a suicide bomber.

I'm spat out the tunnel exit, and the five of us begin the long walk through no-man's-land. We've barely gone twenty yards when all hell breaks loose, as the Israelis open fire from behind us, slamming rounds into the Hamas vehicles parked on the far side.

We hit the dirt, and the 2-inch mortar rounds start howling down. What follows is twenty minutes of a full-on firefight, with us lot trapped in the middle. By the end of it the five of us have been smashed by chunks of shrapnel and blasted rock, but at least we're still alive. The Israeli soldiers know the shit they'd be in if they gunned us down in cold blood, and fortunately Hamas has managed to distinguish between shooting up the Israeli border post, and the five of us. But it's our not being turned into white-eye puree by a mortar or two that's the real miracle here.

With the shooting done, we dust ourselves down and make our way to the waiting vehicles. We do a road move across Gaza in the UN Toyotas, with Hamas gunmen riding shotgun, and we're dumped at our destination.

At first glance the power station compound seems reasonably secure. There's a wall at head-height all around the perimeter topped with barbed wire, and a vehicle track next to that where we can cut around to get to all parts of the complex.

There's a gateway shielded from view, a decent accommodation block, plus a four-storey admin building, from the roof of which there's a panoramic view across Gaza city. The roof is flat, with a knee-high wall running around the perimeter. It's a good location to spend time on stag, although there are no sandbags available to reinforce it.

The five of us break down roles. My job is to sort the local guard force. There are forty-odd blokes that Hamas have waiting for us in the power station dining hall. Thankfully, I've managed to get Hassan from the Karni Project in here as my translator. Of course, we've got to hide the fact that he's a Fatah bloke, or Hamas will more than likely line him up for a walk-on part in their next pink-mist video.

We've also got to hide the fact that a few weeks back four of us white-eyes were training Fatah, or we figure it'll be pink-mist video performance time for us lot, too. We just have to hope that none of the Hamas bunch recognize us, or any other Gazans for that matter.

The forty local recruits are all grizzled Hamas veterans. Each and every one of them has been involved in the recent fighting to oust Fatah, and they know how to handle their weapons. One bloke has scars stretching from ear to ear, from where he was shot by the

Israelis. He proudly tells me he's spent most of his life in Israeli prisons.

I sense that I've got to grip these guys hard and control them from the very get-go. If not, they won't respect me, and if they don't respect me there's no way that I'm going to be able to order them around, or make use of them as a guard force.

All around the exterior of the power station Hamas fighters are dug in, with proper sandbagged positions, and with clear arcs of fire into the neighbouring areas. I train up the guard force so as to provide an inner cordon, and a last line of power-station defence.

Almost right away we realize there's firing going on, right behind the power station. Via Hassan I ask Hussein, the local Hamas commander, what's happening. He tells me it's a Hamas training camp. Knowing that we have that smack on our doorstep isn't exactly a top fluffy feeling. It makes us a prime target for the Israelis.

Hussein is the Hamas commander tasked to liaise with us white-eyes. Whenever he visits he does so completely unannounced, and with this massive security escort. The first day we ask him for some AK47s for the five of us private operators. We've taken the contract on the understanding that we'll be armed.

Hussein tells us that there's no way we'll be needing weapons. With Hamas protecting us, plus our local guard force, we're as safe as houses, he reasons. We tell him be that as it may, we'd still like our weapons. He makes a token gesture: he gives each of us a Beretta 9mm pistol, complete with mags.

The Beretta's a half-decent pistol, and I check out my weapon, making sure it works. *At least we have something to commit suicide with, if they come to drag us off into Gaza and torture our souls.*

The three Swedish engineers are brought in to start working on the turbines. It strikes me that they have to be paying these guys more money than God to be doing what they're doing here. The oldest is a grizzled engineer called Lassen, and he's running the show from their end. He explains that they plan to work very long hours – dawn to dusk – to get the job done as quickly as possible, so we can all get the hell out of there.

The power-station manager is a fat, creepy Palestinian called Naqi or some such name. We nickname him 'Mr Creosote'. I start working the day shift with the guard force, whilst Paul does the night shift. Trouble isn't long in coming.

It's our third or fourth night, and I've sent the chef into Gaza city to try to find us some scoff. Mr Creosote is a waste of space when it comes to managing a power station, and feeding the staff, plus us white-eye operators, seems to be one of the last of his priorities. The chef's gone for hours searching for some scoff, and eventually we lose patience and hit the sack.

It's past midnight when I'm woken by a hammering on my door. I can hear the chef yelling in alarm; 'Mr Phil! Mr Phil! Come quick! Come quick!'

I grab my pistol from under my pillow and tear open the door. The chef takes one look at me in my T-shirt and boxers gripping my weapon, and he runs off screaming. I have absolutely no idea what the fuck is going on, but I figure I need to go and investigate. I'm just getting my kit on when Paul appears at the door. He's got such a flap on he looks like he's about to take off. 'The guards are going to kill you! The guards are going to kill you!'

I tell him to calm down and explain himself. Apparently the chef reacted badly to me in my state of undress with pistol in hand. He rushed off to the guardroom in a total panic. He's told the guard force that I'm coming after him to shoot him, 'cause he was late with the food.

The guard force has got all hot under the collar, and has decided to hunt Mr Phil down. Paul's done nothing to calm them, and he seems to think I'm bang out of order opening my door with pistol at the ready. I'm having none of it, so he heads off to Eddie's room to complain.

He bangs on Eddie's door, and when Eddie opens up he's got a blanket draped over one arm. Paul starts complaining that I've been opening doors and brandishing guns, and that I'm 'well out of order'.

Eddie shuts him up. 'Stop there, mate. What's under this blanket? A pistol. It's there 'cause that's how we work – at the fucking ready. And we certainly don't leave our pistol in the fucking drawer, like you wankers.'

Gazans being the way they are, the chef has gone completely over the top. Paul being what he is has said: *Yes, you're right, how threatening – I'll go and speak to Mr Phil.*

I speak to Eddie and we figure the only person who can sort this out is me, 'cause I'll lose face otherwise. I grab Hassan and we head for the guardroom. There's angry, hostile glares all around as I step inside. You can cut the atmosphere with a knife here.

I take a seat, so I'm in a non-hostile pose. I get Hassan to ask the guards to calm down and like me to take a seat. Then I start talking and telling it like it is.

'Listen, I am a professional soldier,' I begin, 'and if I have someone pounding on my door and screaming blue murder, then I open it with my weapon in my hand. That way, I'm ready for any threat that may be out there. I'm ready to defend the power station and staff if need be. Is there a man amongst you who would have done otherwise?'

There's lots of umming and aaahing, and then they have this Chinese parliament, where they go into a huddle and they're gabbling away in Arabic. Eventually, blokey with the scar from ear to ear starts speaking for the lot of them.

'Yes, okay, we understand,' says Scarface. 'You are a soldier in a foreign country, and it's understood that you are worried.' Scarface tries a conciliatory smile. 'We understand that you are a top-notch combatant, and that you need to protect yourself, and the other foreigners.'

I ask the chef what all the fuss was about. He explains he'd come running to my room and started hammering on my door, because he was so proud of the fact that he'd managed to find some food. He'd travelled halfway across Gaza to find a kebab shop still open, and he'd managed to score a dozen 'shwarma', these gorgeous Gazan kebabs.

'Well, shwarma or no shwarma, you'd better not come hammering on my door again, Mr Chef,' I joke. 'Anyway, where's all the scoff? I'm Hank Marvin.'

There's a little loss of face on both sides – I'm the jumpy foreign operator, and Chef's the jumpy Gazan civvy – before it's all squared away and sorted in an acceptable fashion. We end up having a brew and a laugh about it, and then we demolish the scoff.

But I figure we need to run things differently from now on. I'll take the night shift with the guards, as I don't think Paul is up to task. He's acting as if he's on some UN peacekeeping mission. He's not. He's here on a maverick, covert, Special Forces-type tasking. Except that I doubt if even the SAS would take on a tasking such as this one. In fact, that is what defines the kind of operation that we're on now.

There's no one else crazy enough to take it apart from private operators like us.

CHAPTER 43

At first light a few days later Paul comes to the guardroom to relieve me. I've just got to bed when I hear a deep, booming burst of fire. It's some distance away – definitely outside the compound walls – but near enough to make me think: *What the fuck is that?*

I hear another thumping burst, and I know it's something of a large calibre. I leg it onto the roof, only to see plumes of smoke rising across Gaza. I can see an Apache helicopter gunship swooping low over the city, and pounding targets below with 30mm cannon fire.

There's a column of dust rising in the near distance, and a ponderous snake of Merkava main battle tanks emerges from out of it, crawling slowly towards us. Their thick black 120mm cannons are swinging slowly from side to side, scanning for targets.

We can't see Israel from the power-station roof, so I know immediately that we're in the middle of some sort of major border incursion. The Israelis have sent their state-of-the-art armour, plus their warplanes, deep inside Gaza. The question is: Whom or what have they come for?

I feel a presence beside me, and Eddie's joined me. He briefs me that Jack's in the office, warning the UN that we might be breaking out of here. But Paul has abandoned the guardroom so he can go fetch his weapon, for he's worried now that he can hear gunfire.

It goes without saying that all five of us white-eye operators are supposed to carry our weapons with us at all times. Today is the day we discover that both Paul and Panama Plod are leaving their pistols in their bedside drawer. They are coppers, not soldiers, and each is apparently uncomfortable carrying a weapon.

The sinister, clanking column of Merkavas keeps creeping closer, the metallic rattle of the tank tracks clearly audible above the battle noise. We've got Apaches swooping in low, and malleting targets all around the power station with ten-round bursts of 30mm cannon fire.

The booming noise is deafening, and Eddie and I can see the cannon of the Apaches spurting fire beneath the aircraft's nose. Spent brass shell cases go tumbling through the dawn air as the Apaches thunder past, giving the targets below them a right good hammering.

The Apache's M230 30mm cannon fires armour-piercing high-explosive rounds as fat as your wrist. They're easily capable of punching through the walls of the power station, and tearing it apart. Eddie and I reckon that the Apaches are targeting the Hamas forces that surround the power-station complex, guarding us lot. And that means we're in the centre of their ring of fire. 30mm rounds start punching into the power-station grounds now, the thud and crack of the explosions echoing around the walls. It's clear that one of us has to go check on the clients – the Swedish engineers – and get them into whatever cover we can find.

I opt to go, leaving Eddie to keep watch on the carnage playing out below us. My biggest worry now is the Apaches circling overhead. If they spot me moving they'll likely mistake me for a Hamas operative, and turn me into Mr Phil puree. There's nothing I can do about it other than try to keep to some cover and leg it fast.

I make the inside of the accommodation block without having my arms and legs ripped off by a 30mm cannon shell, which is nice. I grab Lassen and his fellow engineers and stuff them under the lowest flight of the concrete stairwell. There they should have just enough reinforced concrete above them to stop a 30mm cannon round.

I get Paul and Panama Plod stuffed under the stairs with them, to 'keep the clients calm'. In truth, I want them as far out of the way of any fighting as possible. It's just better that way.

I head back to the roof. Eddie's lying prone behind the wall, as the rounds continue to fly. I scuttle over to him, keeping as low as I can.

'What's happening, mate?' I yell.

'Same old,' Eddie yells back. 'Apaches malleting anything that moves. Not a lot from the armour yet.'

I risk a peek over the top of the wall. I see an Apache swoop in low, and then it's pumping rounds into a target just east of the complex. One of the lead Merkavas is spitting fire, as its 7.62mm machine guns start hosing down the same target area.

There's the boom of something firing at ground level, and a trail of dirty blue smoke lances across the sky, as whatever rocket Hamas has fired streaks skywards. The Apache pilot under attack throws the gunship into evasive manoeuvres, as a trail of flame like a firework display blooms in his wake – the aircraft releasing its decoy flares.

I drop back behind the wall. 'Fucking hell! Happy days. Any sign of anything targeting at us lot?'

'No mate,' Eddie replies. 'I reckon they've got to have seen there's fucking UN vehicles, which means UN types, in here. If not, they'd have seen us on the roof and pinged us as Hamas spotters, and we'd have been malleted.'

It's clear this is a major push by the Israelis, and that the fire-fight around the power station is only going to get worse. With all the Hamas fighters positioned here, it's like a magnet for the Israeli airpower and armour. And we're going to catch a cold every time Hamas sneeze.

It's time to get the clients out of here. We've got to get them into the guardroom, from where we can run them out to the UN Land Cruisers. We'll get them into the vehicles, batter our way out of the compound, and make a run for UN headquarters.

One hour in and there's a lull in the ferocity of the fighting. We see the Merkavas go into hull-down positions, where they've basically dug themselves into cover. They're about a kilometre away from us in some open waste ground, and they're all pointing our way.

They've gone firm, and they're clearly not going anywhere. We figure they're the spearhead of a ground assault by Israeli troops, one that's coming sometime soon. In which case it's time to get the hell out while we can.

Eddie and I leg it off the roof, grab the engineers, pile into the guardroom and get everyone ready. We explain to the guard force that dead engineers can't repair the power station, so we're evacuating them. We brief the guards to cover us as we move the clients out, then hold the fort until us lot of white-eye operators can make it back in again.

We pile Lassen and his boys into the Land Cruisers, the guards throw the gates open and we're accelerating out of there. The streets around the power station are littered with bullet casings. We take the main road east, and gun the vehicles. On empty roads like this it should be a forty-five-minute drive maximum to the UN building.

Almost at once we're getting buzzed by a pair of Apaches. Like giant black birds of prey they come swooping low, the powerful blast of the rotor blades beating a rhythm through the roof of our speeding vehicle. I tense myself for a burst of 30mm cannon fire tearing us apart like a giant tin opener.

But nothing comes. Instead, they buzz us for a good ten minutes more, before finally we're allowed on our way. We reach the UN complex only to find the gates locked shut. It's totally closed and deserted. *Fuck it.* Either they've evacuated completely, or they're locked inside deep in their bomb shelters.

There's nothing for it but to head for the one hotel that still seems to function in Gaza. It's hardly the UN, but what choice do we have? In the circumstances, it's the best we can manage. We reach the Al Dira Hotel and bundle the engineers inside. The clients aren't going anywhere until whatever mission the Israelis are on is over. We get Lassen and his boys some rooms, head for the bar and order a large non-alcoholic drink, as that's all there is on offer.

Twenty-four hours later Eddie and I are back at the power station. We've returned for two reasons. One, we need eyes on the scene so we can make the call when it's safe for Lassen and his boys to return here. Two, we need to show some solidarity with the guard force.

There's the column of Merkavas still hull-down in the position where we left them, plus Israeli fast attack jets are screaming overhead. And there's a permanent fleet of pilotless drones hovering in the airspace above the power station. But apart from the odd engagement, the fighting seems sporadic and lacking in focus now.

It's like the Israelis can't determine who or what their target should be, so they're playing the waiting game.

We decide to call the rest of the guys back in, plus the clients. By that evening we're all safely back in again, and Lassen's preparing to work a full shift the following day. We hit the sack early and have a relatively quiet night of it, bearing in mind we're trying to kip in the midst of a war zone.

But at dawn the following day I'm woken by this almighty explosion that rocks the entire compound. No doubt about it, whatever we're being attacked by now has scored a direct hit on the power station.

I'm out of my room pronto, to be met by Eddie in the corridor. We're convinced we've taken a hit from a 120mm tank shell, fired by one of the nearby Merkavas. Question is, how many more 120mm rounds are on their way?

We head out to investigate. We see this thick, angry plume of smoke pooling above the guardroom. It looks like the Israeli tanks are opening up on our guard force, and maybe this is the start of the final push to drive Hamas out of the power station. In which case us lot are fucking toast.

We leg it across to the guardroom. All forty of our local lads are hunkered down behind whatever cover they can find. There's a massive crater some thirty metres away, where the 120mm tank shell has ploughed into the hard earth of the power station grounds.

Eddie and I wonder why there's not been a second round fired after the first. The drones orbiting overhead would have spotted where the first 120mm shell hit, and radioed in corrections to the Merkava gunners. In which case the guardroom is most definitely not the best place to be standing.

Eddie and I leg it over to the crater, to see what we can find. Scarface follows after us, along with some of the other guards. When we reach the crater rim, the weirdest sight ever meets our eyes. In the centre of the crater there's this one, lone smoking boot.

It's got half a human foot still in it, but where the rest of the figure is that was attached to the boot we've no idea. Plus scattered around the crater boundary we see some fragments of what look like the tail fins of a rocket.

It turns out that it's not a 120mm tank-shell crater at all. Instead, the boot and the foot are all that's left of a Qassam rocket operator. Some Hamas fighter has tried to launch a Qassam from inside the cover of the power station itself, presumably targeting the Israeli tanks outside. But the rocket's malfunctioned, blowing itself and the operator sky-high.

Scarface and the rest of the guard force seem to find it all uproariously funny. They're pointing at the Tom and Jerry smoking boot, and cracking their sides laughing. Eddie and I don't find it quite so amusing.

It strikes us that the Qassam's malfunction is very, very fortunate for us. Had the launch gone as planned, we'd have had a bloody great smoke trail flaring out from the power-station grounds, and ending where the rocket slammed into the column of Israeli armour. And that would have been the perfect excuse for the Merkavas to unleash hell upon us.

Paul decides that this is the final straw, and that he's leaving. Jack runs him out of Gaza in the UN wagon, and picks up a replacement flown out from London. Taff Owen's a tough, experienced ex-Regiment operator. He's also a fluent Arabic speaker who's worked all over the Middle East.

He's exactly what we need on a mission such as this one.

CHAPTER 44

The day of the Tom and Jerry boot incident, Hussein the Hamas commander comes to have words with us. He explains that there's a major Israeli incursion taking place within Gaza – as if we didn't know – and that he's not happy. It's us lot, it seems, that he's not very happy with.

He points out that Hamas fighters are dug in all around the power station, to protect us, yet we chose to lift off and evacuate the clients. Hussein is seeking reassurances that we're 'on-side' with Hamas, and not secretly in cahoots with the Israelis.

'We need to see some better presence from the *feringhi*,' Hussein tells us. 'Some real meaningful presence. My men are here on duty spending long hours under fire, and they want to see those they are protecting alongside them. Otherwise . . .'

Hussein shrugs. I figure he has a point. Maybe we do have to balance the safety of the client with keeping Hamas on side. But only up to a point

'Hussein, we appreciate your blokes' efforts to protect this place,' I tell him. 'But our priority has to be the safety of our clients, the engineers. In fact, their safety has to be everyone's priority, 'cause dead engineers can't fix a power station.'

'Plus we returned to the power station just as soon as we'd got the clients out,' Eddie chips in. 'So that proves that we were here with your guys just as soon as we could be.'

'Anyhow, if you're worried about how it looks, what about this,' I volunteer. 'Say we go out on a joint patrol with your blokes. Let's go out with your guys publicly on the streets to show some solidarity.'

Eddie gives me this look: *Blinding idea, mate.* 'Nice one,' he enthuses. 'We'll do a joint patrol. Show a united front. We'll show we're standing firm with your Hamas guys, which'll boost their morale.'

Jack seems pretty mellow with the idea too. But Panama Plod is staring at the lot of us as if we are totally insane. As for Hussein, he's gazing at Eddie and me with a puzzled expression, as if he can't quite believe what I'm suggesting.

I suppose he's got a point. A joint Hamas–white-eye patrol under the very noses of the Israelis: it's either a mark of genius, or we've got a death wish.

I offer Hussein a reassuring, manly arm around the shoulder. 'Hussein, my friend, you know Hamas is still a "terrorist organization" in the eyes of the world. But this way we'll show the world that you are standing firm and doing the right thing to defend us.'

Hussein cracks a smile. 'I like this idea. And you will really do it? You will really patrol with us?'

I give him a grin. 'Does a bear shit in the woods, mate?'

Hussein doesn't quite get the bear shitting in the woods sketch, but he does order a gun truck to be brought to the power-station gates. It's a white pickup with a CSW – a belt-fed heavy machine gun – mounted on the back, on some sort of anti-aircraft pivot. Without another word Eddie jumps in the cab, so he's riding shotgun, and I clamber into the rear.

Bearing in mind the way Hamas move around town at all times

trying to hide from the air, embarking on an overt patrol like this is fairly suicidal. But if we're going to get the job done properly this is what it'll take. *If you're gonna be a bear, be a grizzly.*

With a growl of the pickup's motor and a splurge of thick diesel fumes we lurch off heading east. We have no idea where they're taking us, and we're in clear sight of the drones orbiting above us, and the Merkavas' 120mm guns. I'm tensing myself to jump, as I'm fully expecting us to have to take cover fast and under some savage fire.

We make first for a nearby orchard, where the Hamas fighters are heavily dug in. We're rumbling past and giving it wide smiles and raised-fist salutes, to show our solidarity with the Hamas lot's cause. At first the fighters are staring at us like we're cracked, and then they start waving their guns about and cheering wildly. They even pluck Eddie and me a handful of apples.

From the orchards we head for the training camp and the ranges, where we do a similar performance. Then we're in the camp behind the training camp, and zooming around all their dug-in positions, taking a wide loop back towards the power-station gates.

The Hamas soldiers can't believe we've joined in an overt Hamas patrol, with the Israelis in spitting distance from us. The Hamas fighters seem to be getting the message now that the white-eyes are on-side, and prepared to show it.

Somehow, we make it back to the main gate without being smashed by a 120mm tank shell, or getting a long burst of 30mm cannon fire down our necks. As far as Hussein is concerned this is a show of unity like no other, and we have restored good karma to the operation.

We dismount, and it's handshakes and smiles all round. We even do a proud souvenir photo with the Hamas blokes that did the patrol with us, posing beside their wagon.

Often in war, you don't know why you've not been fired upon. War's like that. It's long stretches of confusion and boredom, interspersed with insane, adrenalin-pumping bursts of action. It's unpredictable, and there are no set rules. That's just how it is.

That evening, the Israeli forces begin their withdrawal. They pop smoke, and under cover of fire the armoured column starts to crawl back the way it came. By the time they're gone the city is largely silent. There's the odd crackle of gunfire, but we figure that's the IDF soldiers having one last crack before they pull back into Israel.

For the next couple of days it's pretty much peaceful in our part of town. We're taking the odd burst of incoming fire, but Hussein and his boys try to convince us that it's only Hamas out on the ranges, test-firing their weapons.

We know that it's not. We know what gunfire going both ways sounds like. It's a two-way range out there, and someone's attacking someone. We presume it's some remnant Fatah fighters having a go at Hamas, or maybe it's some Islamic Jihad nutters having a pop.

Either way, I decide that the show of solidarity with Hamas needs to be made more permanent somehow. We've lost Hassan, our ex-Fatah interpreter, as he can't stand to be around here any more. Apparently the Hamas lads kept telling all these gruesome stories about how they blew away Fatah, and what they did to those they captured.

Hassan couldn't stand to hear it, so he got out. I take my new interpreter and start doing a daily solidarity drive around the power-station perimeter. We do a meet and greet with all the Hamas gunmen, and it's smiles and handshakes all around.

My new terp is the spitting image of Mr Bean. I haven't even bothered to try to learn his real name. From the get-go he's 'Mr

Bean'. He has no idea who Mr Bean is, of course, and he does seem a little bemused at his new nickname.

I tell him Mr Bean is a famous British TV character, and that appears to cheer him up a little. The Hamas warriors seem to find it hilarious that the *feringhi* calls his terp 'Mr Bean'. As we drive around the perimeter, they're crying out 'Mr Bean! Mr Bean!' at the tops of their voices.

I figure we're building a good rapport with these guys now, but a bit more hearts-and-minds stuff wouldn't go amiss. From the roof of the power station there's this dusty football pitch visible in the distance. Every Friday, in between outbursts of gunfire there's this tournament between what must be three Gazan youth teams. I've taken to watching the matches from my rooftop position. It's clear that whilst two of the teams have a uniform of sorts, there's one that's lacking any kind of kit at all. There's a yellow team, a blue team, and one other that appears to be playing in rags. I sense here an opportunity, and I get hold of Mr Bean and tell him what I'm thinking.

Then I get in touch with my mate Woggie who runs the kit room at Southampton Football Club. He knows me well, as I've played a couple of charity matches at the club ground. I explain that I'm in Gaza, and there's this youth team with no strip. If he can get me an old set of Southampton kit sent out, it'll be a good, charitable thing to do.

Woggie's a great bloke. He thinks it's a mad idea and he loves it. He manages to sort sixteen sets of shirts, shorts and socks from their under-14s, to be couriered out to Gaza.

When the kit arrives, I ask Mr Bean to get the team together that plays every Friday in rags, 'cause I've got a surprise in store for them. That Friday I don my own Southampton shirt, Eddie and I stick our pistols in our belts, grab the boxes of kit, and with Mr Bean in tow we wander down to the football ground.

It's halfway through a match when we get there, but play stops just as soon as the lads realize what the *feringhi* have brought with them. We hand out the strips to the kids who are playing in rags, and they go crazy.

Their coach seems completely overcome with emotion, and he's trying to give Eddie and me these big slobbery man hugs. Via Mr Bean I tell him there's one condition attached to the donation. He's got to rename his team 'Southampton United In The Gaza Strip'.

Play is resumed, only now the Rag Team is sporting gleaming Southampton kit. They're proud as punch, and they're playing like it too. Eddie and I can't hang around to watch the match for long. We've gone way out on a limb coming down here already, and we're sure to be in someone's sights by now.

But we do wander back to camp with a top fluffy feeling. Hassan tells us that Southampton United In The Gaza Strip go on to win the match, and in time he reckons they'll win the local trophy. I send a letter from Gaza to Southampton Football Club, thanking them for the donation, and including a photo of me posing with the team. I do the same with several British newspapers.

A few days later I get a call from a mate of mine telling me he's just seen my fat face in print. Apparently, *FHM* have made mine 'letter of the week'. In my letter I explained the security work I'm doing out here, and I mentioned that I'm armed.

'Southampton aren't playing great,' I wrote, 'so I'm probably the only guy in a Southampton strip with a bit of firepower this year.' The editor of the letters page picks up on this, and has added his own comment: 'So, not only has this Gazan youth team got a miserable life in a shit part of the world, they're now Southampton supporters to boot!'

As part of our Hamas solidarity campaign Eddie, Taff and me have taken to walking to the front gate every evening, to shoot the shit with the Hamas fighters manning the checkpoint. We drink endless cups of tea, and do our best to build some rapport.

There's always something we find to laugh about. One evening this guy goes past riding a donkey. There's nothing so unusual about that in this part of the world, but this donkey is towing a car. I manage to grab my mobile phone and film it plodding past, whilst Eddie, Taff and the Hamas lot are rolling around in laughter.

I draw the line at sharing their scoff though. Their idea of top nosh seems to be a cauldron of goats' intestines fried in chilli oil, and mopped up with chunks of unleavened bread. The bread I can manage: the chunks of chewy, rubbery goat's innards and white plastic-like tubes I can well do without.

After all this Hamas solidarity work, Hussein reckons we're flavour of the month. He invites us white-eye operators over to his place for a formal dinner. I just know we're going to be served goats' intestines seasoned with dogshit, and I figure I've got to find a way to get out of it.

Next evening at the checkpoint, I 'accept' some of the Hamas scoff. I proceed to smear it all over my mouth and chin, as if I can't actually eat properly. The Hamas blokes are staring at me in disgust. The following day I get the nod from Mr Bean: Hussein has withdrawn the dinner invitation, because 'Mr Phil has such disgusting table manners'.

Over the next few evenings it strikes Eddie, Taff and me that the Hamas fighters are starting to look increasingly worried. For the first time they're actually looking scared to be there. They spend less and less of their time joking around with us, and more and more of their time praying. Something's spooked them.

One night we go up to the gate, only to find the entire Hamas force has been replaced. Instead of the young, green recruits that we're used to, there are some proper heavy-looking meatheads around. There are more Hamas wagons than normal, and they're manned by grizzled, gun-toting warriors who are tooled up to the nines.

Hard eyes stare out of massive beards, their faces marked by the scars of battle. With these guys their webbing looks like it belongs to them, rather than it's been hung on a pair of reluctant shoulders. Compared with the Hamas lot that were here before, these are lions to their lambs.

There's not a word been said to us, but the ante has clearly been upped. There's a dark and sinister feeling in the air.

It doesn't take a genius to figure it's about to kick off.

CHAPTER 45

At dawn next day we're in the midst of changing shifts, when the attack comes. Taff's just hit the sack, having done the night shift with the guard force. Eddie is taking Lassen and the engineers down to the main turbine building, to start work. Jack's over in the office, checking in with the UN, and I'm heading for the guardroom.

Just as I reach the entranceway, there's this savage burst of automatic fire. Rounds go screaming over my head, just inches off target, and slamming into the compound's wall. I go diving through the guardroom door, being fully aware of just how close I've come to getting my head blown clean off.

As I hit the deck, I can hear further bursts of fire coming from the direction of the turbine rooms. That's where Eddie is with the clients, so I figure they're getting some too. I leg it for the stairs, so I can make the roof and get eyes on whoever it is that's hitting us.

I'm charging up the stairs and I run into Panama Plod coming down. I grab his arm: 'Make your fucking weapon ready, mate, 'cause we're under attack.'

'I don't have it,' he admits. 'I left it in my room.'

I slam him up against the wall. 'Okay, mate, you listen good: you get a set of that fucking body armour on that we keep for the clients. You're about as much fucking use as one of them with no fucking weapon, so you just keep 'em quiet, okay.'

Panama Plod nods his agreement and I'm gone. I tear past Jack, who's in the office, and I can hear him working the phones and trying to raise the UN. I hit the roof, and I can hear burst after burst of automatic fire sweeping the compound below me.

I stick my head and my useless Beretta over the parapet, and there's Eddie with the three clients making a mad dash for a patch of cover. He's got bullets snarling all around him, and kicking up the dirt at his heels. He's sprinting from one patch of cover to another, dragging Lassen and his lot after him, and he never stops moving. Stop, and they're all dead, and Eddie knows it.

I'm sweeping the compound perimeter with the Beretta, trying to spot the source of the gunfire. Somehow, somebody fucking evil has breached the Hamas lines, plus the compound's own defences. But I can't seem to locate their muzzle flashes, and with every burst of fire I'm imagining Eddie taking a round to the head.

Eddie makes a last, desperate dash for the office block, and he's shoving the clients inside. He's last in, kicking the door shut behind him, as a burst of fire chews up the doorframe. He'll be linking up with Panama Plod to get the clients into body armour, and into the cover of the concrete stairwell.

In the meantime, I've got to do something to stop whoever it is that's attacking us from breaking into the building. I turn for the entrance into the stairwell, and there's Mr Bean standing frozen in the doorway. I grab him by his lapels and practically throw him back inside.

'Get out of the fucking line of fire, you twat!' I'm screaming in his face. Then I slam him against the wall. 'And while we're at it, you tell me what the fuck is going on here! Fucking now!'

Mr Bean knows I mean business. 'It's Islamic Jihad.' His lips are quivering as he starts speaking. 'And they are coming after you.'

For a moment I'm almost shocked. 'What, *me personally?*'

He nods. 'Yes. They are coming to get all you white-eyes.'

I drop Mr Bean, and I leg it down the stairs. I've got to warn Eddie and Jack that Islamic Jihad are inside the compound. As I'm hammering down the staircase I'm thinking: *Fuck me, if I live through this I'll never forget those words: 'It's Islamic Jihad and they're coming for you.'*

I'm working through in my head how we're going to defend ourselves. We'll have to fight it out at close quarters, as we've got no longs. We'll have to lure them into the close confines of a building, where we can use the Berettas to best effect, and even up the odds a little.

Trouble is, Hussein the Hamas commander has only given each of us the one magazine with the pistol. We each have one nine-round mag, and that's it. Nine bullets each, forty-five between the lot of us. We'll have to make every round count. Especially as Panama Plod has forgotten to bring his pistol. So correction: make that thirty-six rounds between the lot of us.

I warn the lads that we're being hit by Islamic Jihad, Eddie gets the clients sorted in their body armour, and Jack's still trying to raise the UN. We leave Lassen and his blokes with Panama Plod, and Eddie and me head back to the roof. If we can just see where the attackers are, we can work out what building to lure the fuckers into.

I raise my head above the parapet, and phuut!, a round ricochets off the brickwork not an arm's reach from my skull. Eddie pops his head up, and gets the same treatment. Every time we try to get a look in, there's the whine of a round shooting past just inches from our heads.

There's a fierce fight sparking at the eastern end of the compound now, with long bursts of fire going backwards and forwards. We figure Hamas must be trying to beat back the assault by Islamic Jihad. We're lying there wondering what to do, when Eddie glances at me in alarm. It's rare to see him looking ruffled.

'It's Taff,' he yells at me. 'He's still in the accommodation block. He's got to be.'

Our standard operating procedure if attacked is to get everyone into the office building. The accommodation wing is on the far side of the compound from there. And it's from that direction that we're taking all the incoming fire. Taff must be pinned down and isolated there, with a useless Beretta pistol and one nine-round magazine.

Eddie starts crawling towards the stairwell. 'I'm going to fetch him,' he yells at me.

'You want back-up?' I yell back at him.

'No mate. Keep an eye and watch our backs from up here.'

'What – with this piece of shit!' I yell back, waving the pistol like a rotten banana.

Eddie's pissing himself laughing as he goes charging down the stairwell.

A few seconds later I hear the roar of an engine, and Eddie's off. He's grabbed one of the Toyotas, and he's doing a Top Gear impression as he screams it around the compound. It's a smart move: unless you're very highly trained, it's next to impossible to hit a vehicle when it's moving at high speed.

With Eddie gone I try to work out what's going down with the firefight. There are still savage exchanges of fire going on in the direction of the main gate. I figure that maybe the Hamas meatheads we saw there are starting to win the day.

A couple of minutes pass, and Eddie comes screaming back in

the Land Cruiser, bullets chasing the vehicle as it swerves and weaves through the grounds. He's got Taff riding shotgun, so we're all present and correct in the office building now.

Eddie's also managed to grab Panama Plod's weapon and ammo, which we disperse amongst the four of us. We don't trust him any more even to handle his own weapon.

An hour later and the fighting has all but died down. It's around now that the UN decide to respond to Jack's calls, and send in their Quick Reaction Force (QRF). We see a column of white UN armoured wagons turn up at the power station's main gate.

Eddie, Taff and me run the clients over to the UN APCs (armoured personnel carriers). As we're shovelling them inside, there's still the odd burst of gunfire echoing around the place. We're just throwing Lassen into the last vehicle, when who should rock up but Mr Creosote, the power-station manager.

'Please, not to evacuate the engineers!' he starts howling at us. 'I am begging thems not to leave. I have big pressures on me to get the power running again, so I am begging thems not to leave.'

'Listen, mate, if Islamic Jihad are coming for us lot that means they're after the clients,' Jack tells him. 'And that means they're out of here.'

'No, no, no,' he tries saying. 'Not a big fight, this one. Not even a real fight. This one only training exercise. Only training exercise.'

It's a fine act by Mr Creosote, but we tell him we're out of there. Jack has sorted it with the UN to get Lassen and his team out of Gaza entirely, 'cause with Islamic Jihad after your clients you don't fuck around.

As we exit the power station, there's a barrage of rounds pinging off the armoured skins of the UN wagons. It's like being in some massive steel drum inside. *Some training exercise, Mr Creosote.*

After a long and bone-jarring ride across Gaza city, myself, Eddie and Taff opt to get dropped at the Al Dira Hotel, so we can get back into the power station as rapidly as possible. But Panama Plod is sticking with Jack and the clients. In fact, this is the last we ever see of him. He gets himself well out of Gaza, which is no great loss as far as the rest of us are concerned.

The three of us sip our non-alcoholic beverages, whilst a series of Hamas military-style funerals take place in the city that day. We ask the hotel manager who the dead are, and he tells us they are 'Hamas martyrs'.

We presume Hussein has lost a good number of men back at the power station. And for sure, Eddie, Taff and me were lucky to escape without having our heads turned into pink mist by Islamic Jihad's lunatic fighters.

Mr Creosote keeps sending blokes down to the hotel, in an effort to persuade us to bring the engineers back in again. We tell his messengers that unless Hamas guarantee our safety, the clients are not returning any time soon. Finally, Hussein himself pitches up to see us.

He stubbornly refuses to admit to having been in a firefight. He's got some UN guy with him who seems to have gone completely native. The UN bloke keeps trying to tell us that it was a 'Hamas training exercise', and that we've got nothing to worry about security wise. The guy's a fucking idiot.

'Listen, mate, you weren't there, were you?' I tell him. 'And you weren't the one whose head was all but ripped off by a burst of rounds that hit the wall. Bollocks it was a training exercise.'

Hussein still won't admit the truth – that Islamic Jihad all but took the power station, whereupon they would have skinned us alive, and forced us to eat our own testicles.

But bearing in mind we still want to get the job done, we agree to cut a deal with Hussein: in three days' time Eddie and I will return, and spend a twenty-four-hour stint at the power station. If Hamas can keep the peace for that twenty-four hours, we'll make the call that it's safe enough, and we'll pull the engineer team into Gaza again.

Three days later Eddie and I are back at the power station. We go to check things out, with Mr Creosote dogging our every step, and blathering on again about a 'training exercise'. I walk him over to the wall where I almost had my head blown off, and show him the fresh bullet marks.

'No, no, no,' Mr Creosote shakes his head vigorously. 'Bullet holes already there. Already there.'

We ignore the stupid fucker, and concentrate on checking out how well Hamas have the placed secured. They've beefed up numbers and weaponry considerably, plus they've improved their sandbagged defensive positions. We figure it would take the entire Israeli Defence Force to blast their way in here now.

We tell Hussein we'll bring the engineers back in, but only in forty-eight hours' time. In the meantime, we want to see his men with their fingers on their triggers day and night, in case Islamic Jihad try anything nasty again.

Hussein has stopped going on about a 'training exercise' now. He figures we know the truth, so what's the point in bullshitting us.

I wake very early the following morning to one of the most eerie sounds that I've ever heard. The voices of young kids are singing out in Arabic, and being broadcast over the loudspeaker systems on the minarets that are all around the power station.

On and on it goes, these spine-chilling, yet angelic voices – all boys, of course – chanting out this litany for hours and hours on end. I'm used to the call to prayer being broadcast by the imams, but this high-pitched, quivering wail of children's voices is weirdly disturbing.

What if Islamic Jihad has taken over the mosques? I ask myself. What if they're using the kids to call for the final assault, and the slaughter of the white-eye infidels in the power station?

I go and find Mr Bean, and demand to know what the hell is going on. They do this every year, he tells me. The kids do the call to prayer for six hours solid, to celebrate the end of Eid, the Muslim festival that rivals Christmas in the West. There's one more hour to go, Mr Bean reassures me, and then the eerie racket will stop.

I tell myself that maybe I'm getting a little too jumpy. Or maybe I've been in this crazed hellhole for more than long enough, and I need to get out and get me some down time.

Jack arrives that evening with the engineering team. Everyone's looking properly shaken, and I wonder why. Jack tells me they got into a bit of a dust-up as they went across the border. It's the usual, with the Israelis shooting up Hamas to provoke a firefight, and Jack and the engineers caught in the middle.

Luckily, they've got Raymond Barclay with them, as the replacement for Panama Plod. Raymond's a top bloke if ever there was one, and he was a legend whilst in The Regiment.

From starting this op with two ex-SAS blokes on the ground – that's Eddie and me – we're now all ex-Regiment, apart from Jack, who's ex-Royal Marines. Which just goes to show what a heavy tasking is this one.

In the following days there are dozens of sporadic firefights, but the second big push by Islamic Jihad never comes. After two more weeks under siege in the power station, we figure we've had enough. It's time to get out whilst we can still walk, and are not being carried in a coffin.

In any case, the job of refitting the power station is pretty much finished, and the power's coming back on line.

We leave Gaza as we entered it, sandwiched between the Israelis and Hamas trading fire with each other, as we scuttle across no-man's-land heading into the tunnels.

Still, we've manned it out and we've got the job done. It's mission accomplished. Who dares wins – no matter what the odds are against you, or how much of a shitfight there might be involved. I never have been one for half-measures, even when the tasking is a totally insane one like that Hamas mission.

If you start something, you see it through to the bitter and bloody end.

CHAPTER 46

It was during deployment to the Falklands that I'd first earned a reputation for being the bloke who just wouldn't quit. One evening myself and some of the Royal Hampshire lads – now renamed the PWRR – were queuing to get into a bar called Timmy's, in the Islands' capital.

We'd been drinking, there was a bit of aggro and we got into a punch-up. My favourite people, the Royal Military Police (RMP), arrived to break it up, and one of them accused me of being the chief troublemaker. He and I had prior form.

A few days back I'd been on the lash in the main camp, and I was caught pissing in the corridor. Basically, I'd had enough beer to sink a decent-sized ship, without the bladder to match. I offered to clean it up, and I did so in front of the RMP bloke who'd caught me. But still he reported me to my CO, and got me fined fifty quid.

At that time all my money was counted out in terms of beer and nights on the piss, so fifty quid was no small issue. And it was the same RMP wanker who'd run into me at Timmy's. He shoved me into the rear of a Land Rover, along with a couple of big RMP mates of his.

He kept giving it 'Mr Big', and shoving me in the back. He was trying to tell me that the RMP were the hardest bastards on the island, and that once they got me in the cells I was done for. I warned him that if he pushed me or threatened me again, he was going to get some.

We arrived at the police station, a prefab hut with just the one front door and a corridor leading to an interview room and the cells. As I stepped inside the RMP wanker shoved me, and started taunting me with what he was going to do to me once he got me behind bars.

Being locked up in a place staffed by abusive bullying bastards: *not good*. Bad memories of the kids' homes. The RMP bloke shoved me in the back again, sending me stumbling through a second door. So I spun around and dropped him.

He went down hard, and I didn't care if I'd knocked him out or not. The RMP guy behind the desk sprang up, so I dropped him too. I threw the second guy on top of the first, and shoved the both of them into a third RMP idiot who came charging in from outside.

As they struggled to get to their feet I shoved all three of them out the door of their own police station, and locked and bolted it. All their weapons were in the gun cabinet, in the room that I was in. I now had the guns in the office with me, and they were locked outside.

They tried talking to me through the barred window, to get me to open up. 'Come on this isn't helping anyone,' RMP wanker number one said. 'You're only making it worse for yourself.'

'Shut up,' I told him. 'I'm not talking to you.' I glanced around the tiny police station. 'This is what I'm going to do instead.'

I sealed up the door completely, blocking it with a desk and chairs. Then I proceeded to urinate on their casebook, flick cigarette ash in all their drawers, and generally cause havoc in there. I knew it had gone so far that it didn't really matter what I did now, I was in so much trouble. *If you're gonna be a bear, be a grizzly.*

They had one bloke stationed by the window, and I figured the others had gone off to fetch reinforcements. He kept saying stuff like: 'Come on, lad, open up. What will this achieve?'

I ignored him, and stayed awake smoking. I told myself that I was stagging on, and to fall asleep would be a dereliction of duty. I got these wire coat hangers, and wrapped them around my fists, like knuckledusters. *This is my fortress, and I am defending it.*

It was me holding off the entire RMP unit of the Falklands.

Result.

Their move.

I remained where I was until the morning, when my Troop Commander came to talk me into surrendering. He was a Royal Marines officer attached to the PWRR, and he was a sound bloke. I could tell he found my single-handed occupation of the RMP police station funny, though he was trying not to show it.

He talked to me through the window. 'Come on, soldier, it's time to open up.'

'I am not going anywhere until those RMP wankers are out of here,' I told him, 'and there's a car to take me back to my lines. If not, one of those guys is going to get seriously hurt.'

'You lot, make yourselves scarce,' my Troop Commander told the RMPs. 'You've made a serious mess of this already. Leave it to us, and we will discipline our own.'

When I finally pulled down the barricade and unlocked the door, there wasn't an RMP in sight.

I was carted off to Mare Harbour, where the Commander in Chief of the Falklands ordered I be kept under lock and key until I could be taken off the Islands. He was waiting on the next available flight to get me out, but he'd seriously underestimated Mr Phil.

I figured I might get thrown out of the Army – *the only home*

I've ever had – for good for this one. So I was determined to go out with a bang, and take some of those RMP fuckers with me.

I told this crow (new recruit) who shared my Mare Harbour cell to get into my bed, and to act as if he was asleep. That way, whenever the guards peered through our cell door they'd see a body in my cot and think it was me.

I sneaked out of Mare Harbour and contacted a mate of mine from the PWRR, who picked me up in an Army wagon. He loaned me some money, and I was on my way to the NAAFI to get drinking.

It was late and I was looking to hook up with a gang of the PWRR lads. I went into this bar, and I saw this girl that we knew well being given a hard time. She was surrounded by these lads from the Engineers, who were abusing her verbally.

The girl was crying, they were laughing and I didn't like it. I walked right into the middle of them.

'Which one's the big man here, then?' I announced.

This bloke stepped forward. He was bigger than Ben Hur, but I didn't hesitate. I knocked him down and he was out for the count. But there were more of them than I'd reckoned on. They got hold of me and held me down, whilst one tried kicking me in the head.

Luckily, one of my PWRR mates saw what was happening through the window, and raised the alarm. The PWRR gang – Daisy, Nobby, Stu and the rest – piled in, and soon we were taking those Engineers apart. The NAAFI owner called the RMP, and they arrived at the door trying to pull people out and separate them.

Eventually, we were down to two or three still fighting, in this small corridor leading to the doorway. I was filling in the last of the Engineers, when one of the RMP blokes fronted up to me.

'All right, you little bastard, stop it!' he yelled.

I turned around, and he realized who it was. I dropped the Engineer, and started to advance on the RMP. He backed off.

'All right, mate, we've had enough. Just leave it. Move on. We don't want any more trouble.'

I left without a word, and got my mate to give me a lift back to Mare Harbour. But in the meantime the RMP lot reported to the Commander in Chief of the Falklands that they'd just seen me in the NAAFI, causing total havoc and chaos, when I was supposed to be in my cell.

By the time anyone came to check, I was back in my cot sleeping like a baby. The guards confirmed that I'd been there all night long. Every hour they'd been checking through the window.

The following day I went before the Commander in Chief of the Falklands to be disciplined. I was fully expecting to get kicked out of the Army, but I decided to use the incident with the RMP lot to argue for some clemency.

When the Commander asked me if I had anything to say for myself in response to the charge of taking over the RMP police station, I said the following: 'Sir, you yourself saw what happened last night. The RMP lot have a vendetta against me. They pretended I was out causing havoc, when really I was here sleeping.'

The Commander must have taken pity on me. He busted my stripes off me and kicked me off the Islands. He made it clear that I was persona non grata in the Falklands Islands for the rest of my life. But he didn't throw me out of the Army.

I was handcuffed and flown back to Brize Norton, with a sizeable bunch of RMPs as my escort. I was kicked out at Brizers with no money, and just my small backpack. Word hadn't yet filtered back to regimental headquarters of my Falkland misadventures, so there was no one there to meet me.

I hitched a lift to Southampton and went to my adopted sister's house. Anne and me had stayed in touch ever since the crazed

Audrey days. I got her to phone the PWRR adjutant to tell him that I was ill, and would be off work for a week or so.

I had a long hard drinking session and a good think. I needed a new challenge in life, and P Company was to be the answer. The PWWR formed part of Five Airborne Assault Brigade, and they needed a platoon of men to be jump-trained, which would be designated P (Para) Company.

In spite of my Falklands misadventures, I talked myself onto the team for P Company selection. I was one of the fourteen lads from the PWWR sent to earn our parachutist wings.

Before starting P Company proper, we had to go through 'Log Battalion' – getting beasted by a bunch of Para instructors at Aldershot. The instructors were full of airborne attitude, and treated us PWRR lads as if we were dogshit.

Just as soon as we pitched up the slagging began. The Para instructors told us in great detail how they were going to break us, and that none of us would ever get through to P Company proper.

The worst moment came when all fourteen of us were ordered into the gym, and the instructors started to beast the hell out of us. All the while one of them was reading extracts from someone's diary, and screaming filthy obscenities at us.

Sure enough the diary was mine. Most of what I'd written was how easy 'Log Battalion' was, and what self-important idiots the Para instructors were. In the end they couldn't keep pace with us in the beasting, and the three of them ended up in the sick bay.

We laughed our cocks off, which just enraged them all the more.

They failed to break even the one of us, and we moved on to P Company proper, at Catterick. We shared the grounds with a bunch of Guards recruits. The Guards reminded me of the posh types I'd rubbed shoulders with at Kingham Hill. They had that same head-up-their-own-arse attitude.

The Paras hated the Guards and vice versa. I took to leaning out the window of the accommodation block and howling orders at the Guards recruits on parade. They'd all come to a sudden crashing halt, or they'd wheel about on the wrong foot. It was total chaos, and priceless entertainment.

The P Company instructors couldn't but find it hilarious, and they didn't have it in them to discipline me. There was no bullshit or bullying in P Company. Instead, you had to keep up with the relentless pace of the instructors. Three good sessions of PT every day, on top of the training, and as much scoff as you could handle. Happy days.

P Company lasted three weeks: two of 'beat up' and training, and the final test week. The staff let you know you were being watched and evaluated the whole time.

P Company had started with sixty recruits. It was soon down to thirty, with most feigning exhaustion or injury. By the end of week two we hadn't dropped a single PWRR lad, and all fourteen of us graduated onto the week of jump training proper.

We moved down to RAF Brize Norton, and were assigned bunks in some ancient wooden Nissen huts. We were on the very edge of the base, right next to the dog section. The RAF hated everything squaddie, and they just wanted us kept as far away as possible.

It was a Sunday night, and we decided there was nothing for it but to head for the NAAFI. There were some young Paras in there giving it large. We sensed trouble, but me and the other PWRR lads tried to keep ourselves to ourselves, and enjoy a good few pints.

The mouthiest of the Para lads went to the toilet, came back, and for no reason at all launched into me as he was passing. I picked him up, slammed him through a table, then hammered him in the face. The rest of the Paras were frozen. They couldn't believe that their Mr Large had just got flattened.

We finished our pints, and headed for bed. We'd just got back to the Nissen hut, when the door flew open there was Mr Large and his mates looking for trouble. This time we didn't hold back. Within seconds there was a door torn off its hinges, and a pile of smashed-up Paras lying beneath it outside.

A week of live jumps followed, which was a great crack parachuting from C130 Hercules. P Company ended with a 'milling' session, the instructors' last chance to test us. In the milling you went face to face with another recruit and fought with no rules until one of you went down. Milling is designed to be a test of total aggression, and sheer ability to take punishment and pain.

You had to fight someone of similar size, with no defensive action allowed. In the PWRR I'd earned the nickname 'Big Phil' for a reason – I'm not small. But the guy the instructors pitched me against was at least as big as me, and a trained boxer.

In the first seconds he threw a classic boxing punch and I went down hard. But I was up again an instant later, and I went in with flying fists and total aggression. I was using my head and feet and knuckles, and it was brutal and bloody.

I would have used my teeth too, if I could have just got a hold of the bastard. Eventually, they stopped the fight, as we were battering each other to pieces and covered in blood. At the end of it all I felt my Para wings had been well earned.

Before leaving the Para course, myself and another PWRR guy asked the Brigade Commander if we could transfer to the Parachute Regiment. I'd been itching to move on ever since passing Royal Marines selection. This, I figured, was my chance.

The Brigadier told us to leave it with him. Unbeknown to us he got straight on the phone to the CO of our Regiment, and told him that two of his men had asked to transfer to the Paras. Might the CO enlighten us as to the correct protocol for such requests?

Just as soon as we got back to our lines we were called before the CO. I went in first and the CO hit the roof, berating me over my lack of loyalty to the PWRR. I responded that the system had shown little loyalty to the Royal Hampshires, the Regiment I had signed up to. All I was doing was reciprocating.

The CO was steaming, and he told me that my request for a transfer to the Paras was refused. I walked out without being relieved. The Adjutant collared me next and we had a similar row, closely followed by the Battalion 2iC.

The 2iC pointed out that I'd just reached my 'career ceiling', and that now would be a good time to apply for selection into another unit. I took the hint, submitted my paperwork, and decided to go for gold.

I was going to attempt selection into 22 SAS.

CHAPTER 47

Mostly, I loved working the circuit. It kept the adrenalin flowing and paid the bills, plus it suited my restless, rebel spirit. But after the insanity of that Gaza mission with Hamas, I figured I needed something a little less out there and on the edge.

'Suicidal' was the word that Eddie had used for the Gaza contract, and I couldn't argue with that. For sure that tasking – and Islamic Jihad's burning desire to give us what Mr Creosote had insisted was a 'training session' – had almost been the death of us. So when the offer comes up of a new tasking I jump at the chance, especially as it's a right cushy-looking number.

The rock band Kasabian are planning a tour of Ibiza – the Ibiza Rocks Tour – and my mate from the firm Risk Contained is organizing their security. He invites me to be part of the four-man team bodyguarding the band, and after the Gaza mission I figure a few days sunning myself in Ibiza is just what I need. I mean, why not? It beats playing buddy-buddy with Hamas and Mr Creosote, whilst dodging Islamic Jihad.

We fly out to Ibiza, and we're billeted with the band in this plush, sun-washed villa complete with palm trees and its own swimming pool. The Kasabian lads are a proper laugh, and it has to be said the job's a doddle compared with those weeks of graft in Gaza.

The nearest I come to any action is when I have to hoist the lead singer, Tom, above my head and carry him out of this gig, 'cause he's got surrounded by this overzealous mob of fans.

Once I've finished palming off all these drunken, frenzied groupies, I dump Tom in the tour bus and we're on our way back to the villa. The band's manager comes up to me and he's all handshakes and smiles. He tells me he's never seen anything like the rescue job I've just done on Tom. I tell him it's no big deal. Needs must, old boy.

That night everyone gets just a little bit tipsy. I end up having a belly-flopping contest with the bass guitarist, Chris, to see who can make the biggest splash in the pool. We start from standing on the poolside, then belly-flopping in from a chair, and soon we're up to eight chairs piled on top of each other. I've got to hand it to Chris: for a civvy he doesn't give up very easily, and as far as belly-flopping's concerned, he's nails.

But Big Phil cannot be outdone by the bassist of Kasabian, and so I decide to go for the nuclear option. I scale this palm tree that bends gracefully over the pool's waters. I reach the frond-enshrouded top, and announce to the assembled crowd that all the water in the pool is about to evacuate from it, 'cause Big Phil's dropping in from a great height.

I proceed to do the belly-flop of all belly-flops, but unfortunately I've slightly miscalculated how far over the pool the palm tree is bending. I catch my foot on the edge of the pool and there's a bit of blood, and Chris decides discretion is the better part of valour and that he'll call it a day.

It's fortunate that he does. The only higher point that I could see to top the palm tree is the villa roof, and that's set a good few yards back from the pool. The only way to do it would be to take a massive run-up and launch myself off it in the hope of making

319

the pool's deep end belly-first. And by now I've drunk just about enough San Miguel to want to give it a right good go.

I do a couple more jobs with Risk Contained, one of which is this massive Led Zeppelin gig – one that could have sold out ten times over, the demand is so fierce for the tickets. It's a real experience being up on stage with Jimmy Page, and the celebrity-filled backstage party after promises to be a blast. But it's more cocoa and slippers than cocaine and stilettos for the bodyguarding teams, for we have to remain together and on guard the whole time.

I nickname this work 'hobby guarding', as opposed to bodyguarding, it's so easy compared with what I'm used to. I get to accompany Liam Gallagher to a charity footie match between Manchester City and Tottenham, after which I have to audition for a hobby-guarding gig with Angelina Jolie, for some trip she's taking to India. But I'm told that Angelina didn't really like the look of me, and in truth hobby guarding isn't really my thing.

I'm craving some real action, and I get just what I'm after – in the form of some anti-piracy work off the coast of Somalia. I'll be catching a plane to Muscat and boarding an oil tanker bound for Ukraine via the Gulf of Aden, prime pirate territory. A few weeks cruising the Indian Ocean, doing a spot of sunbathing and fishing from the ship's deck, plus battling some Somali pirates. What could be better? I figure it's the perfect antidote to the weeks of suicidal lunacy that I've just spent in Gaza.

But what I haven't counted on is the odds that'll be stacked against us. For some reason carrying weapons on the high seas is considered a big 'no-no' – that's unless you're a Somali pirate, who is going to be armed to the teeth. So the two-man security team that I am heading will have to brave pirate-infested waters without any weapons.

How many times now have I gone in on a contract unarmed: the Abu Dhabi diamond job; the Kabul embassy mission; crossing the border into southern Iraq; into Gaza with Fatah and then Hamas; and now this anti-piracy mission. *So what's fucking new?*

Having taken the job, the first priority is to build up an intel picture. The pirates' tactics are always pretty similar: an approach in small, fast craft; a few shots across the bows; board the ship when it slows; and take everyone hostage.

Our greatest defence is clearly going to be speed: keep the ship at full steam ahead to outrun the pirate boats. Vessels that make the mistake of stopping are toast. But before setting sail I figure we can take some extra defensive measures.

The first thing we'll do is string razor wire along the ship's gunwales and stairwells. That should make boarding us a little less comfortable. Before leaving the UK I get the PMC who's running the contract to order a load of razor wire to be delivered to the docks.

There's no sign of it when I get there, so I ask the shipping company what's what. They tell me the wire is in the car park. I go to take a look, and all I can find is one roll of green gardening wire. It's not even barbed.

I phone the London office of the PMC, and tell them I have one roll of gardening wire with which to protect a whole fucking ship. The response is: 'Nobody said it was going to be easy.'

I feel like telling them that I'm the one going to sea, and I'm the one that's going to get boarded. But what's the point? They're in London, I'm here, and there's a job to be done. At great expense I manage to source some razor wire locally, and we start working it into the ship.

My fellow operator on this, my first anti-piracy trip, is an ex-Regiment bloke, called James 'Jim' Munro. Jim's an excellent operator, but we figure with the two of us we're just a tad undermanned for this job. We could do with three times our number to run security on a big old tanker like this one.

Jim and I spend two days constructing evil barriers and entanglements, and binding the bulkhead doors shut. We cook up some nasty little nail bombs, and Molotov cocktails – perfect for tossing into a pirate boat, to torch it. Flare guns are carried on all ships, and we each will carry one of those.

Finally, we get some big, official-looking warning signs made up, both in English and Arabic, saying that the side of the ship is 'ELECTRIFIED'. It isn't, but the signs look the part. Then we mount a watch, set sail and sit on the bridge waiting to be attacked.

We rehearse drills with the ship's crew. They come from Burma, and nothing is too much trouble for them. They work like pigs, do as they're told and are very disciplined. Like many a bloke from the developing world, they seem able to make a clay pot from a pile of poo. I've got every confidence in them.

The SOP in the event of an attack is to get the crew together in a pre-identified muster station, and then below decks to a holding area. The holding area is basically somewhere with good cover from fire, where we've cached food, water, blankets and basic survival gear.

The ship's captain is this ancient Russian sea dog called Sergei. He's got to be well into his seventies. If we're attacked, Captain Sergei's role is to remain on the bridge, with engines at full steam ahead. Whatever he does, he's not to stop his ship.

I make it clear to him that I have no qualms about taking command of his vessel, should I have to. I know the basics of how to speed up and steer a ship, and come what may we are not going to stop. Captain Sergei makes it clear to me that no one – Somali pirate, or private security operator – is taking over his ship.

He'll outrun the fuckers if it kills him.

Captain Sergei and me recce this route so that we can climb to the very top of the ship's funnel. He figures we can steer the ship from up there, using a radio link to the engine room, just in case the pirates do board us.

I like Sergei. He's an if-you're-gonna-be-a-bear-be-a-grizzly kind of bloke. I figure he's got some military experience behind him, and he's going to be a key ally in evading the Somali ship-jackers. I explain to him some of the finer details of how we intend to deal with the pirates.

First off, we *want* them to open fire on us. Going like a bat out of hell in a small speedboat on the high seas, they'll have next to no chance of hitting us. All they'll succeed in doing is using up their limited supplies of ammo, plus they'll be burning up scarce supplies of fuel as they keep chasing us.

The pirates may use their small pursuit craft to herd us towards their mother ship. We'll stay alert to that by keeping a close eye on the radar, to ensure we steer well clear of it. If they do get close enough to try to board us, we'll fuck them off with flares, nail bombs and Molotov cocktails.

'And Sergei, once they're out of ammo we'll invite them on board,' I tell him. 'We'll drop a ladder down to them, and I'll stand every one of the fuckers to a fist fight.'

Sergei gives me this evil smile. 'I have the better idea. We ram them with our big tanker and send them to the sharks.'

Jim and I stand staggered watches, four hours on and four off. During one of those I start thinking back over my Gaza gig with Fatah. For some reason the cardboard cut-out AK47s come into my mind. I have a flash of inspiration.

That day Jim and I each make a cardboard mock-up of our weapon of choice, mine being a shotgun. Plus we rig up some mock medium machine guns attached to the ship's rails. From a pirate boat at distance they should look entirely convincing, or so I hope.

For two full days we charge through pirate-infested waters with their boats shadowing us. Now and then we make a show of standing in full view, brandishing our cardboard cut-out 'weapons'. None of the pirates makes a move to attack and the bluff seems to be working.

Or at least it does until we reach the stretch of ocean between the Seychelles and Madagascar. We're ten days into the voyage, and approaching the Mozambique Channel. We're doing 12 knots, it's a muggy old day and the tanker is full to the gunwales with oil.

She's at full steam ahead but heavily laden and low in the water, which makes her an easier target. From out of the heat-haze a vessel appears, steaming straight towards us. It's the size of a large trawler with two fast skiffs strapped to its gunwales. It can only be a pirate mother ship.

We line up on deck brandishing our cardboard cut-out weapons and trying to appear as big, mean and threatening as possible. The pirate ship keeps coming. It's steaming up on our port side on an interception bearing, the decks lined with an evil-looking crew brandishing assault rifles, machine guns and RPGs.

At the last moment the pirate skipper seems to misjudge his bearing, for the ship shoots past a whisker's breadth to our stern. The pirates loose off a couple of RPGs, in an effort to force us to slow down. Fortunately their aim is way off – a heavily pitching pirate boat makes a God-awful fire platform.

The pirate boat comes around in a hard turn. The fact that it's come about to be dead in line astern can only mean one thing: the chase is on. The pirate captain's gauged our speed, and he knows he's less than a nautical mile behind. He figures he's got half a knot on us at present speeds, so he'll gain on us and catch us.

I tell Sergei to put pedal to the metal in an effort to outrun the fuckers. I get the Burmese crew bundled below decks into the engine room, hatches closed and all battened down. I'm up with Captain Sergei on the bridge, with a bloke on each wing keeping watch.

The sea is rough, with a heavy swell running. It's a blessing and a curse for us. It's a blessing because the pirate captain will have trouble launching his fast skiffs to overrun us. The sea's likely too rough for him to do so. It's a curse, because ploughing through the swell laden to the gunwales as we are really slows us down.

The pirate ship keeps coming. I tell Captain Sergei to squeeze some more speed out of his engines, or we're toast. He gets on the blower to the engine room, and he's yelling at them to stoke up the engines.

He starts yelling at his first mate to get the Burmese crew up from below decks, and have them lob any heavy objects over the side – anything that might lighten the load. I can see the tension on Captain Sergei's face, but it's mixed with a grim, stubborn determination that no one's taking his ship.

The Captain keeps sending out these urgent distress signals, but it's pretty obvious that no one's coming to our aid. It strikes me that if only we had a nice, bolt-action rifle – something like the Dragunov I'd picked up in Basra – then we'd be sorted. We've got this great big stable shooting platform from which to pick off the pirates, and they're bobbing about in their boat. They wouldn't stand a fucking chance.

The pirate boat gains upon us until it's down to 200 metres – less than a ship's length – behind us. I can see individual figures on the deck menacing us with their weapons. They're screaming at us, and whilst I can't understand the words I can have a good guess to the meaning: *Stop your ship, or we'll blow you out of the water.*

There are a lot more of them than there are of us, and they've all got weapons. If we stop and they board us, Jim and I know we're in for a good kicking, unarmed as we are. The only option is to keep going, and to try to squeeze some more speed out of the tanker.

The pirates are trying to drop the fast skiffs, so they can launch the final stages of the assault. But the sea keeps slamming the small boats around and threatening to swamp them. They're forced to give up trying to get the skiffs in the water, and they concentrate instead on using the mother ship to catch us.

We start to pick up speed, as Sergei pushes it to 13.5 knots. The pirate vessel is on 13.2, and gradually it starts to slip behind. Then the pirate captain seems to find some more welly in his vessel, for he hits 13.6 knots and he's gaining on us again.

Sergei yells for more power. With our engines thumping away crazily below decks the noise is deafening, and there's no way I can hope to hear if the pirates are firing on us. For an hour or so it seesaws backwards and forwards, us gaining on them, them gaining on us.

We hit the two-hour mark of the chase, and suddenly the pirate captain slams on the anchors. I can only think he's running desperately short of fuel. Jim and I line up with Sergei on deck, and we've waving a mock goodbye to the fuckers. The pirate ship fades into nothing on the horizon, and we know that we've lost them.

We may have shaken the pirates off, but our troubles are far from over. Sergei has flogged the tanker's engines, and sure enough they die on us. All of a sudden we're this massive vessel drifting to a stop in pirate-infested seas.

Captain Sergei's done something terminal to the engines whilst outrunning that pirate ship. Or so it seems. There's thick black smoke drifting up from the engine room, and a horrible smell of burning.

The Burmese crew is racing about all over the shop, as Sergei screams out his orders about how to get the engines fixed. But the minutes become hours and still we're drifting on the open water.

Even Captain Sergei is starting to look worried. Under his breath, I can hear him muttering his prayers.

I figure there's only one thing for it: I go for a sunbathe.

In between scouring the horizon for suspect vessels, I have ample time to sun myself and to think. I reflect upon what led me to joining the SAS, the one part of the military that encourages maverick, free-spirited soldiering, and the kind of lateral thinking that's gone into trying to safeguard Captain Sergei's ship.

After my attempt to transfer to the Paras, the CO of the PWRR was steaming angry with me. In spite of my applying for SAS selection, he delayed letting me go until I'd completed our next operational tour – Omagh. In fact, it turned out to be a blessing in disguise. The Northern Ireland ceasefire was in place by then, and all there was for lads like me to do was bone sangar duty. Other than that there were few restrictions on where we could go, and so I began training in earnest for SAS selection.

Myself and two other lads got permission to head off into the Mourne Mountains. We went out in full civvy kit and with no security, knowing that Paddy wasn't about to keep up with us lot up on the hills.

We carried everything we needed for ten days, tabbed during daylight hours, and laid up at night bivvied out on the moors. We didn't see another soul the whole time.

After that we went to train in the Welsh hills. We stayed in the cricket pavilion at Crickhowell, disappearing into the mountains every day with a small house on our back. In the evenings we'd go for fish and chips and beer in the local village, and then the next day more of the same.

I refused to run anywhere. I argued that all you needed to do for selection was to walk well. Too many guys turned up for selection having overdone things. I decided to train up until December, then go on the lash for Christmas, ready for a January selection.

Winter selection is the worst possible time of year to attempt to get into The Regiment. Sure enough, that winter proved to be one of the toughest ever. The worst day of whiteout, blizzard-like conditions became known as 'Black Monday' for all the lads who were carried off the hills in survival bags.

But I passed selection and I was badged as a member of 22 SAS. Joining The Regiment was the highpoint of my military career, one that I had dreamed about ever since meeting those SAS instructors in the Kenyan jungle. The fact that I had come from the shittiest beginnings imaginable and made it into this elite unit meant the world to me.

This was brought home to me most powerfully when I ended up being the SAS bloke training men from my former regiment – the PWRR – in jungle warfare.

CHAPTER 48

Things had come a full circle in my military career, and they were about to do so in my personal life. On the very day that I was badged into the SAS, I was given an address and phone number of what could be my real, birth mother. For years I'd been trying to track her down, but mostly any leads I followed turned out to be complete dead ends. I presumed this one would be as well.

I'd been out on the lash the previous evening, celebrating getting badged. Once I'd recovered some from the mother of all hangovers, I dialled the telephone number that I'd been given. My hungover mind never for one moment considered that it might actually be my real mother's place.

A woman's voice answered. I asked her if she knew Della Smith, the name of my real mother on my birth certificate. When the woman confirmed that she did, there was silence for a long second. I didn't know what to say.

'You'd better have a sit down, then,' I finally told her. 'If you know Della, that's my mum.'

'Then I'm your grandma,' the woman blurted out.

I was stunned. I'd just been through the toughest trial of my life – SAS selection – yet now I was about to face an even harder one, in meeting my real mother, plus the wider family that I never knew I had.

I jumped into my battered Ford Escort, and set off for London, following the directions that the grandma I'd never met had given me. I was looking for Topsham Road, Wimbledon. When finally I found it, I kerb-crawled up the street searching for number fifteen.

All of a sudden a door burst open and a woman came running out: 'WAYNE! WAYNE!' she yelled. 'Wayne! Welcome home!'

I'd been christened Wayne Smith, so I figured this had to be Grandma. I left the car where it was, raced across to her and was smothered in her embrace. It turned out to be Patsy, one of my mother's sisters. Grandma was right behind her, shaking her head and smiling.

'I knew it!' she kept saying. 'I just knew we'd find him.'

Grandpa Bob was beside them. He stuck out his hand. 'Welcome home, son.'

Then came the biggest shock of all: Tony, my brother appeared. I'd never even known I had a brother. Tony and I hugged, and cried, and hugged some more, and then my mum was there.

There was total hush as I came face to face with her for the first time since she had given me up. For a second or so we just stood and stared at each other, and then we were holding tight to each other as if we were never going to let go.

It was Tony who finally prised us apart. 'Right,' he announced, 'best get down the Club then.'

As we approached the local social club, out walked a bloke that I instantly recognized. It was Jimmy White, the snooker ace.

He gave me this grin. 'Wayne? Welcome home, son!'

It turned out that he was my uncle on my father's side. I'd always loved snooker, ever since wasting away my school days playing it in the kids' homes. Jimmy White was one of my favourite players. Now I had him as an uncle! What a day.

In the club I met a host of uncles, cousins and aunties. It seemed there were a hundred people in there who were related to me. After a good session we retired to my Auntie Jackie's place, where there was more drink and a massive takeaway from the local Indian.

The next morning we went for breakfast in a café on Wimbledon Common, after which I had to return to The Regiment.

On the drive back to Hereford I started thinking seriously about leaving the Army. I had only just got badged into 22 SAS, but I had a burning desire to spend some time with, and to get to know, my real family. Getting into The Regiment was the peak of what I'd spent my entire life striving to do, yet now I also had to deal with finding my real family.

The weekend after our reunion, I went down to London to see my folks again. This time there was even more drink consumed, and a few home truths came out.

There was a massive brawl outside Grandma's place, and eventually the police were called. We closed ranks as a family, and no one had much to say to the coppers. After that, I figured we'd pretty much buried the hatchet.

I continued to grow my relationship with my real family, and at the same time I continued to build a place for myself within my other family, the Army. I'd realized that I'd be a fool to leave The Regiment, having only just got in, and I re-committed myself to building a career within the world's most elite military force.

But my time in The Regiment was not without its controversy. After several very eventful years, and a number of awesome operations, I got into yet another beery scrap in Hereford town. I ended up bashing my quarter up, kicking off with this bunch of RMP blokes, and getting taken to hospital. It was more of the usual, really.

The CO of the SAS had me hauled before him, for a severe interview without coffee. He started banging on about my unruly, disruptive ways. I felt like pointing out that if he'd been knocked about by his adoptive dad, starved and abandoned by his mum, then bunged through a shedload of abusive kids' homes, he might have unruly ways.

Instead, I decided it was time that Big Phil left The Regiment. I paid my money, bought my way out and did the off.

It was the spring of 2001 and I got out of the SAS with my head held high. The view of The Regiment after I left pretty much reflected how one of my Green Army commanders had described me. I was a useful kind of operator, if 'kept in a metal cage and only brought out at times of war'.

Fair enough, I reckoned. Best I go find myself a war then. Afghan, Iraq, Gaza with Fatah, Gaza with Hamas – over the years I'd found some good ones, including fighting my way across the half of Africa.

And now here I was battling pirates on the lawless high seas.

Five hours after Captain Sergei's ship has died, I hear a cough and a roar and the engines splutter into life. *Thank fuck for that.* We get under way and build up speed, and everyone starts to relax a little.

With Captain Sergei powering his vessel ahead, the job turns into very long stretches of sunbathing and boredom, with the occasional spike of action and adrenalin thrown in. I chuck out some lines baited with bits of Coke can, which glitter and flash in the sunlit water, and soon we're hauling in big tuna, barracuda and sailfish.

The Burmese chef grabs the fish, guts and fillets them, throws them onto a barbecue, then a quick flip over and they're ready.

I wolf down half a dozen tuna fillets, and they're delicious. Almost as enjoyable as having Captain Sergei ram a Somali pirate ship.

Still, the trip's far from over: there's plenty of time still to find and smash one.

Sadly, the remainder of the journey is fairly uneventful, and we make it to our destination port without too many worries. I run several further anti-piracy operations, and we continuously refine our tactics. We get ourselves crossbows, to add to our firepower. The range isn't great, but from a distance they even look like real weapons, which is a major bonus. Better than cardboard cut-outs, anyway.

Then I invent the 'bouncing barrel' concept. You get an empty metal oil drum, drill a hole through the rim, and mount it on a chain. The chain is set to the exact length that allows the barrel to hang down from the ship's sides, dangling in the sea. You attach the free end of the chain to the ship, and rope the barrels tight on a quick release knot.

If the pirates try to board, you release the barrels all down the side you're being boarded. There's just enough slack for them to hit the sea, bounce back up again, hit the sea and keep bouncing. As long as the ship keeps moving, the bouncing barrels present such a murderous obstacle it makes it nigh-on impossible to board.

I do this one trip with an Indian crew who are so into the bouncing barrels, they are actually disappointed when the pirates don't try to hit us. They want to see the A Team roar into action, and the pirates getting exactly what they deserve – a large steel barrel in the head.

We've turned a potentially terrifying situation into something quite enjoyable and exciting for the crew. But all such defensive techniques and weaponry are useless without good operators to man up the anti-piracy missions.

I'm midway through a trip off the Horn of Africa, and I'm leading a team of six blokes on this one. I'm on a cargo ship carrying these giant wind turbines. The massive towers and turbine blades are piled two-up on the open deck, which means it's impossible to see from the bridge to the bow of the ship, or vice versa.

Of more concern, the turbines' bulk obscures our view of the sea. We've got blind spots from where the pirates can sneak up on us unseen, if they're in small enough boats to do so. As a precaution against that happening, I've got a couple of sentries posted right on the vessel's bow and a couple on the stern, plus we've got radios linking ourselves to each other and the bridge.

I happen to be coming up onto the bridge halfway through a guy called Pete's watch, and as soon as I'm there I automatically do a quick 360-degree scan of the horizon. Right away I see what looks like a pirate mother ship powering directly towards us.

I check the radar, and I can see there's this tiny island not ten nautical miles to the west of us. From the radar scan, I can see that the island is surrounded by a flotilla of small boats, which are typical pirate craft. I can also see that someone on that island has installed AIS (Automatic Identification System), a piece of kit that can identify all ships steaming nearby.

If your vessel is over 50 metres long you have to carry AIS by law. It broadcasts the name of the ship, plus details of the cargo and crew to all other vessels in the vicinity, as a navigational aid. Unfortunately, AIS also provides perfect information for any pirates who might be considering targeting your ship.

When steaming off the Horn of Africa ships have started turning their AIS systems off. The pirates on that island must be using an AIS system from one of the ships that they've captured, to scan for maritime traffic passing by. We've still got our AIS switched on. Pete's done nothing to get the Dutch captain, Andreas, to stop it. Our vessel will appear like a hulking great invitation to a hijacking upon the pirates' AIS system.

I'm team leader on this mission, and I've discussed our vulnerabilities with Andreas. The main problem is that our ship can do about 10 knots max, and there's a real danger that a pirate mother ship will be able to catch us. We've taken some extra defensive measures to try to warn off any ship that may try to overrun us.

We've put dummy 'soldiers' around the bridge, dressed in army combat fatigues. We've got them roped to the railings, to give the impression that we've got a contingent of commandos permanently standing watch. We've welded shut the doors giving entry into the vessel, and we've welded bars over the windows and across the gangways. The ship's a real fortress, but that doesn't make us any the keener to get boarded, and for the pirates to test our defences.

Pete, the guy who's been on watch, claims a long and distinguished military pedigree. Whatever the truth of it, he's totally missed a boat steaming fast onto the horizon, plus the wealth of evidence upon our radar screen of a pending pirate attack. Rather than sussing all of that out, he's done jack-shit: he's failed to raise the alarm, failed to stop the AIS from broadcasting, and he's failed to get Andreas to take evasive action.

Pete's faults here are legion. I've learned the hard way that in certain situations you are given no second chances. Survival depends on decisive and immediate action. It's better to risk making the wrong decision than to make no decision at all, or to vacillate for so long that a decision, once made, comes too late.

Even if you do make a wrong call, if you see it through with total determination you can still adapt and evolve it as you go. In the elite units that I'd trained and served with we used to call this 'using The Force'. Better to use The Force, to get it wrong, but still have a chance of winning through, than to do nothing at all.

To do nothing is to condemn yourself to the worst. Pete has opted to do nothing. He deserves to suffer for it, 'cause he's endangered all of our lives. He deserves to get locked in some stinking Somali cell and become some scummy pirate's ransom demand. The way things are going he may just end up there, and us with him.

I opt to act. Immediately. It could just be a regular fishing boat. The island could be some fisherman's tropical paradise, with a bunch of fishing skiffs moored to it. But somehow, I don't bloody think so.

I get the lads lined up on the deck pronto, brandishing crossbows and flare guns. The pirate boat is going a good deal faster than we are, and it closes fast.

Once it's within range I give the word on the radio, and the four of us loose off with our weaponry. There are flares flaming across the pirate ship's bows, and the odd crossbow bolt winging it across the seas towards them. They ping! as they hit the pirate ship's metal deck, making a half-reasonable impression of bullets ricocheting off steel.

The pirates must find it fairly convincing, for first their vessel slows, and then it shies away. The bandits must have seen all the razor wire strung over our decks, and the dummy commandos, plus us lot. And they've probably heard what they figure are bullets hitting their ship, and so they likely think that we're properly armed. *If only.*

I figure the pirate captain has decided that discretion is the better part of valour on this one, and to wait for some easier prey. But had I not raised the alarm and got us into battle stations when I had, it might well have gone otherwise.

The pirate vessel turns from its line of attack, and falls away to our stern. But unbeknown to us, it has only done so in order to launch a second, much more covert and concerted assault. We steam on for another hour or so, and all seems to be quiet. The pirate ship's fallen a good nautical mile behind, and we look to be in the clear.

I'm just starting to relax a little when I catch the distinctive crack-crack of small-arms fire. Rounds go pinging off the steel superstructure of the bridge, and I know for sure we're under attack. At the same time I see a couple of flares being fired by our guys up ahead on the bow, so I guess that's where they must be hitting us.

My radio goes wild: 'Pirate craft on the port bow! Pirate craft on the port bow! Coming in fast alongside.'

It's one of my team from up front, and I can sense that his voice is tight with fear and tension. The canny bastards must have come in using their fast skiffs, which can keep below our radar level. They've snuck in to hit us in our blind spot, where the wind turbines block the view from the bridge.

I glance at Andreas, the Captain, and he's gone white as a sheet. I can see him struggling to get into his body armour, whilst trying to steer the ship with his one free hand.

'Keep dead ahead!' I yell at him. 'Do not turn one degree to port or to starboard! You deviate from course we'll lose speed and they'll find it far easier to board, and then we're fucking dead! And give her all you've fucking got!'

Captain Andreas seems to have heard me, and he's back concentrating on steering his ship.

I yell into my radio: 'All stations, get the fucking bouncing barrels going! Then hit 'em with flares, Molotov cocktails, whatever you've got! DO NOT LET THEM BOARD US!'

If they board us, we are well and truly fucked. We have no proper weapons, and going hand-to-hand against Somali pirates armed with AK47s isn't my idea of a fair fight.

I grab Pete and yell into his face: 'You fucking missed the pirate mother ship, so make up for it by smashing the bastards trying to board! COME ON!'

I sprint out and onto the far edge of the ship's wing, the flat T-like structure that protrudes from the side of the ship's bridge. Immediately I see a skiff below us, crammed full of pirates. It's about 100 feet away from our vessel and closing fast. Every second brings them nearer to the range from which they can swing a grappling hook up onto the side of our ship.

My two guys from up front are sprinting down the ship's gunwale, releasing the bouncing barrels as they go. I glance behind and my two blokes from the rear are dashing forward releasing bouncing barrels on the way. Each steel cylinder plummets towards the sea, hits the first wave, and cannons off it in a massive shower of spray.

The guys are nearing the point directly below the bridge when they hit a problem. The design of the ship's superstructure, coupled with the way we've lashed it up with razor wire, means they're prevented from getting any further, and so they're unable to unleash any of the bouncing barrels directly below the bridge.

Right underneath me there's a good part of our vessel's side that's unprotected by the bouncing barrels. There's a gap in our defences, and the pirates are onto it. I start screaming into my radio for the lads to cover the gap.

If the pirates are going to breach our defences, this is where they'll do it.

CHAPTER 49

I grab a flare from out of the magazine that I've got jammed in the map pocket of my combat trousers. It's a Chinese-made standard ship's distress flare, and it's about 12 inches long and an inch and a half wide. It's packed full of nasty explosive chemicals, and I figure it's more effective than a crossbow bolt against a skiff packed full of pirates.

I slide it into the stubby black flare pistol, sight down the cylindrical length of the barrel, getting the pirate skiff bang in the line of fire. I pull the trigger, and there's a blinding red fiery explosion right in front of my face. The useless piece of shit of a flare has blown up in my hand, badly burning my palms and scorching my face.

I ignore the pain, grab another flare, load it and go to fire. Beside me Pete unleashes one himself, and it roars over the pirates' heads. My second flare goes fizzing into the water just in front of the bow of the skiff. Every second that we keep missing the pirate boat keeps edging closer and closer to the unprotected side of our vessel.

I can see this big-limbed, impossibly tall Somali guy getting ready to swing the grappling iron up and over. He's dressed in a motley collection half of combats and half of Arab dress, and he's got this evil kind of grin on his features. I do not want that bastard – or

any of his half-a-dozen well-armed pirate buddies – getting anywhere near our ship's deck.

The pirates have got bandoliers of bullets wrapped around their
waists and looped around their necks. They are heavily armed, and
I can't understand why they aren't malleting us with more fire. I
figure maybe they're trying to conserve their ammo until they've
boarded us, and they can start hunting us down at close quarters.

Suddenly a flare streaks out from one of my guys below, and he
scores a direct hit. The thing explodes right above the pirate skiff,
just a couple of feet behind the tall guy's head. For a second the
tiny craft is enveloped in fierce, scorching fire, as the magnesium,
potassium perchlorate and strontium nitrate ignite into a red-hot
fireball.

The craft swerves and veers away from the vessel, before the flare
falls away behind and is doused in the sea. There's a badly burned
and very angry bunch of pirates in there now, and for a second
their fire-discipline falls apart. They unleash long bursts of fire at
us, and rounds come ricocheting and screaming off the thick steel
of the ship's superstructure. It's only the fact that they're bouncing
about so wildly in their tiny craft that's keeping them from hitting
us.

I turn to check on Captain Andreas. He's digging himself into
the floor of the bridge to avoid the fire. He's down so low he could
wriggle under a snake's belly with a top hat on. I yell at him to get
back to his post, and to squeeze some more speed out of the rust
bucket of a ship he captains.

I turn back to the battle. The skiff's captain has ordered his men
to cease fire, and get back to their main task – which is boarding
us and seizing our ship. He directs the skiff back in towards our
side, and I can hear him screaming at the tall geezer to throw the
grappling hook.

Tall pirate bloke swings and releases. The three-clawed hook loops up towards us, trailing rope in its wake. I grab for my last flare, as the hook falls just short, clanging against the steel side and dropping into the sea. Tall guy starts pulling it back in hand-over-hand, as the skiff's captain keeps yelling encouragement.

By now they know we're not armed, or at least not with anything truly lethal, like the sniper and assault rifles we so desperately need. What I wouldn't give for a real weapon now. A couple of half-decent AK47s and we could finish the lot of them.

Tall guy is preparing to swing again. I slot my last flare into my flare gun, sight and fire. It goes sailing harmlessly over tall guy's head, and ignites way beyond the skiff. I'm fucking beside myself with frustration.

A tiny, wiry pirate is standing beside tall guy, legs braced against the swell and an AK47 slung across his back. He's readying himself to go shimmying up the rope. A thickset, powerful-looking pirate with a machete tucked in his belt is behind him, ready to follow up the rope, and there's four other guys queuing up to follow. They've all but got us.

Tall guy starts swinging the rope. I turn and charge back into the bridge. I can remember the time Captain Sergei got his crew to hurl stuff off the oil tanker, in an effort to outrun the pirate ship that was after us. It left an indelible impression on my mind, and it's given me a flash of inspiration borne out of sheer desperation.

I grab the first thing that I see: a big, heavy fridge. It's full of chilled cans of drink, and it weights half a tonne. I heave it up above my head, ripping the wire out of the wall as I do so. Captain Andreas is staring at me wide-eyed in fear and surprise, as I go running out of the bridge with the fridge perched on my shoulders.

I pound out onto the ship's wing. Pausing only for as long as it takes me to aim, I hurl the fridge over the side and down on top of the pirates. The oblong white projectile impacts at tall guy's feet, halfway in the water and halfway on the skiff. It smashes onto the tiny vessel's side, and for an instant the skiff is swamped.

Pirates go piling into the sea, before the skiff somehow manages to right itself. Half of them are in the drink, and the vessel's taken on a lot of water and has lost its speed completely. A few seconds later we're leaving the pirate skiff, and the fridge that I hurled at it, bobbing about in the sea well behind us.

We remain on action stations for twenty minutes, but there's no more sign of any pirates in pursuit. Captain Andreas is down one fridge full of cans of Coke, but at least he's still at liberty and in command of his ship.

But no one's kidding themselves that we haven't just had a very lucky escape. By not being alert to the presence of that pirate mother ship, Pete let the bastards steal a march on us, and they all but took our vessel.

I double my own watch and I relieve Pete of duty. No way can I trust the guy on such a heavy tasking as this one. He's along purely for the ride now, but he's still drawing his wages, which irks me. It turns out that Pete has a huge mortgage to pay, and once again he's taken it out at the height of the Baghdad security boom.

Like many now working the circuit, Pete is desperate. He's banking that push never comes to shove, and that he'll never have to use his weapon in anger. Guys like Pete have skill sets, but not the ones you need to deal with the heavy situations like we're getting into on these anti-piracy runs.

There's a second operator on my team, Geoff, who hasn't distinguished himself greatly in the battle with the pirates. As we cruise ahead, Geoff offers to show me some footage on his mobile phone.

He'd been in the Green Army, but got out before the wars in Iraq and Afghanistan kicked off. He'd found his way onto the circuit, and started working security contracts in Baghdad.

The footage shows him somewhere in the Baghdad Green Zone – the city's safe area – doing weapons drills. At first he's firing his long, but then he has a stoppage. He throws it onto his back on its sling, and pulls out his pistol. All good drills so far.

He goes to pull the pistol's trigger, and all you can hear on the video is a hollow 'click'. He's failed to make ready the weapon and to have a round in the chamber. He's shown me this film with great pride. I wouldn't have shown it to my dog. It's a case of all the clobber, what a nobber. Period.

Once he's finished screening me his war movie, my only comment is: 'Nice one, mate.'

I am not into criticizing people to their faces, or upstaging them. I may be the team leader on this job, but when people ask me what my background is, all I ever say is Royal Hampshires. But God forbid if we get boarded by Somali pirates with Pete and Geoff on watch.

As far as Geoff is concerned, he's living the dream. He's a nice enough bloke, and a loyal family man with a huge mortgage to pay, one that he'd taken out during the purple patch that was Baghdad. But the bottom line is he should not be messing around with Somali pirates, who are only a few steps removed from Al Qaeda. Those guys do not mess around, and they do not take prisoners.

You need specialist training for this kind of work, and a special kind of awareness and mindset. You need to read a situation, and to be able to react in an instant with total aggression. You also need to use maverick, lateral thinking – a bit like I did with the fridge-hurling trick. With guys like Geoff on the job, the client is paying for one thing but getting very much another.

Those guys are hungry for work, and the PMCs who hire them keep driving the prices ever lower. The fallout from Baghdad means that some blokes are willing to work for next to no money. The PMCs are still charging the same rates to their clients, so they're making a killing. Too many of the blokes with guns come cheap these days, and they are pretty much expendable.

The only jobs that seem to pay properly now are those that insist on certified ex-Special Forces. In effect the circuit has become a two-track operation. There are those of us with provable track records and a cast-iron pedigree; and there are those who might have earned a stripe in Iraq, and are floundering around trying to get work.

In my teams I try to get the guys with the bona fide, provable track records, no matter what their nationality might be. I'd rather have a Fijian guy who is ex-Hereford than a Brit who is an ex-copper or a nightclub bouncer.

When the Somali pirates are poised to attack, they don't give a fuck about your skin colour, or what passport you might carry. In fact, to them a white-eye is the promise of a higher ransom. All that will deter them is blokes who can think and act lightning-fast, and face down an enemy who outnumbers them and is far better armed.

I can barely think of an operation I undertook with the elite units I served with when we weren't outnumbered and outgunned. It came with the territory. It was our superlative training, our unbreakable comradeship and esprit de corps, combined with our willingness to try the unexpected, that won through every time.

If you're gonna be a bear, be a grizzly. And when all is said and done, the same rules apply on the circuit. Or at least they should do, for anything else is an invitation to a kidnapping or a beheading.

I get contracted to do this next anti-piracy mission, and it's a highly unusual tasking. We're to take delivery of the *Vixen*, a ship that's been held with all her crew for many months by Somali pirates. A ransom has been paid for the vessel, one of several million dollars, and the US military has taken her into their custody.

They're sailing her down to the Kenyan port of Mombasa, where we'll take over. Our role will be to sail her from there to her home port in the Far East, which involves navigating the *Vixen* through hundreds of miles of pirate-infested waters. No one wants a ship that's just been ransomed falling into pirate hands for a second time, so the stakes are super-high on this one.

En route to Mombasa I stop off to say hello to the ex-prime minister, Tony Blair. One of my ex-military mates is running Blair's security. I know Blair has a soft spot for ex-elite forces operators like me.

Tony Blair strikes me as being remarkably tall. He's eye-to-eye with me as we shake hands, and no one's ever called me small. We reminisce over various elite forces missions. Had any of those gone tits-up – and there was every chance they might have done – it would likely have spelled the end of his political career. To me that's one of the highlights of his time as Britain's prime minister, and I sense Blair feels likewise.

I tell him about the contract I'm on to take the *Vixen* back to her owners, and he lets me know I've got his full support in battling piracy on the high seas. He gives me a copy of his book, and a signed photo of the two of us together. He signs the book 'to Big Phil . . . yours ever, Tony'. We agree to meet for beers next time I'm passing through his neck of the woods, and I'm on my way.

The *Vixen* is in a right state by the time it reaches Mombasa. One of its engines has packed up, and it stinks of shit and piss and general neglect. The pirates have squatted in the vessel whilst guarding it and their captives. They have used it as their toilet whilst standing watch over the ship and her Thai crew.

I've heard all the reports of pirates torturing their captives, so as to raise the stakes and the ransoms paid. I figure the Thai crew must have suffered horrendously.

We're allowed onto the ship to prepare her for the next leg of the journey, where we'll be in control of the security. In the ship's mess I discover this battered-looking plastic calculator, which is the very one the pirates used to work out the sums of money they were demanding in ransom, and being offered. It's even got the pirates' names scratched into the back of it: *Mohammed, Faizal, Abdul* and another *Mohammed* . . . I decide to keep that calculator as a macabre souvenir.

In between rigging the ship with razor wire, I sit in on some of the debriefings that are taking place with the ship's crew. I'm less fascinated to hear how they've been abused. I figure it's better not to know, in case the bastard pirates ever make a go of capturing me alive. I reckon a bullet to the head is a better option than being taken alive, if only we could carry guns.

I'm more interested to hear how the pirates dealt with the vessel and the hostages, once they got them into their pirate stronghold. The ship's crew talk about how the first thing the pirates did once they got the ship into their harbour was to strip it of anything useful to them. Fuel, food, fixtures and fittings – anything valuable or usable was removed and divided amongst them as the immediate spoils of war.

The pirates then used the ship to practise and rehearse similar takedowns, so as to better refine what they do. They used the vessel to carry out mock climbing assaults from the sea, and to refine the design of their grappling hooks. They've left one of those grappling irons on the ship by accident, and it turns out that it's made from an old metal ladder, with the rungs bent into three claw-like hooks.

The pirates have been refining and rehearsing their ship pursuit and assault tactics – not to mention their methods of torture – just as we've been refining and improving our defences and our SOPs.

They've also started selling the hostages up the chain, from 'simple' pirates like themselves towards the real bad guys, like Al Qaeda. Each time a hostage has been sold up the chain, they've been moved further and further away from the coast and the point of any easy access for an assault force that might come in to rescue them.

No doubt about it, the pirates are getting better and better at the evil business that they practise, which means we've likewise got to up our game. And on this job to take the *Vixen* back to her home port, we've just been given the biggest-ever improvement in our security provisions that I ever could have wished for. At last we've been issued with weapons. We can properly defend our passage through the high seas.

Each of us has got issued with a brand-new AK47, the ultra-modern version with the forward-mounted pistol grip. As we prepare to set sail in our razor-wire-fortified ship, I have this ultimate sense of wellbeing now that we're finally, properly armed. The pirates are welcome to have a go now. Bring it on. Come get some.

We've not long set sail from Mombasa when one of the team comes up to have a word with me.

'So what's the SOP with engaging the pirates?' he asks. 'Are we firing warning shots first, or what?'

I say: 'Sure we're firing warning shots: bang into their heads.'

He looks a bit confused. 'But how's that a warning shot if we shoot 'em?'

'It's a perfect warning shot. They'll be deader than a fried chicken, which is the perfect warning to their bastard pirate mates.'

The guy gets the message. We're not fucking around here. When dealing with Somali pirates – who love nothing more than a bit of kidnapping, pillage and torture – you are only one remove from Al Qaeda, and you play by big boys' rules.

When the next pirate ship steams onto the horizon, we'll unleash the bouncing barrels, grab our AK47s, brace ourselves on the gunwale and prepare to fire. And inside I'll be smiling, for I'm never happier than when I'm behind a weapon.

Needs must, old boy.

INDEX